HOW TO KISS

CU00642725

An Inspirational Spiritual and
Metaphysical Narrative about
Human Origin, Essence and Destiny

JOZEF SIMKOVIC

Dedicated to the Memory of Robert Monroe

This non-fiction real story is based on many meditations, and it has been written by a former professional reporter. However, a fiction style has been used to make the story easily understandable and more entertaining.

While all efforts have been made not to offend any living person, the author sincerely apologizes to anyone who would be distressed or feel uncomfortable during the reading of the story. Stories and views expressed in this book have not been reviewed nor endorsed by The Monroe Institute and do not represent the policy or views of that institution (TMI).

The explanations of terms used in the book may be found in the *Glossary* at the end of the narrative.

Copyright © 2018 by Jozef Simkovic
Edited by Dr. Juanzetta Flowers
Cover Artwork by Aldren Gamalo
ISBN-13: 978-1-7325957-1-2
Library of Congress Control Number: 2018953435
How to Kiss the Universe Press, Washington D.C.
Printed in the United States of America
First Edition

CONTENTS

1. QUESTIONS   9

2. DAWN   13

3. KICKOFF   17

4. CASTLE   21

5. FIVE MESSAGES   24

6. NO TIME   27

7. FEAR   30

8. MACHO   33

9. FIRST KISS   35

10. GROUNDING   37

11. KUNDALINI UNLEASHED   39

12. FLYING GRIZZLY   41

13. REINCARNATIONS   44

14. PARK   47

15. THE MONROE PROTOCOL   50

16. GRAND THEFT IN STOCKHOLM   53

17. SHAMAN   57

18. BACK ON THE ROAD   63

19. RETRIEVALS   66

20. ELENA   70

21. BELIEF SYSTEM TERRITORIES   73

22. KUNDALINI MACHINE   76

23. LOOSH AND GARDENER   79

24. ATLANTIS SURPRISE   81

25. MISTER Q   84

26. EDUCATION   86

27. GUARDIANS   89

28. RA AND HADIEN   92

29. DREAMS   96

30. LUCID DREAMS   99

31. OUTINGS   102

32. MENEV THE GREAT   107

33. WEDDING   111

34. INTRUDER   114

35. BEYOND THE EARTH   118

36. VOYAGER AND ALPHA SQUARED   122

37. HADIEN THE FRIEND   125

38. RA THE COP   130

39. COUNCILS   133

40. RUALA   136

41. GUESTS   139

42. MIDNIGHT, THE STARS AND YOU   141

43. CONTEMPLATING STARGATE   144

44. MICROWORLD   146

45. MULTI-EYES   148

46. DECEIVER   150

47. LOVE AND STARGATE   154

48. PAUL OF TARSUS   159

49. SOUL TRADERS   163

50. MORE RETRIEVALS   167

51. SOLDIER   172

52. FIVE RESOLUTIONS   175

53. HEARTGATE   178

54. ROTE   180

55. CHALLENGE   183

56. SPIRITUAL DEVICES   187

57. TRANQUILITY OF TIME   190

58. CHILDHOOD REVISITED   193

59. PAST AND DYING   196

60. GARDENER THE TEACHER   201

61. LOVE THROUGHOUT THE AGES   204

62. SILVER CORD   209

63. GOING TO SCHOOL   212

64. DIVINE STRUCTURE AND EVIL   215

65. GRASSHOPERISTICS   219

66. UNDERSTANDING OF DREAMS   221

67. MIRACLE ON HIGHWAY 95   224

68. LURE OF THE STARGATE   227

69. SPIRITUAL CHILDREN   231

70. PLANTS, ANIMALS AND EARTH   234

71. STORY OF ALENKA   238

72. AVATAR   246

73. ONE AND MANY   249

74. REMINDERS AND WARNINGS   252

75. CANALING   255

76. BIRTHDAY   258

77. LOCALITY OF CREATION   260

78. STILLNESS AND MOTION   263

79. AWARENESS AND BALANCE   265

80. SPICE OF LOVE   268

81. BUBBLING AND ELOHIM   271

82. MISSION HAS BEGUN   274

83. HEADING TO THE ROOTS   277

84. IN MENEV'S COUNTRY   281

85. JUANZETTA'S HEART   284

86. WITH OLD BUDDIES   286

87. COUNCIL OF STAR FRIENDS   290

88. STRINGS AND IMMORTALITY   293

89. DIMENSIONS AND UNIVERSES   296

90. LIGHT BODY AND RAMA   300

91. REWARD   305

92. GOODBYE   309

EPILOGUE   314

GLOSSARY   320

ACKNOWLEDGEMENTS   336

REVIEWS AND MESSAGES   339

Chapter 1
QUESTIONS

"Judge a man by his questions rather than by his answers."
(Voltaire)

There are many questions puzzling people on this planet, regardless of whether we want to or do not want to ask, whether we are busy, afraid, or too lazy to ask. Here is just a little sample of them:

Why? Why am I here on this planet? What am I supposed to do here? What is the purpose of my life? Where did I come from? Was I here before? Or am I here only once? Why do I have to die? Why do I have to fear? What happens to me after I die? Is there a God? How did it all begin? I bet that you, Dear Reader, ask not just these, but many other comparable questions.

Some of us, whether female or male, start to ask such questions as soon as we learn to talk. Others are cruising through life without considering these questions or are even afraid to ask. Yet others have hardships which do not allow them to stop and think even for a little while, for they were not born in such a good place as you and me. But much of mankind on this beautiful planet simply believes what others have told them. They proclaim, as my dear Slovak friend on the other side of the ocean says:
"I shall leave that for the smarter ones."

Most of us are members of, or at least affiliated with some religions and other organizations. Ministers, priests, rabbis, imams, gurus, lamas, political leaders, scientists, philosophers, and others are those "smarter ones" trying to explain everything to us. They may inspire us in their genuine efforts, but they can also indoctrinate us and manipulate us for whatever motivations they might have.

And then, when time is closing the window of life and we are getting ready to depart this world, many of us realize that all our knowledge and destiny are literally hanging on a hook in the air, connected to nothing. We do not know how to die and often we beg for more time here, even if there is no good reason to stay here anymore.

Yet, there is another way to try to find the answers to these questions, to gain true spiritual knowledge, to become completely free for a full and rewarding life on this planet, and then finally be ready to die when the time has arrived. I have learned in my spiritual experiences that physical death is merely a change or transition to a different place. When you have finished your life, it is the same as graduating from a school. One day all this beautiful experience of yours and all your misery will be over whether you want it to be or not, or whether you believe or not that you are more than your physical body. Your time simply has arrived. If you hold the belief that you are indeed more than your physical body, on that day you will simply just lose the physical body you have temporarily occupied.

Most of us believe that we somehow continue after a physical death on the Earth. According to numerous surveys, most people on this planet believe that we have a Soul. They believe that there is a heaven where we will reside after death. Then there is a question of whether we come back again into another physical body on our planet or not. What is amazing is that most of us are not trying to understand just what might happen; we are simply expecting to figure it out after we die. Or we hope that maybe someone will be there to help us and even take our hand. Or some believe there will be nothing there, just complete darkness and the definitive end of everything.

I have a better proposition for you. How about taking a little trip with me into my spiritual world which may then inspire you to take a similar journey yourself? Human progress has always been accelerated by individuals who discovered and pursued revolutionary innovative ways of thinking. Throughout history such individuals have found and gained knowledge never seen before. This also applies to spirituality.

At the beginning of my spiritual voyage, I quickly discovered and further developed a unique way of diving into the deepest corners of my mind. That opened the door for me into the Unified Mind of the whole Universe and beyond because everything is interconnected. Then I developed a very effective way to record and bring gained new insights back into the physical world. They not only will benefit me after I die, but they have also already created benefits for me in everyday life on this planet.

The spiritual beings I have communicated with throughout this process have clearly let me know their desires. They have wanted me to bring such information back to our physical planet to be shared freely with all mankind. Yet, there are also other forces in multiple dimensions of the spiritual world who have been trying to prevent my doing so. When I finally decided to start to write my story, their efforts to stop me intensified and became despicable.

You can say:

"Wait a minute, Jozef Simkovic! What are you trying to say here? Who are you? I have never heard of you! Who told you that you are The One who knows such things? Why should I read someone else's subjective experiences? You made it all up, didn't you?"

It is true, Dear Reader, that if you are looking for proof about the existence of the Soul, God, or the Other Side in my book, you will not find them. I am neither a scientist, philosopher, nor priest. I am simply a storyteller who rather reluctantly has agreed to bring this testimony to you in exchange for a promise given to me by a highly developed spiritual being.

What is described in this book is the most fascinating chapter of my life and it can equally fascinate you also. You can choose sooner or later, Dear Reader, whether you could perceive these experiences as real happenings in a very real spiritual world, or as my dear skeptic friend would characterize them, "fictional stories created by a wishful thinking motivated brain."

All that is described in this book happened exactly as written. I do not consider my stories to be just beliefs, or even airy-fairy tales; they are the knowledge gained through my experiences.

I recognize only the things I know already and the things I do not yet know. My journey has been full of fascinating discoveries and profound revealing messages. I have completely freed myself of all kinds of conditioning. I have reached an incredible freedom of mind that I never dreamed possible, and I am a very happy man.

After you read my book, then you can judge and decide what was in it for you and maybe, likewise, possibly immerse yourself in an experience like mine. Your own personal experience can give you the definite proof of spiritual reality you might need and desire. I am sure you are looking for such proof. Remember, you can fully understand your essence only with your own experiences.

And now you must decide for yourself, my Dear Sister or Brother, to read or not to read. All I am suggesting, just as the great Robert Monroe suggested, is for you to consider the possibility that you might be more than your physical body. Then this book is for you, and I wish you a good ride and lots of fun and surprises. But, if you believe up front that things like the topic of this story are just hogwash and hallucinations, maybe you should put it down right now. However, if you have just the slightest bit of doubt about your beliefs, then I am inviting you to reconsider. This just might be your chance to modify and beautify your life.

Chapter 2
DAWN

"Life can only be understood backwards; but it must be lived forwards." (Soren Kierkegaard)

The time in our life when we start to ask those questions depends on our personal individuality and our desire to find the answers. But frankly, only a very few of us would ever venture to tackle the genuine effort necessary to accomplish such a seemingly vague and undefined task. Ask yourself how many times you have tried.

When we are young, we really do not care; we believe that we are going to be healthy and live forever. When we are starting to get older, we suddenly become aware of our mortality and the fight against the inevitability of dying begins, sometimes at all costs. Antonius Block, in the famous Ingmar Bergman movie "Seventh Seal," tried to beat Death in a game of chess. For most of us, as the end is nearing, fear is growing.

Several years back I loved a woman who was very strong, always in charge, and literally not afraid of anything. Yet when she became mortally sick and she knew the end was coming, all of her being was overtaken by fear. She was begging for anything that could prolong the misery she was in. I could not help her no matter how hard I tried because she was not receptive to understanding the course of Nature and inevitable departure. A Slovak proverb says:
"He who is drowning would grab even a straw to stay above the water."
I hope, Dear Reader, that after you read my book most of the fears you might have will disappear.

I have struggled with these questions since an early age. While a freshman in college, I even became suicidal because there were no persons or resources to turn to for answers. Even though I read everything I could find, there

were no answers in those texts either. The Communist dominated schools in Czechoslovakia (the country I originally came from) required believing in and praising only The Party. The official church was not the answer either because it was so often corrupted. My dad once said about our village Roman Catholic priest:
"I think he is a Communist, even his hat is red!"

I was raised as a Roman Catholic in a country governed by the Communist party. And frankly when I tell you why I believed in God, many of you can relate to it. I just wanted to make sure, that if God were out there somewhere, God would not punish me after I died for not believing and behaving. But several times in my childhood I had dreams about Jesus on the cross giving me signs such as moving his eyebrows, blinking his eyes, or even slowly moving his head. Waking up, I always felt euphoric about such a magical experience. It was also like having a secret or being chosen or special.

At college, I became a member of the martial arts club and continued be very active and successful in all levels of the martial art of karate for the next eighteen years. My friends and I tried to understand the spiritual backgrounds of the eastern martial arts and related Zen Buddhism. We tried to meditate, even though we did not really know how. But even then, my intuition was telling me that such a way was not entirely enough for me. The Zen premise about suffering being a postulate of our existence did not speak to me. Finally, after my myriad experiences, I now understand that such a premise is only for those who either decide to believe that way, or because they were raised in a different culture. However, I always respected their beliefs.

After college, my job, taking care of my family and karate activities successfully pushed those why questions into the back of my mind. After immigrating to the United States, life became even busier. I literally became a workaholic as a journalist at The Voice of America, believing that I fulfilled my life mission and dreams. And in this beautiful country of ours, I completely changed my world view. The American attitude of optimism and love for one's fellow human beings infiltrated my Soul.

I continued to keep contacts with my dear Slovak friend on the other side of the ocean. He had inspired me to escape from communist governed Czechoslovakia, yet he himself had stayed behind. This dear friend of mine, a diehard skeptic about spirituality, had also continued to look for answers to the same questions I had, but in a separate way in a radically different environment. Thanks to him, I read a Czech translation of a book by the world-renowned Russian eye surgeon, Ernst Muldashev, with the title: *Where do we come from?* After reading this magnificent work, I suddenly realized for the first time in my life:
"We must have a Soul!"

Another friend of mine who helped me to begin my spiritual journey was my colleague at The Voice of America, Native American Eugene Taylor. Eugene is half Cherokee and half Sioux. He brought me the book *Adventures Beyond the Body* by William Buhlman, told me about The Monroe Institute and gave me a book about chakras. The chakras are energy centers in our body which enable us to exchange energy and information with nonphysical realms. These two friends helped me tremendously to start my spiritual journey in diverse ways. For sure, these fellows did not appear in my life just by coincidence.

In October 2007, I spent three days in the hospital after receiving a stent into my widow maker artery which had been ninety-five percent closed. After recovery, I realized there was not as much time left as I thought for my physical life on our planet. I suddenly felt the spiritual void in my life with new urgency and decided to seriously study all those questions, and more. In July 2008, I received my very first two impressions about my past lives with the help of binaural beats developed by William Buhlman.

I learned that I was a Roman soldier being killed by the spear of another Roman soldier next to a stream of water. That explained my love of sandals in this life to me. In another vision, I was a medieval Spanish courtesan named Isabella who was secretly in love with a knight with a moustache. Without knowing anyone by that name, Isabella had been coming into my head all my life and I simply cannot imagine my face without a moustache. I also had often thought throughout my life that it would really be interesting to be a woman. I was hooked.

All my life I have had very intensive and vivid dreams. Now, I felt compelled to record them even though I did not know why or what use I could have for them. During the summer of 2008, I had several variations of dreams about being shot right in the middle of my forehead, with a subsequent burning pain there when I woke up. Only after being in an intensive meditation regiment much later, I finally understood that those dreams meant that my third eye chakra was opening.

After reading all three of Robert Monroe's books: *Journeys Out of the Body, Far Journeys* and *Ultimate Journey,* I finally decided to sign up for the famous Gateway Voyage program at The Monroe Institute founded by him. During the next several years, the Monroe programs led me to the discovery of the deepest mysteries of our existence and the secrets of the Universe and beyond as I know them today. The dawn of my spirituality had begun. I was starting to learn everything I needed to know. I was awakening.

Chapter 3
KICKOFF

"They say to me in their awakening: "You and the world you live in are but a grain of sand upon the infinite shore of an infinite sea." And in my dream, I say to them: "I am the infinite sea, and all the worlds are but grains of sand upon my shore." (Kahlil Gibran in Sand and Foam)

What is meditation? Most people who are not practicing it generally believe that it is a way to relax the mind and eventually bring relief and peace into the body. Those who occasionally meditate or read more about it naturally start to understand that there are many other benefits. Regular and experienced practitioners will tell you that it is the way to reach a higher state of being, whether you call it Nirvana, Samadhi, Satori or otherwise, or you are not even giving a name to such a state of mind. Then we could argue whether the purpose of such a state is a euphoric feeling, or nothing, or a tool enabling you to know more about yourself, the Universe and everything.

The basic steps of meditation are the same regardless of the kind of meditation method or school you use. You must get quiet and relax your mind. Then you must disconnect yourself as much as you can from the physical environment you are in. Then you can open and direct your mind to go wherever you desire. It took me quite a while to understand the simplicity of these principles. But let me tell you, Dear Reader, an effective spiritual journey leading you to the highest and most profound secrets of yourself and the Universe requires a tremendous amount of discipline and determination. It especially applies when you are busy with your everyday life and its duties and demands. Ask yourself: "Do I really want to know these things?"

If you have a hunger to know as I had, I have no doubt what your answer and decision will be.

I was rather impatient, so instead of looking for a way to meditate regularly, I decided to go to The Monroe Institute to get "out of my body," see my physical body from the spiritual world and, thereby, have immediate proof about existence of the Other Side. That was the primary reason I signed up for the Gateway Voyage. After all, it is a very attractive proposition indeed for anyone who flirts with the idea of leaving the physical body and going to the Other Side. In my excitement, I had an earworm in my head all the time reminding me that I was going to the "Get away voyage" because it could "get me away from my body." I do not have dyslexia; "gateway" did not meet my expectation, but "get away" did. But after my subsequent participation in 15 different programs at the Monroe Institute, I can tell you that I learned that there are much, much more meaningful adventures than just trying to reach an out of body state. For me, I could not have made a better choice of how to proceed in my spiritual journey than by going to The Monroe Institute.

The Gateway Voyage in September 2008 completely changed my life. The Monroe Institute is a unique place, probably second to none on this planet. When you go to their program, you have no guru. They call their highly skilled spiritual teachers the facilitators because that is what they do; they are there to facilitate your progress. And they provide the tools for you to use in your development. The basic tool is an audio product called Hemi Sync. It produces different tonal sounds into your left and right earphones. The difference in frequencies stimulates your brain and helps you quickly get into a higher altered state. You carry out these programs in your own private booth called the CHEC unit. Each program has specific tools and exercises. Robert Monroe created a classification system for the distinct levels of states of mind when you are in an altered state. He named them Focus Levels and I will describe them in detail later. These are the basics at The Monroe Institute.

On Saturday evening when the program had begun, before we went to our CHEC units, the facilitators Karen Malik and Lee Stone explained to us the first tools we could use for quieting the body and mind and isolating disruptions as we aligned ourselves in tune with the harmonies of the Universe. Then, in our units, we were practicing resonant tuning. It seemed to me that we sounded like Buddhist or Hindu monks. Next, we placed all that could be disrupting and bothering us mentally into a security repository box. Anything could be put in there. The design and construction of the box was completely up to the individual. The facilitators also strongly emphasized the importance of the Gateway Voyage affirmation. You can follow it in your mind during the preparation process or even speak it aloud if it would help you more that way. Lastly, they explained to us the enormous difference between intentions and expectations.

They also warned us about the possibility of an upcoming emotional cleaning. They said some of us would cry. Sometimes, according to them, there were classes when participants simply could not deal with the overwhelming emotional issues that might come up with this exercise. Some would leave the program and go home. I thought that I would not. I assured myself that I would not cry and, for sure, I would not go home prematurely. I was planning to go out of my body and that was all I wanted.

Next, we learned the ten points of body relaxation leading to the first level of an altered state. Robert Monroe defined this state as Focus 10. I want to emphasize here, that the names and numbers really do not matter. They are just helping us to be oriented in the distinctive levels of altered states according to Monroe's model, and I found them very helpful. The number 1 in Focus 10 meant that the mind was awake and 0 meant that the body was asleep.

Very quickly I learned to recognize when I was in Focus 10 by the feeling of having my body lightly paralyzed and pleasantly tingling and humming except for being aware of my breathing. As the week progressed, I was often very entertained to hear myself deeply snore. With all this new fun, I was feeling very uplifted and expected something to happen when I finally went to sleep that first night.

Very vivid dreaming had just begun. From the literature, I already knew that separation from the physical body and returning to it would be accompanied with vibrational feelings. I was not surprised to wake up dreaming about sitting in a large auditorium where my seat was violently shaking like an electric massage chair roaring at full power. I went back to sleep and woke up from another dream. I was pointing my gun at someone's forehead, but he was doing the same thing and he was faster. I was sure I had been shot to death. I felt the bullet passing through my skull, but after waking up the pain quickly disappeared. Ahaa...! Now I remembered that my third eye chakra was supposed to open even more. Apparently, the opening was not wide enough yet. Variations of this dream were repeated several more times at various times afterwards. But when my spiritual journey picked up speed, they stopped.

The next day as we shared our experiences with the group, I found it quite difficult to recognize myself as being the shy dude from a small Slovak village who spoke with an accent. I wanted to tell the group everything, and I did it vigorously because it was so coooool...! It continued like that throughout the whole program until I had to start to deal with my overconfidence and ego. But let's leave that for a little bit later.

First, let me insert a funny story here. Participant Brock had a problem with his security repository box. Someone continued to steal it and throw it down a hill. As he was trying to get the perpetrator, he finally realized that he himself was the one who was trying to get rid of his box with all his obstructions in it. We had a lot of fun trying to analyze all the possible explanations for such an activity. The exciting spiritual games had just begun.

Chapter 4
CASTLE

"Most people on planet Earth try to change themselves by changing their external world. And that is like trying to change the picture on a TV screen by rubbing it with a cloth." (Rosie McKnight in Soul Journeys)

We were progressing quickly in our Gateway Voyage. Next, we learned to understand Focus Level 12. Every Focus Level was supported during the exercises with a very specific mix of patented Hemi Sync technology signals which were stimulating our brains and helping to open our minds in every possible direction in space and time. Focus Level 12, called the state of expanded awareness, represented the first higher level of the mind in an altered state. In Focus 12, most of the higher centers of the brain supporting physical life are suppressed and minimized to keep the body in physically muted harmony and relaxation. But the awareness of the mind miraculously widens, and we are suddenly able to dive into our inner beings and send out, as well as receive, signals and messages from the Universe itself.

During the first exercise, with almost total concentration on it, I could quickly reach complete darkness. There was nothing out there, just heavy, and vast darkness. I had tried many times before to reach this state when practicing yoga or martial arts. But my so-called monkey mind was always strongly present. With Hemi Sync and under good guidance, the monkey mind was suppressed very effectively. There is a story often told at The Monroe Institute about Tibetan monks who were shocked at how quickly they could reach such a state while participating in the programs. When they were asked to express their shock, they supposedly reluctantly stated:
"We sometimes meditate 20 years before we are able to reach

such a state of complete darkness."

But after the initial enjoyment, I did not like the mere empty blackness I had in my mind. I asked for a change, and everything became blue. Now, I really wanted to know what was going on.

"Hey, is anybody or anything there?" I sent the question into the blue vastness.

The blueness was becoming foggy and soon, amid it, I recognized a massive door to a castle. In awe, I heard a series of questions in my mind without any control exercised by my brain:

"What is this? Elena, are you doing this? Did you build this big castle, so I would see it right away and find you for our talk?"

I suddenly heard my mind reaching out to my deceased wife, Elena, whom I had hurt badly years ago in a way she did not deserve at all. Elena answered:

"No, My Love, it is the castle we were supposed to build together."

With this, I started to cry. For the rest of the exercise, I cried like never in my life, like a baby. That crying contained everything: guilt, sorrow, shame, pain, but also understanding, accepting and hope. The emotional cleansing, they warned us about had arrived. It was so overwhelming that I could hardly take it, I wanted to go home.

After the exercise, I realized that I was not the only one who had cried. At lunch, I could see the red watery eyes of the other participants. But because the issues were apparently very private, there was not much sharing. Only one lady at our table told us about meeting with her daddy on the Other Side. She had longed for this encounter for a long time. They could resolve issues which her father had taken with him to his grave.

Later, I asked Karen for a private consultation. She explained that almost everyone who was accessing the higher states of consciousness had to go through something similar.

All of us are carrying some unpleasant baggage we regret. When you decide to start your spiritual journey, you can expect a rising urgency to deal with it. Once you do deal with it, you can commute your emotions into understanding and knowledge, and you can proceed.

Elena disappeared and left me to deal with my castle. My progress in meditation slowed down a little bit. I wanted to learn what was hidden behind the door to the castle, what was really inside the castle. The door was locked, so I constructed a spiritual key. It was small, and I had to enlarge it several times until it fit. Then I got scared of what might be behind the door and it took me a while to get the courage to open the door. When I did, the answer was there:

"You cannot continue effectively because a disrupting evil is hiding in your heart."

Later in the program I found that evil and fired it far away into space. After a while the castle just crumbled; I saw only rubbish and, finally, beautiful green grass grew on its site.

Three weeks later in a dream, a small boy and girl dressed in white like little angels appeared on that same meadow holding hands and walking around. Afterward, whenever I would visit this spiritual place, there were always zillions of kids like them walking around. Innocence, compassion, and understanding had replaced guilt and sorrow. The main emotional issue of my life which had bothered me deeply for a long time was finally over.

Chapter 5
FIVE MESSAGES

"Ask and it will be given to you; seek and you will find; knock and the door will be opened to you." (Matthew 7:7)

Expanded awareness defined by Robert Monroe as Focus 12 is the state of mind where we suddenly discover that we can go outward, recognize, confront, and hug all that exists out there, outside of our brains. And, likewise, we can go inward, immerse ourselves in our brains, minds, hearts and whatever else is inside of us. It really does not matter how we call it. It is there waiting for us to recognize it and understand it. When you have suppressed your monkey mind, have put your body to sleep while your mind is awake, and have disconnected yourself from physical reality, little miracles can start to happen. A similar state of mind in martial arts is known by the Japanese phrase "Mizu no Kokoro," which means "mind like water." You are present, you are at peace, and you are calm like water when there is no wind blowing and disturbing the surface. In such a state, you can start to send and ask questions in both directions, inside of you and outside of you, and you can receive answers. Everything we want to know is out there; we just must find the way to access it.

The Gateway Voyage at the Monroe Institute has a wonderful tool with which to start your inquiry. It is called "Five Messages." You can simply ask these important questions after reaching Focus 12 and stabilizing your mind in that state. Here is what I used:

"At this moment in my life, what are the five most important things I should know? Give me number five first and the most important number one last, please."

Express gratitude and wait and you shall receive. My messages came into my brain crisp and clear in plain English just as if they had been dictated directly from a script:

5, "That which you think is important for you and what you are dealing with right now is not important at all."
I immediately understood this was a reference to my internal struggle with The Castle. Reasonable, I thought; if you want to run fast, you cannot carry a lot of baggage. What is message number four?

4, "Yes, there is a God Creator, and you will get closer to Him, but not enough that you would know who He is and what His intentions are."
This answer made me wonder what more important message there could be than that. And that is number four, not number one? Wow! What could message number three be? Now I was curious.

3, "You will help many people on your way to get closer to God, and you will be helped likewise by many other beings."
This was overwhelming, and I was crying again. I had no doubt that there was much more out there, and this was just the beginning of the beginning.

2, "You will also penetrate deep into your Soul. You shall access The Akashic records with your mind, and you will know who you were, who you are and who you are going to be."
Now, I was impatient to hear number one.

1, "Yes, everything in the spiritual world is as Robert Monroe described it. He chose you to be the One who will fully understand his message and you shall widen his legacy."
That message hit me truly hard at that time because I thought:
"Who am I, this little me, and what do I know? What am I supposed to do? The Monroe Institute is already here for widening Robert Monroe's legacy and spreading his teachings, and I have only just begun some little experiments!"
An interesting side note here was the take of my skeptic

friend on all that I had received in my messages. When I described my messages to him, especially the last one, he immediately said:

"You had headphones on your head, who knows how they were influencing and manipulating you!!!"

No matter how I tried to explain to him that there was no way someone could implant those kinds of thoughts into my head, either technically or otherwise, he remained skeptical.

Only now I do fully understand that there were forces that had somehow discovered my possible abilities. And they steered me into the direction about which I had not had the slightest clue for most of my previous life. I was obviously chosen to accomplish something far bigger than my wildest imagination could have foreseen. Those Five messages became the most important highlight of my Gateway Voyage.

Chapter 6
NO TIME

"It is meaningless to ask what God was doing before He made heaven and Earth, because there is no time." (Saint Augustine)

There are many ways we can understand the distinct stages or levels of altered states of mind. The method that Robert Monroe created is a system of Focus Levels which enabled those who wanted to communicate and share experiences with others to quickly identify similarities between individuals. It is also usually generally understood that with the higher Focus Levels we are talking about higher and higher frequencies of our vibrations. Everything that exists in the physical world is in motion and vibrating. Regardless of how we perceive it, nothing in the world of matter or energy is static. Let's say you magnify a piece of wood, plastic, metal, or anything many times, what would you see? You would see only molecules, atoms with cores and electrons moving around with incredible speed and the rest is just vast empty space.

Focus 15 in Monroe's model is the state of mind where we raise our vibrations high enough that we are not aware of, nor do we consider it important to be aware of time. When you can detach yourself from time, you can start to observe and study it. In studying it, you might conclude that time has been created and developed for the material world to be able to function. In truth, the reality is that present, past and future are just illusions. I will have much more about time later in the book. But, in the Gateway Voyage, we just began to use the simple tools developed by the institute for investigating time. At the beginning of this series of exercises, we simply went to Focus 15 to see what waited for us there.

After settling into Focus 15, I perceived an infinite

sea of flying sheets as large as big clouds. After a while, I recognized that they contained windows. In each window, I saw the silhouette of a head and one hand waving at me and inviting me to peek in and see what was above the sheets. When I say, after a while here, it means in the earthly understanding of time as a sequential flow. In the no time environment, everything is parallel and in the same timeframe. (I will explain this later when I will be talking about another one of Robert Monroe's marvelous discoveries called ROTE.) Basically, the transfer from parallel perceiving into an earthly sequence is enabled by the interpretation executed by our brain's coordinating its right and left hemispheres.

I decided to accept the invitation and popped up through one of the windows. I could see an oval track frame, like those used in a dry cleaner, holding numerous hangers with white robes on them. All the robes were plain white except for two. I reached out to move them around on the oval frame. One of them showed a Roman soldier and the other one a courtesan; and I got it. I was now browsing through my previous lives. I could take these two off the rack, I could put them back and shuffle things around, but nothing was changing, all the others remained plain white. I could see in this display only those I had already discovered. I understood there was a lot of work ahead to see who else I had been throughout the ages.

In one of the other exercises, we learned to construct a time wheel to enable us to project our mind forward or backward. It was September 2008 and I wanted to see what would happen in December 2012. But the wheel was letting me go only backwards; it stopped at 2003. Apparently, it was not time yet for more elaborate research.

My subconscious mind was reminding me to appreciate the last five very happy years in my life. I spent them with my friend and lover Alenka. During those five years, I had also pulled myself out of financial troubles and traveled with her to many beautiful places in the world. But, best of all, I had finally put myself on the right track. I was now finally doing something which was making more sense than anything else in my life before.

Chapter 7
FEAR

"Love is what we were born with. Fear is what we learned here." (Marianne Williamson)

The next level in Robert Monroe's model that we learned to understand was Focus 21. We were raising our vibrations even further, and we were reaching the borderline between our Earth Life System state of mind and the universal state of mind without Earth's conditioning and limitations. We were flirting with the unknown beyond time and space. There are obviously many interpretations and understandings of what such a borderline can be. One of them might be a description of the spiritual belt around our planet where the souls or spirits of dead people reside as they decide whether to reincarnate or move on beyond the Earth Life System (ELS). The following is what happened to me when I reached Focus 21.

I encountered zillions of little silhouettes flowing like snowflakes and singing in beautiful heavenly tunes. It was obvious that they recognized my presence, and they were ready to communicate.

"Who are you, beautiful ones?" I was curious.

"Souls, Souls, Souls..." the heavenly cacophony started.

"Souls of whom?" I insisted.

"We cannot tell you yet, we cannot tell you yet, we cannot tell you yet..." and they continued in their incredible harmony seemingly not paying much attention to me.

The guidance on the tape had said it was time to return my mind fully into my body, but suddenly I realized that the window in the sheet through which I had sneaked up had been closed, and there was only a vast infinite membrane preventing me from seeing where I came from. I panicked, what did this mean, what was going to happen now? Then I cooled down and created a pickaxe and started digging, because I wanted to return down to my body. I was digging and digging, and the snowflake souls were singing: "You better do it, you better do it, you better do it…"

Having difficulty returning to reality happened to me so many times afterwards that I ended up building a metaphysical bulldozer to make sure I could always return. When I was sharing my story in the group session, Karen calmed me down by saying:

"We have not lost anybody yet, Jozef."

But I was still a bit fearful, so I asked Lee for a private consultation. During a quick light hypnosis, Lee helped me to create an Internal Self Helper (ISH) whom I could ask for advice when in trouble. I opted for a female and gave her the name, Kamaláska. She always carried a silhouette of a heart with her. The name, Kamaláska, was created by the Slovak singer Pavol Hammel. It means more than friend, but less than lover. I subconsciously felt that this would be what I might need. Only later could I fully appreciate Lee's help, when I learned that the concept of ISH would be explained during another Monroe program called Guidelines.

Kamaláska used to wait for me in the armchair in my living room whenever I returned home. She always indicated that she was there to support me and help me. She liked to take the form of Elena, the mother of my two sons. However, it was only the shape of Elena; I hoped that the true essence of my former wife was somewhere in a good and peaceful place.

This story illustrates the fear encountered by many, if not most, spiritual, and out of body travelers when they are beginning their journeys. It often causes them to lose courage and stops them continuing in their efforts. It is also the most frequently asked question by those who are interested in the topic but, at the same time, are scared to try:

"But what if I don't come back into my body?!"

This represents our ages old conditioned and

cultivated fear of death, which keeps us from having enough courage to venture beyond the temporary earthly vehicles that our physical bodies are. Later I understood that in my adventure, I had only touched the bottom of a vast ring of stacked souls hovering around our planet. For a long time, I needed a lot of effort to pass through this ring. Eventually, I developed mastery in passing through. It became exceptionally pleasurable to swish through quickly, because that ring is really like a deep pile of mud.

I now have much less physical fear in this life than I ever had before. I am not afraid of dying. Physical death is just like a graduation indeed. But beware of those who claim that they are not afraid of death at all. Here is what I learned much later about fear in a meditation when I was told:

"Fear will stay with you on a small residual level even when you are approaching zero. But you shall never reach zero. Fear can be missing in your spiritual existence, but a little bit of it shall always be with you in the physical realm. It is part of your earthly experience."

Chapter 8
MACHO

*"The highest form of human intelligence is to observe
yourself without judgment." (Jiddu Krishnamurti)*

As I wrote in the Chapter, Kickoff, during the
Gateway Voyage I became very confident because I started
to intuit that I was up to something big. I literally did not
recognize myself and started to have feelings that maybe I
was the "star" of the program. Being a shy guy from a
faraway country speaking in accented English, I obviously
started to suspect that something was very wrong with my
ego. I had not put any brakes on my desire to share my
stories in the group. I thought maybe I had been sharing them
just to shine and impress others, like that would be very
important.

Later, while in an altered state, I asked the Universe
for help. I sent the signal that I wanted to suppress my ego
because it had soared too high. Suddenly from somewhere in
the distance, a silhouette appeared. When it got closer, I
recognized a big six and a half feet tall muscular guy with
Mexican looks and a huge moustache. He was wearing a
large sombrero and brandishing a huge baton, and looking
straight into my eyes with a challenging posture, he
proclaimed:

"Hi, my name is Macho, and they sent me here to correct
your behavior. I will beat your ass you megalomaniac, just
bend over. How much you want?"

I reluctantly complied:

"Just give me twenty-five please, that should do it" was all I
was able to say in my state of shock.

"I'll give you fifty and you can call me anytime you need
me," and Macho really beat me up.

The feeling was the same as if he had really beaten me up in
the physical realm.

Obviously, sharing this story caused a lot of laughter from my fellow voyagers. But Karen let us know that we should never allow such an abuse. She also recommended that I let Macho know that he was not wanted. She emphasized that there was nothing wrong with ego if it was properly used as a positive and compassionate driving force.

Macho continued to bother me for quite a while even after I returned home from the Gateway Voyage. Whenever I would look down from my apartment's balcony, he would be standing in front of the entry gate waving at me with his baton and letting me know that he was there and ready for me. Finally, with the help of Kamaláska, I found the courage to put him on a bridge to another energy level and then shoot him far away deep into outer space.

As I learned from this story and many others later, we must be very careful about what we are creating with our mind. Every thought, every creation is shaping energy and it stays somewhere forever unless it can be returned by us, or without us, to the Source of Everything. But that is another story for later. You can always get what you want with your mind, what you wish for. As you will see later in the book, a mind and Love are the most powerful forces in the Universe and beyond. And that does not only apply for doing good, but also for doing bad.

The biggest addictions many of us have in our earthly lives are not alcohol, cigarettes, drugs, porn, sex, coffee, or anything like these. It is merely our need to be right in our opinions about everything. This need is driven by the ego. It can not only lead us into troubles of our own making but may cause us not to be liked by others. Ask yourself now if you, too, could benefit from some lessons about your oversized ego as I learned from the eager and willing Macho. I do suggest however, that you not allow such a harsh punishment as I experienced with him. But entering an internal dialogue with your ego can surely bring you some benefits for your life on our planet.

Chapter 9
FIRST KISS

"All the powers in the universe are already ours. It is we who have put our hands before our eyes and cry that it is dark." (Swami Vivekananda)

One exercise of the Gateway Voyage program was an illustration of what the power of the mind can do to self confidence and trust in ourselves. At first, we watched a video of beautiful imagery about the Earth, our planetary system, stars, galaxies, and clusters. Then we were told to use this imagery to take our minds on a trip out of our CHEC units up beyond the Earth, throughout our planetary system and the stars to the borders of the Universe and beyond.

After lifting out of the bed, I was passing through the roof and seeing the scenery of the surrounding mountains. The Monroe Institute became just a small point and soon flying much higher, I recognized the North American continent. The speed was getting faster and faster. Soon, our blue planet and Moon were just two small dots in the distance. When passing Pluto, I had the feeling that this little member of our solar system looked like a lost and forgotten child.

The incredible speed was changing our entire galaxy into a small dot of light, and soon I realized I was out of the entire known Universe. And I realized with stunning surprise:

"Our Universe does have boundaries!!!"

When the Universe had shrunk into the size of a soccer ball, I stopped my acceleration. I came back closer to the Universe and took all of it into my hands. I thought for a while what to do, and then I started to toss it from one hand to another. I was playing with the Universe just like Charlie Chaplin did with the Earth in his famous movie "Dictator."

Then I put the ball of the Universe on the

ground (which mysteriously appeared) and I was thinking:
"I can step on it and crush it if I want to."
I even raised my right foot ready to do so. Suddenly, I had a
bright flash of light in my head, and I heard:
"Oh no! You are not going to step on me, are you?"
I picked up the ball and put it in front of my mouth. Like
being hit by lightning, I immediately understood what I
desired and what I wanted and needed to do. I kissed the
Universe!

Our mind has incredible power, but we must be
careful and wise in how we use it. Those who regularly
meditate know that it is better not to have any expectations,
irrespective of how elaborate or masterful your intentions
may be. The products of meditation are almost always
unexpected, surprising and mind boggling.

After I kissed the Universe, the idea of writing this
book about my experiences was born, even though I had not
the slightest idea where my intentions would be going to take
me. I did not know yet that I would be able to kiss our
Universe much later in my journey in a much more powerful
way. At this point however, my still very short journey had
suddenly gained a completely new meaning and direction.

Chapter 10
GROUNDING

"I'm very much down to earth, just not this earth." (Karl
Lagerfeld)

After six days being immersed in Gateway Voyage, it
was time to go home. And that was not easy when you have
just been inspired to think about who you truly were. You
had forgotten about the outside world and time because, at
the beginning of the program, the facilitators had taken your
watch away and asked you to try not to cheat and check out
the time in other ways. During the week, you were away
from realities and confusions of everyday life, you were in a
wonderful environment with wonderful people, and you were
fed and otherwise completely taken care of. Now, it was time
to wake up and return to work, families, and friends. But our
minds were still levitating, and our vibrations were high.

That was why at the end of the program, we were
getting important instructions about grounding, about the
way to normalize ourselves back to everyday life. We were
watching a video about a guy returning home from Gateway.
He put his suitcase on the top of the car while talking or
checking something. Then, he got behind the steering wheel
and drove away. The suitcase was completely forgotten and
slid down from the roof onto the road. We also heard a story
about someone driving home to Texas but finding himself in
California. How funny! I laughed knowing it could not
happen to me since I was for sure in my full senses.

Then, I was driving home from the Charlottesville
area where the Monroe Institute is located. I was taking
route number 29 to the north toward Washington D.C. My
driving was very safe and enjoyable and all that had
happened in the program was going over and over through
my mind. I saw a gas station and stopped for gas and a drink.
As I was looking around, the environment was somehow

unfamiliar to me. I stepped into the convenience store and asked:

"How can I get back to route 29, please?"

"There is no route 29 here. Where do you need to go, Sir?" the lady asked me.

"Home to Washington, D.C."

"Oh, that is easy. Just continue to drive for several miles, hit the Richmond Beltway and it will take you to 95," was the answer.

Instead of going north from Charlottesville, I apparently had taken a wrong turn somewhere and drove southeast toward Richmond. The facilitators knew what they were talking about.

When you take courses such as Gateway Voyage or similar programs somewhere else, you must be aware that you are going to be changed and excited, unless you are in complete denial or ignorant. You also should not try to excite your friends by trying to make them share your enthusiasm. They will not. You will be on a high for a while. So just wait and let them come to you if they show interest. You accomplish much more if you are not pushy and allow possible communication about spirituality to develop naturally.

Chapter 11
KUNDALINI UNLEASHED

"True spiritual leaders have little need for the beliefs of others, for they are self-directed by spirit." (William Buhlman in Secret of the Soul, p.118)

Only two weeks after completing Gateway Voyage in September 2008, I headed to Poland Springs in Maine for a workshop with out-of-body explorer and teacher William Buhlman. My intention for this workshop was the same and very clear: to try to reach an out of body state as described in his books; not yet understanding a wider implications of an altered state of mind. I obviously had not grown up enough yet; I was obsessed, as many beginners are.

The workshop was held in a golf resort which was full of golfers and other tourists. It was a three-day workshop and William (Bill) was teaching all kinds of techniques and mechanics on how to separate one's mind from the body.

One of the techniques we were trying was called Pond. After entering a light hypnosis with the support of his own binaural music, Bill led us into an altered state. We imagined a path through a forest leading to a clearing in the woods with a small pond. We laid horizontally on the water and began to rotate our astral bodies around our third (solar plexus) chakra, first slowly, then speeding up more and more. Suddenly, a pipe with a diameter of about five inches touched my third chakra, and I was sucked into it with a powerful vortex like force. I was shot high into the sky. It was as if someone up there was very thirsty and had sucked me up with a huge straw. All my physical body started to shake uncontrollably; I forgot who and where I was.

Then I felt Bill's hand on my feet, and the shaking slowly weakened and stopped. He said he had to stop me. He asked me if I was out of body, but I could not confirm that absolutely since I had conditioned myself for an image. He said he had never seen anything like that before.

After that experience, I suggested in the follow-up discussion that maybe my astral body was so desperate to leave that it started to shake out of my physical body. Bill opined that it might have been a kundalini experience. At that time, I did not know what kundalini was and I did not want to admit it. But soon I learned that kundalini was the hidden energy sleeping at the base of our spine, coiled like a snake waiting to be unleashed. Once it is unleashed, you can utilize it for spiritual enlightenment.

On that afternoon in Poland Springs, subconsciously and without intention, I created a channel to my Higher Self which, after that, became ready to be activated whenever I needed it. It opened a way to get quickly to the higher levels of my own spiritual essence with relative ease and enabled me very effectively to continue in my magic quest.

Chapter 12
FLYING GRIZZLY

"I think that if you have a horse, pegasus, qilin or unicorn, you should sit on it! You should stroke its hair, whisper in its ear, be one with it! And you shouldn't feel sorry if other people don't have one." (C. Joy Bell C.)

After returning from Poland Springs, I decided to continue going to The Monroe Institute's programs after my life changing experience with the Gateway Voyage. I signed up for another program entitled Guidelines. It intrigued me, especially when I read in the description that it contained a portion described as "initial stages of out of body training." My obsession with the form based astral projection was still there, even though I had already intuitively started to feel that it was not where my future focus in spiritual research would be or should be.

I already knew that I could talk to my Internal Self Helper, Kamaláska. But I was also a little bit familiar with the concept of guides and helpers as beings who appear when we are in an altered state. Many religious people often call them guardian angels or just simply angels. I did not know the difference between Monroe's concept of ISH and guides and helpers described in other sources. Only later did I start to understand the distinction. I learned that I needed to build my relationship with my Internal Self Helper. I recognized that she would always be helpful, but never be a servant. She would help only if I would ask and be ready to receive.

But I had not the slightest idea of how to look for the guides, how to contact them or how to develop an effective communication with them. I had not yet discovered that the most amazing things in an altered state would be happening when I expected them least.

In the week before going to Guidelines, I tried to repeat the exercise, Pond, where I had the kundalini experience described in the previous chapter. My clear intention was again to reach a classical out of body state. I had been lying on the water and trying to form a vortex from my astral body and shoot it up. Instead, I suddenly saw next to me an animal head with teeth showing. It was slowly twirling up and pulling its body out of the water. I recognized the form of a grizzly bear. He started to talk to me:

"I want to warn you not to have incorrect expectations when you go to Guidelines. What you would most like to happen is not going to happen the way you expect. The purpose of your quest is very different. I guarantee you that a lot of amazing things will happen to you. I can be your Guide, if that is the name you would like to give me. I will be there for you anytime you would need me and ask me to help."

My not completely comfortable relationship with my first guide began. The grizzly later developed wings and was flying like Pegasus, because he figured out that I liked flying. He taught me a lot. He taught me to be polite, thankful, appreciative, as well as confident and curious. I often argued with him and asked for explanations and clarifications. Sometimes I even begged. Part of the Guidelines program was a laboratory exercise which used an isolated chamber with a waterbed. You can communicate with the facilitator through a microphone and headphones. My conversation with the Flying Grizzly was recorded by Skip Atwater. When I was listening to it later, I felt pathetic. All the time I was still arguing with my new spiritual friend about my unfulfilled desire, even though he had told me upfront it was not going to happen the way I was imagining.

Instead, later in the program he said:

"I am going to show you what you are missing by not concentrating on your main task."

Suddenly, something like a big bubble broke in front of my eyes and an unbelievably blue shining void opened with a completely euphoric feeling. The whole effect lasted only for several seconds, but even now whenever I think about it,

I feel a complete connection to God or Source of Everything.

Another time in Guidelines, the grizzly showed me an infinite sea of elliptically shaped clouds under one huge cloud with no boundaries to be seen. I later understood that I had seen zillions of spiritual beings on a very high level of vibrations with very loose forms hovering under and separated from the Ultimate Creator.

Chapter 13
REINCARNATIONS

"Whether or not we believe in survival of consciousness after death, reincarnation, and karma, it has very serious implications for our behavior." (Stanislav Grof)

Another fascinating struggle for the spiritual beginner, besides trying to get out of the body, is looking for past lives. Many esoteric researchers stop their quest right there. I am not talking about professional hypnotists and regression therapists, but about those who would merely like to discover their essence.

Identifying my reincarnations was fascinating for me just for a while. Ask yourself what human history of a regular guy like me or a girl like you reincarnating throughout the ages up to today would usually be; struggle for survival, looking for food and shelter, constant fear of enemies, fighting disastrous forces of nature, being tortured by the more powerful and mentally sick, and, at the end, often a violent or slow and horrifying death. I learned to understand this quickly. After discovering my most important reincarnations, I continued in uncovering others only occasionally. I was getting more and more similar senseless violent past lives. After a while, this research even became boring.

It is not difficult to learn about your past lives. You can ask many past life hypnotists for help, or you can do it through your own altered states, or as most would say, through meditation. You just need to disconnect from the present time and physical reality, open to the Universe and let the impressions start coming. Do not question their validity; what it is, it is. But ask for further details and clarifications as much as you can. Everything that has happened in our earthly past is recorded somewhere. Some call that somewhere the Akashic or Akasha records or library. The major thing is, if it happened it must be remembered and recorded somewhere. All your experiences and even your thoughts in this life and other lives are somewhere. Or do you think they are not? If not, they did not happen, and you were not having thoughts. And if they do exist, then there also must be a way to access and retrieve them.

In one of the inquiries about past lives, for example, I received an impression of being a clown in Saint Petersburg in Russia in the 17th century, standing in front of a window and thinking how I would entertain the guests when my daughter was at home gravely ill. Another impression I had was about a monk practicing stick fighting on a small plateau in the mountains. During a tactical retreat as that monk, I was not careful enough and fell into a deep ravine to my death. I was also an old, apparently sick, and weak female living more than thirty thousand years ago trying to die by walking into water.

But very soon I just wanted to have an overview, so I asked how many reincarnations I had on this planet. I did not question the validity of the answers. I learned that I have been here seven hundred times with ten possible reincarnations to go. I came to Earth approximately 91,000 years ago and the average turnover between lives has been about one hundred and thirty years.

The Guidelines program in January 2009 had only eleven participants with one facilitator, Patty Ray Avalon. She led us into an exercise called "Three most important reincarnations." Results from that exercise enabled me to focus on what has really been important in my spiritual journey on the Earth to date. I learned how to blend experiences from them into a complex picture about my mission in the few remaining years I must live in my present incarnation.

My most important life happened in the 15th century in Rhaeto Romansh Switzerland. For the first time, I received a name related to a specific incarnation. The name was Menev, and I have continued to use it without any further questioning. As Menev, I was a folk healer helping the sick and comforting the dying, solving arguments, pacifying fights, making love connections, and educating and guiding children. I was the guy bringing joy and peace to everybody wherever I went.

In my second most important incarnation, I was a Viking Shaman in the middle of the 9th century. Later I identified my name as Skjoerg. I was the keeper of spiritual discipline in our village, but my most important task was motivating and preparing soldiers for battles. When I received this impression, I did not know anything about shamans. Later when I learned about who they were, I was really surprised that the Vikings had them too. For the third most important past life, I received only the name Platus. Later in a series of meditations, I was able to clarify the name to be Titus Maccius Plautus, the Roman comedy playwright.

It is not my intention to write a lot here about reincarnations. There are many books describing the topic in detail and giving more guidance on how to proceed. I just wanted to illustrate another small step leading me to the essence of my quest. But looking at my three most important incarnations makes perfect sense when I compare them to the three most powerful drives in my present life. First, like Menev, I love to give people various healing advice related to their physical conditions and advice which could help them mentally and emotionally. I am trying to bring people together and I simply love people around me. I have often acted as a natural peacemaker. Second, I love to investigate and explain connections between our physical world and the Other Side. Shamans do that. And third, I like to tell and write stories, and I also try to be funny as much as I can. That is what Titus Maccius Plautus had been doing a long time ago.

Chapter 14
PARK

"Knowing yourself is the beginning of all wisdom."
(Aristotle)

During the program, Guidelines, we also learned to visit a spiritual place called the Park in the Monroe model. It has the Focus Level of 27. It is the state of mind where you can evaluate your life which has just ended on the Earth. Your guides, helpers, spiritual teachers, angels (or however you call them) are helping you to understand your development in your previous life and they are preparing you for your next conscious reincarnation. You do not have to call this place The Park, but I will use that name for the sake of an easy discussion. To get there after you die, you must find the way. You can prepare yourself for that during this life, or someone can help you after you die. But be aware that there are unwanted states of consciousness between a physical life and something like The Park.

There is a very dense nonphysical ring around our planet described by Robert Monroe as Focus Levels 22 and 23. Focus Level 22 is usually occupied by people still physically alive on Earth, but who are mentally disturbed in many ways like having dementia, Alzheimer's disease, heavy drug dependency, or schizophrenia, etc., or they may be in a coma. Large parts of their earthly minds are out of their bodies most of the time without being controlled or influenced by their left brain.

Focus 23 is the equivalent of what many esoteric researchers call the lower astral plane. People who are dead reside there if they have lost connections to their higher selves and do not know their spiritual identity. Most of what they remember is their last finished earthly life, its pleasures, and struggles. They are either in a hurry to go back or they are reluctant to go back depending on whether they liked their earthly experiences, or they did not. One way or the other, they are stuck. All they want to do is to hibernate there or quickly recycle back to Earth without any notion of what they would like to accomplish. As I wrote before, developed spiritual beings will have no attraction to this Focus Level when they are passing through it.

Other obstacles to a smooth transition of souls trying to reach a reconnection to their higher selves are the areas of consciousness inhabited by likeminded departed souls. These souls are still under the strong influence of their religious or other types of leaders from their earthly lives. In Monroe's model, they occupy Focus Levels 24 to 26, which Robert Monroe defined as Belief System Territories (BST). Myriads of souls can reside between the dense ring of stuck souls and the Park. There is much more organization in the BSTs than in the Focus 23, and they are usually separated from each other. They look a bit like spiritual islands. You can find the departed souls of members of as many kinds of organized groups as you can imagine.

When I was returning from the Park for the first time, an interesting thing happened. At first, what I recognized was a choir loudly singing "Soyuz nerushimij," the national anthem of the former Soviet Union. I observed buildings full of diehard communists continuing to believe in their cause. During my countless spiritual travels into the Park and higher vibrational levels, I observed the variety of BSTs where people were enslaved, controlled, and manipulated, as well as those organized very loosely and kept together only by the free will of the participants. I shall have much more about them and BSTs in general later in the book.

The Park itself seems to be very old, according to some researchers, more than three hundred thousand years old. It is situated on a plateau with a lake in the middle and forested hillsides all around. At first look, you notice immediately that many people are also walking around with their pets. The guide at the entrance station told me that the woods are designed for those who need solitude during their recoveries from traumas caused by their earthly struggles and tragedies.

The plateau has a variety of buildings, each with a different purpose. The Recovery center where rescued or retrieved souls are led on arrival has two main parts; the first one is for those with sudden traumas caused by deadly accidents, and the other one is for longer traumas caused by a lifetime of troubles on Earth. The other buildings are for continuous study and preparation for subsequent reincarnations.

We were told that we would spend much more time in the Park during another Monroe Institute program called Exploration 27.

Chapter 15
THE MONROE PROTOCOL

"A dream doesn't become reality through magic; it takes sweat, determination and hard work." (Gen. Colin Powell)

Whenever we decide to systematically engage in any repeated activity leading to established goals, it is usually very helpful to develop a routine practice. Such a routine enables us to quickly reach those areas where we have already been. Imagine doing underground research by building a system of small tunnels, passageways, and hallways. Once you have dug them out, they are there, and you can quickly approach your intended target from the starting point of the system. We can do the same with the passageways we have built in our minds through meditating practices where the starting point is our physical realm. The Monroe system calls our physical realm Consciousness One (C1). After learning how to reliably reach an altered state, I started to call my way of preparation the Monroe Protocol. What is the Monroe Protocol?

I always use the preparation just as we were taught in the Gateway Voyage. Even after all my experiences as described in this book, it still works very well for me in its original form with only a little bit of modification. That is why I call it The Monroe Protocol. Before every meditation, I set up an intention concerning what I want to ask and with whom I want to communicate. Usually, I have three questions for one meditation. However, what happens in the target area while I am communicating with the desired or just appeared entity is another story altogether.

Sometimes, nothing happens, or I get an answer to only one question. Other times, it can be a whole truckload of information. I always carry my intention with me into higher vibrational levels because meditation without intention feels to me like driving without a destination. Obviously, you can argue that you can just enjoy driving for pleasure without going somewhere in. I agree with you that meditation without intention can be very relaxing, calming and rewarding. I just prefer otherwise.

I always meditate while lying on my back in a flat bed with my hands on either side of my body. That way, I am not distracted by even the slightest tensions in my body muscles. The first goal is to reach a state of deep breathing and general relaxation of the whole body.

Then I imagine opening my Security Repository Box and putting away everything that could distract me during meditation.

Next, I follow up with resonant tuning to bring my body and mind into higher vibrations. After that I do the affirmation, sometimes reciting it in my mind, sometimes just listening to it from the recording.

Next, I activate the chakras, beginning with the heart chakra. Then I move down the spine to the three lower chakras and then back up to the three upper chakras, with the crown chakra coming last. After that, I create a protection balloon all around my body with rays coming out of the crown chakra and entering the base chakra.

The last step in the preparation is the ten-point relaxation of the muscles of the whole body, beginning with the toes and ending with the top of the head. This leads me to Focus 10 where the body is asleep, but the mind is awake.

When all this is done properly with a clear intention and affirmation, an altered state appears almost immediately, characterized by muscle paralysis and slight vibrations all over the body. The so-called monkey mind is suppressed, and my awareness is centered on the intention. I know very clearly if I am there or not. If I am not, I give up.

There is no guarantee of being able to enter an altered state at will. But at the very least, I can always effectively use the guidance from the recordings to move myself into different Focus Levels.

Depending on what I want to accomplish, I look either for my Internal Self Helper, my guides, or other higher beings whom I shall call Star Friends. Or I just simply go to a spiritual place and see who is available or shows up there to help me.

ISH usually shows up at Focus 15 or 21; the guides like to hang around in the Park; and for the star friends, I must look well beyond the Earth Life System.

With communications, you must be free of any expectations, you must be completely open minded and polite and grateful. Then, the possibilities for learning and growth are boundless and the downloads of information will flow smoothly.

All I have described here was working wonderfully and I thought I was building my spiritual growth very well. But then one month after Guidelines, something happened that brought me to my knees and threw me into a deep depression.

I traveled to Stockholm.

Chapter 16
GRAND THEFT IN STOCKHOLM

"If Satan wasn't around, churches would go out of business." (Marilyn Manson)

My lady at that time, Alenka, and I arrived in Stockholm, Sweden in February 2009 for an elaborate celebration of the birthday and life achievements of her friend who was a prominent Swedish lawyer. We arrived at the Hotel Rica across from the train station early in the morning. We had to wait in the small lobby because our room was supposed to be ready only in the afternoon. We were tired after the overnight trip from the United States.

When they finally called us to go to our room, I realized that during the moving of our luggage toward the elevator my backpack had disappeared. Even though the taxi driver in front of the hotel confirmed seeing a young man running away with my backpack, it was too late to pursue him. Hotel surveillance tapes showed that the job was done by three apparently professional thieves. One of them was pretending to look for something on the lobby computer for tourists, the second guy was distracting Alenka next to the elevators, and the third one was on the watch to signal the right moment.

My travel documents, important medications, several hundred dollars in cash, a digital camera with hundreds of irreplaceable pictures from other travels, and expensive audio equipment were all gone. The Police came and took the report, but they were unable to find the perpetrators even after several weeks had passed.

The thief who calmly walked and then ran away with my backpack wore a woolen hat with purple and white horizontal stripes each about an inch and a half wide.
"That is interesting, purple is the Miranon color for Focus 20 and white is the color for Focus 21", I thought to myself.

Miranon colors are the colors associated in the Monroe model with the Focus Levels between Focus 15 and 21. Focusing on colors when rising through the vibrations is very helpful in the transition to 21 (15 is blue, 16 is red, 17 is yellow, 18 is pink, 19 is green, 20 is purple and 21 is white). I almost immediately suspected that the theft had something to do with my spiritual quest. But now I had to move on and get replacement medications and travel papers and continue with the trip program, even though my whole festive mood was gone, and I felt miserable. But the worst was yet to come.

Two days after the theft, I woke up very early in the morning and wanted to record my dream in my diary which I always carried with me wherever I went. But that morning in Stockholm, I realized that my diary with everything else that I have already described, and much more, was gone. My irreplaceable Diary was in the stolen backpack.

Before I continue, I must explain the importance of keeping a diary for every spiritual explorer. If you want to progress either just with your dreams or with your meditations, a handwritten diary is a must. Never mind how sophisticated your computer, smartphone or tablet is, it cannot replace the importance of the intimate process of recording by hand into a good old-fashioned diary.

I had been recording my dreams sporadically for years, but when I started my spiritual journey, I intuitively knew that I had to record everything. I mean everything. Even now, when I wake up in the middle of the night from having a dream, I get out of bed to record it. When I meditate, I use the simple command, Remember, to help me carry information back to the physical realm (C1). Then I immediately write everything down upon awakening.

When I found out that my precious diary was gone, the world around me just crashed down. I felt like my Soul and heart had been ripped away. I was devastated, like never in my life, and I literally wanted to die. Alenka woke up, too.

She told me that something very heavy was all around me and she knew that something very bad had happened to me. The TV set was on with a scrambled picture, and it did not react to the remote buttons in any way. I had to pull its plug from the wall to shut it off.

Alenka was a devoted Roman Catholic, and she was not interested in my spiritual journey, or as she used to call it, "that satanic stuff." She tolerated my Monroe trips, but we were unable to have any sensible conversation on the topic. That morning she said:

"Maybe Jesus wants you back."

It was pointless to try to explain to her that I had not run away from Jesus. On the contrary, I was already understanding him much better because I had started to go inside my Soul. (For behold, The Kingdom of God is within you; Luke 17:21.)

It took me a long time to truly recover, especially because I thought I would never be able to fully recollect all that had happened since my journey had begun up to the theft in Stockholm. That is also why, eventually, you might notice that the previous part of my book might be different from what follows. The part up to now has been written based on what I remembered from the Monroe programs and other meditations, and what I was able to recollect without the support of my stolen diary. Obviously, many dreams and other recordings were lost without the possibility to recover them. The next part of this book is based more on my diligently written diaries and experiences, and especially dialogues, which are presented exactly as they happened.

Ten days after the theft, I had a dream about a small child falling from high rocks into the sea. I was able to save him and hold him in my hands. The child was around three years old but talked like an adult. At that time, I did not have my current methodology of understanding and analyzing dreams as messages from nonphysical realms. But it was obvious to me that the child represented a new spiritual me and that it needed more protection and guidance while growing up. Those who were helping me from the Other Side, even though I did not know them yet, had sent me the dream. And I was slowly getting back on my feet.

Chapter 17
SHAMAN

"Your vision will become clear only when you look into your heart. Who looks outside, dreams. Who looks inside, awakens." (Carl Jung)

After the theft of my diary, I started to struggle with a dilemma. All information seemed to point to the fact that it was just a perfectly organized common crime. On the other hand, I had no doubt that there was a connection with the spiritual realm and that the initiation to commit such a despicable act could have come from there.

Many religions on our planet are teaching about how the devil, in one guise or another, seduces us from the Other Side. We are subjects not only inspiring spiritual forces enabling us to do magnificent, good, but we are also the targets of evil forces who want us and others to cause harm. Did this happen in my case? Were the thieves manipulated from the Other Side? It took me a while to pull myself completely out of my depression to the point that I was able to start to recollect my experiences as described up to now.

In April 2009 during my visit to Sedona, Arizona, I met M.I.T. trained scientist Pete A. Sanders Jr. He founded an educational non-profit organization called Free Soul, and he also conducts guided tours into the energetic vortexes around Sedona.

Sanders promotes a so called "Soul stretching." According to his explanations, we can tap into targets with only a fraction of our Soul. Whereas in "Soul traveling," only a silver cord is holding the Soul bound to the physical body. He also maintains that we can meditate with open eyes or while walking. He recommends frequent grounding in order, as he says, "not to bliss out." It is a completely opposite approach to the conscious out of body techniques.

Meeting and having a conversation with Pete helped

me later to create and form my own understanding of how consciousness can partially leave the body for effective exploration without the need to be fully out of body. I can now simply say that consciousness can be stretched out of the body like a giant piece of chewing gum without the need to have any defined diameter or length of connection with the body.

After returning from Sedona, I signed up for the program, Shaman's Heart, at TMI mainly because it had that magic word, Shaman, in it. I already knew that I had been a Viking Shaman. But I also had an intention to either resolve my struggle or, if nothing significant would happen in that program, to simply quit the whole thing and live my life like anybody else. I had spent not only almost all my vacation time to go to these programs, but also a lot of money. Monroe courses are not cheap, but they take complete perfect care of you, and I am not sorry for even one penny that I have spent there.

I arrived at the Nancy Penn Center of the Monroe Institute in June 2009 and again immediately felt the peace and magic of the place. My vibrations obviously jumped up. In a dream in the first night in my CHEC unit, I was out of body and back in my workplace at The Voice of America. In the dream, I saw my physical body sitting in one armchair and my astral body in another chair. The astral body was talking to someone I did not recognize. Then my astral body went over to my physical body, and I was amazed to watch how they merged. At first, the head of the astral body slowly merged with the head of the physical body and then the rest of the astral body slipped in. My coworker Phil came to the room, and I told him:

"Phil, I was just out of my body."

"Oh Joe, Joe, you always have some interesting stuff to tell," said Phil in his typical posture of the distinguished gentleman he always was.

He started to laugh, waved his hand over me, and left the

room. In waking up from my dream, I became aware of our multidimensional nature for the first time. I had been in three different dimensions at the same time. And, in one of them, I had met Phil's other body, because apparently at that time, his physical body was also sleeping in his Maryland home. My recovery process was going full steam.

The Shaman's Heart program was led by Byron Metcalf. He is a long-time musician, drummer, percussionist, recording artist and producer, but also a shamanic practitioner, researcher, and teacher. He was assisted by facilitator Karen Malik, whom I met for the second time. Unfortunately, this wonderful course is not included in TMI programs anymore. Byron created an excellent mix of traditional shamanic techniques and Hemi Sync technology supported by his and Steve Roach's award-winning music. I think he set the standard for how outside teachers should adapt into the TMI environment.

Byron led us into a synchronization of our heart energy with fifty-five beats of music a minute in a group setting. We were doing invocations and inviting spirits into our group. It was here that I learned to start any activations of the chakras from the heart chakra. We were practicing the opening of our hearts with intentions to focus on forgiveness and tenderness.

At that time, I was already working with several guides of mine and three of them were taking the forms of my three most important reincarnations. In one of the meditations, Skjoerg the Shaman suddenly arrived sitting on a Flying Grizzly. He slid down from the bear and said to me: "Do not be so tight, I am going to teach you how to establish a connection between where you are and where I am. Relax and dance with me!"
But I was not in the mood for something like that:
"Stop that, Shaman; what are you drunk, or what? I need to talk to you!"
I answered with my body shaking heavily and feeling my

physical heart wildly beating all the way up into my throat, but Skjoerg jumped back on the grizzly and left.

Next time, I tried to invite the Shaman to talk to me, but instead the scenery appeared with soldiers and horses gathering near water for preparation to go into battle on anchored long ships and boats. I saw myself as the shaman giving the soldiers drinks from a wooden kettle. They were eagerly drinking and then wildly slaughtering goats. Blood was everywhere, and soldiers were leaving. My wife came to help me cut out the goat's hearts and line them up on the long wooden table.

I felt that something was trying to pull my physical mouth apart and I tried to leave the scene and go back to my original intention. It had been vividly and morbidly annoying. But I saw carts carrying dead soldiers and decapitated heads of enemies despite my effort to leave the scene. The cohort was heading to the village. As Skjoerg the Shaman, I was dancing around the carts and rattling chains. Soon a wild celebration with eating and drinking threw the whole village into a frenzy. I felt like I needed to throw up all the sludge accumulated inside of me. I did not know yet that it was going to happen later.

When I was later sharing the story in the group, a fellow participant, Karl, told me that I was dealing with berserkers, an elite group of Viking warriors often going into battle while in a trance.

Wednesday was the day set aside for learning holo-shamanic breath work. An expert in this field, Sandy Phocas, was also present to help Byron and Karen with the group. They divided the group into couples. When the traveler was doing the breath work while lying on an inflatable mattress, the other one, called the sitter, was assisting with whatever was necessary. Then the roles switched for the second half of the day.

The technique was simple: breathe as fast and as deeply as you could; be open minded and see what was going to happen. But we were not supposed to expect anything specific when going into the trance. For those taking their turns in the afternoon, lunches were not recommended.

In the morning, I was the sitter for my partner, Nancy. She was very quiet during her trance, but everyone else had been behaving very wildly in theirs. I wondered why they were doing that. Some of them were twisting their bodies and limbs into all sorts of positions like giant worms. Others were shaking, screaming, turning around on mattresses, moaning, or even grumbling. Nancy was licking her lips like she was extremely thirsty. After the exercise, everyone drew pictures representing their experiences. They then shared them with the sitters.

In the afternoon, it was my turn to be on the mattress. During the breathing leading into the trance, I tried to follow my Monroe Protocol. But shortly after I finished the activations of chakras, my body was taken into the same worm-like dance; I was turning around, violently throwing my limbs into the air. Now I understood why the others did the same in the morning session. I had completely forgotten my intentions. I was cursing someone in Slovak and soon I saw why.

The thief from Stockholm had appeared wearing his purple and white striped hat. My hatred for him soon magnified itself into contempt for all those who consciously hurt other human beings. I needed to vomit, and I was glad that I had listened to the recommendation and had not had lunch. Sandy Phocas made sure that I was okay, and she held a bucket for me. When I cooled down, I asked ISH to take me to the Akashic Library. I had no reason for that; I just intuitively felt that it was what I needed to do.

We were walking between the shelves, and she pulled out a file on the thief from Stockholm. I learned he was a fellow Roman soldier who had killed me next to Hadrian's Wall in England. Now in our present reincarnations, he had found me again with the intention to kill me again, or, at least, destroy my life. I felt like getting angry again, but instead I heard my ISH:

"No, you do not want him to get you again!"

I cooled down and the trance faded.

Finally, relief came as I recognized why the Stockholm theft had happened. Apparently hate, like love, is not limited by distance or time. The thief probably was not aware that he might had been driven not just by the desire to commit a common crime, but also by forces from beyond our physical reality. I understood that, and I was trying to forgive him. I was cool, peaceful, and suddenly completely euphoric. I wanted to sing.

Beautiful imagery followed. I was flying over many of the beautiful places I have flown over in my physical life. From above I saw again the North Carolina Outer Banks, Kilauea lava fields and the Hamakua Coast of Hawaii, Buenos Aires, Croatia's coast, Prague, Kosice, Ljubljana, and Paris. Serene and peaceful flying brought me back into the physical realm. Byron and Sandy made sure I was fine and that all was okay. I knew that I wanted to hit the spiritual road again.

Chapter 18
BACK ON THE ROAD

"A man contains all that is needed to make up a tree; likewise, a tree contains all that is needed to make up a man. Thus, finally, all things meet in all things, but we need a Prometheus to distill it." (Cyrano de Bergerac in The Other World, 1657)

I became eager to know more about everything. I was back home in Washington, routinely getting up very early in the morning when my mind and everything around was peaceful and quiet, and when meditation was most effective. I was still operating in the Earth Life System for ninety-nine percent of the time. I was only occasionally crossing beyond its boundaries, but I did not know yet how to connect with higher beings. Sometimes when I was passing through the ring of the lower astral plane, I was detecting my wider family members, friends and schoolmates who had died and left the physical Earth. I was not sure yet how to contact them or how to communicate with them.

I quickly signed up for the TMI program, Lifeline, to be held only five weeks after Shaman's Heart in July 2009. According to the brochure, the tools of Lifeline should enable participants to contact departed ones and eventually help them if they are stuck.

Meantime while waiting for Lifeline, I continued in my effort of asking very fundamental questions about our creation and purpose.

In my most important reincarnation as Menev, I was able to routinely communicate with nonphysical realms, guides, and creators. I learned from my guides that these creators were created by the Ultimate Creator. Such creators, besides other activities, also cultivated our planet. Not only do we need creators, but they also need us. Like us when we want to learn and develop, they need challenges. And our physical environment is the densest end of the manifestations created by God.

As such, it is the most difficult existence a spiritual being can experience while incarnated. I am proud to be here where everything is so difficult, and I am proud to be a human. This planet is not for sissies! I no longer want to rush to go back "home" to the spiritual world; I do not want to die yet. We here on this gorgeous little piece of rock might very well be at one of the most beautiful places in this Universe. We are a highly developed manifestation of God, and as such, we are always protected. Our planet is protected by our creators as much as they can in the face of the incredible and, at times, destructive powers of Nature.

But the creators and God also need us for another reason which lies at the core of our entire existence. Robert Monroe named that reason the Loosh. What is it? It is a non-form substance created by the emotions and experiences of sentient living beings. The Loosh is flowing back to God, the Ultimate Source; and it is our payback for the gift of our creation, and the gift of Love we are receiving from God.

Some misunderstand this very important relationship and mistakenly say that Robert Monroe described us as if we were animals in a Zoo. Not so fast my friends, stop and think! God gives us the driving force which enables our existence. God is also constantly sending us Love. Are we not supposed to give our Ultimate Creator something in return? Are we not supposed to at least cherish and magnify that Love? There is no doubt that the Love from God and the Loosh produced by us are interconnected in a loop and are intended by the Ultimate Creator to be in perfect harmony.

But as spiritual beings get farther away from the Source, the manifested environment becomes denser and denser. And godly Love is pouring into more and more difficult conditions. The Love itself becomes compromised. We must relearn how to love because, by incarnating into this denser and material world, we tend to forget more and more just why we were created. These were the first conclusions about the magic of creation that I received during conversations with my guides, but I had no idea that it would be just the beginning of revelations yet to come.

Chapter 19
RETRIEVALS

"If Heaven ain't a lot like Dixie, I don't wanna go!" (Hank Williams, Jr.)

I attended The Lifeline program at the Monroe Institute in July 2009. Out of nineteen participants, five were Japanese, with some of them not even speaking English very well. One lady came from Holland and one from Saudi Arabia. I had the wonderful opportunity to see Karen Malik for the third time. The other facilitator was the remote viewer Paul Elder from British Columbia in Canada.

The primary purpose of Lifeline is to inspire those of us who are living on the planet to help those who have died and are not physically present on Earth anymore but are generally stuck in Focus 23. But again, this is just the name in Monroe's model. We can also call such area of consciousness: limbo, bardo as in Tibetan Buddhism, purgatory or otherwise.

Even though there is no satisfactory explanation as to why it is possible, certain humans on Earth are able during their spiritual journeys to help these lost souls to move on to better places. In the Monroe way, we learn tools that are useful for trying to help them reach The Park. At the same time, we can also retrieve parts of ourselves, because as I shall report later, we are very complex multidimensional and structured spiritual beings.

During the Lifeline program itself and afterwards, I performed dozens of such actions whether we call them rescues, retrievals or otherwise. I helped many departed family members, friends, coworkers I knew, but also some known personalities and unknown departed souls from our planet. But I will keep the describing of such actions to a minimum to keep the focus of this book on spiritual information and discoveries about our human essence and the essence of Divinity not yet published anywhere else.

According to the suggestions at Lifeline, the most effective way to approach retrievals requires a relaxed, focused and determined mind of the rescuer. The facilitators suggested that we go to the Park first and ask for a guide and then go back to Focus 23 to look for souls needing help. That was what I always tried to do, but often I would detect subjects for retrievals on my way to the Park. I had to promise them often that I would come back.

During one of my first rescue trips, I even had a brief conversation in Focus 22 with my somewhat mentally challenged brother who was wandering there even though he was still physically alive on Earth. Such personalities still alive on Earth hang on here while large parts of their earthly minds are stretched into Focus 22, just below Focus 23. In the time of our interaction, my brother was apparently physically sleeping in Slovakia. The whole conversation just made me very sad, and I cried deeply.

Regardless of whether I was on a direct mission or I just met someone in Focus 23, I would go to the Recovery Center and ask an official there to give me a rescue vehicle, sometimes with a crew, sometimes without. The official was originally introduced to me as "Morphon." At that time, I had no idea that his name was connected to the "morphogenetic field," about which I only learned later.

Some souls in the lower astral plane just hibernate, others can create environments around them that are reflecting and reminding them of their last earthly lives. If they died unexpectedly, they may be in a cycle of playing their departing situations again and again.

For example, I encountered a group of fifteen Roman and Celtic fighters viciously continuing in their battle killing each other and then rising again in a cycle. During my intervention, I screamed at them trying to explain the absurdity of the situation. Some of them looked at me and immediately spread their hands and flew towards higher vibrations. Yet others continued in their senseless fight.

In another example, a young man who had died by crashing his sports car into a tree continuously cried and cursed himself more over the totaled vehicle then his own death. Only when I had persuaded him he was dead was he able to leave the scene and head on to higher realms. Likewise, a young girl who was the victim of the big tsunami of 2004 was desperately holding onto a tree terrified to be let go even though she was dead. She was very relieved when I helped her.

Remember, time from our point of view means nothing there; there is no time, all is in the present. We can see situations in time because we are able to transfer parallel information from our right brain into a sequence in our left brain.

I found a deceased former coworker from Czechoslovakia. She had created a beautiful beach and a lovely piece of the Dalmatian coast because it was the most pleasant environment she remembered. But she was alone and bored, and after she recognized me and accepted my appeal, she also "flew" up.

The deceased former chief of our sport umbrella sponsoring group told me he was hibernating most of the time because he was unable to find connections. In his life, he had been an admirer of the antique world. Now, he was impressed by the Latin spoken to him by the Plautus reincarnation fragment of my Soul, so he finally stepped into the rescue vehicle.

The deceased father of my first wife was tremendously enjoying his ability to get rid of his huge belly caused by liver disease. Now he obviously looked much younger than he had when he died. But I had some difficulty to persuade him to go to the Recovery Center. He told me that he "would not want to go to any nuthouse."

The father of my second wife had been an artist and he was fascinated by the sudden opportunity to be easily creative in any manner he wanted. He agreed to move on only when I described to him the incredible variety of colors in the Park.

My Grandfather had some contacts in Focus 23, but he did not like that everybody was telling him that he would have to go quickly back to Earth. He had died of cancer, and he remembered the pain very well. Now he was relieved when I told him there was no need to hurry and that he could plan everything in the nice environment of the Park.

And, finally, when we were passing the Belief System Territories, my former boss from Slovakia was passionately cursing both communists and Catholics, because in his life on the Earth he had hated them both.

Later, sometimes in following trips, I would check on those people whom I helped to get to The Park to see how they were doing there.

Chapter 20
ELENA

"Look at everybody through the eyes of love, not the eyes of judgment." (Joel Osteen)

Not all departed souls are hopelessly stuck in Focus 23 on the lower astral plane. Many of them are enjoying a continuation of their earthly ways even if they do not have their physical bodies anymore. Some of them discover that they can create practically anything with their minds; they create environments they remember from their last incarnation on the Earth and try to enjoy them. They do not have physical pains, but they cannot have their earthly pleasures like sex which require physical bodies. Sooner or later, they realize that they are stuck, even though not in such a hopeless way as those who do not know where they are or what happened to them. Many of the souls on the lower astral plane are staying there for a variety of reasons, such as waiting for relatives or friends to join them when they die.

That was the case of my deceased wife Elena, the mother of my sons. I have to say here that, when you start to play with your vibrations and openly accept the possibility of the existence of the spiritual world, many things can start to happen. My guides told me that I could expect sensual contacts from the Other Side. You might hear sounds and voices when no one is around, you can be touched, teased, or gently pulled. Things like that have happened to me countless times during my spiritual journey. Your dreams become more vivid and diversified. One day I was awakened by someone touching me gently on the inner side of my left thigh and I clearly heard:
"Jožko, what is the title of the book you are reading now?"
No one was in my bedroom, and I was touched exactly the way my departed wife Elena used to do, and without doubt the voice belonged to her. That was my first contact with her

without realizing its tremendous impact on me at that time.

I have already described Elena's showing up at The Monroe Institute when the castle appeared in front of me. Elena was not only able to move around in Focus 23, but she also lowered her vibrations to meet me. She had no intention of moving into any higher vibrations beyond those of Focus 23. Here is what happened when I found her in July 2009 during a retrieval exercise in Lifeline:

"Come on, My Love, you should not stay here, I want to take you to a better higher place!" I suggested, and she answered: "Here we go again; you are trying to fool me again. You always thought you were especially smart and often you were making things up. I do not believe that there is anything higher. I believe in what I have here. I have my home now and my friends. I can go to sleep whenever I want and as much as I want. I have rest and peace. I still love you; I never stopped, and you know it very well. I know you are going to tell me again that you need to go somewhere as you did many times before. But I am going to wait here for you until you decide to stay here with me all the time, not just visiting as you do now. And then, we will wait for our boys to join us."

"Sweetheart, you are much more than you think you are, you had many other lives, and you have other husbands from those lives and maybe thousands of children. I do also!" I tried again.

Soon I knew there was not time yet for a retrieval of her Soul. I returned to the Recovery Center with the vehicle and its crew. Morphon just said:

"Oh, another no show. Do not worry Menev, we have plenty of no shows. You can try another time."

I knew already that I had also hurt Elena in one of our common previous lives, when she was Hilda. I could only speculate whether she knew about it or not. After my rescue attempt, I was asking my guides for advice for how I could help her. The usual answer was that nobody could force the issue and her will should be respected. But I was not going to give up.

Later in August during a meditation at my home, I found her again. I knew I had to listen to her first. She talked a lot and she expressed sorrow that I left her, and she said she knew I was missing her very much afterwards. She said if I had not left her during our marriage on Earth, she maybe would not have died, and we could have a good and happy life. She insisted she would have fulfilled all my fantasies and she would have been loyal despite all my shortcomings, and she would have continued to make me happy. I could not argue with that. If she had not died, I would probably be with her today, if she would also want it while in her physical body, of course. After she finished I said:

"Please My Love, come with me right now. All that you have here is just illusion. I shall get you to wise spiritual beings who can really help you to understand who you truly are. And after that if you would still like to be with me, we can fly all over the Universe holding each other's hand."

She surprisingly and reluctantly sat down in the rescue vehicle. I had to hold her attention by hugging and kissing her form as we were passing the Belief System Territories. It did have happened to me before that souls would suddenly jump out and disappear after being attracted by a spiritual island in that area. When I woke up after the meditation, I cried and cried. Only later, I realized how important the rescuing of Elena was for me. Now I did not have to worry about her eventual efforts to block my spiritual development.

Months later, I visited her in the Park. She said she was learning a lot and she thanked me. She said she never had doubts that I would find her. Her love for me had always been simple, straightforward, and genuine. I was the one who did not walk the line.

Chapter 21
BELIEF SYSTEM TERRITORIES

"I dreamed I was there in hillbilly heaven, Oh what a beautiful site!" (Country song with Tex Ritter)

You already may understand these territories from previous chapters. During our life on this planet, most of us experience a variety of affiliations to different religious, political, spiritual, or other groups. Others of us might be loners or we just did not build any such connections. When we die, the law of attraction also applies in the nonphysical world. We might end up with the group of souls we are most attracted to in those territories, unless we become stuck in Focus 23. Other more highly developed spiritual beings might shoot up quickly and directly to something like the Park.

During my spiritual travels, I discovered that the Belief System Territories are very vast. Most beings have safe feelings when they encounter people and environments that remind them of their earthly lives, so they go to the familiarity of those to which they were attracted. We are naturally afraid of the unknown; therefore, we select what is giving us a sense of security, even though it can be very deceiving and misleading.

Some might argue that the Park is also a Belief System Territory, and they might have a point. But there is a stark difference. The Belief System Territories are usually controlled by beings who have an agenda. Unfortunately, the leaders there are often driven by the desire to keep power over other beings. I encountered many such BSTs, whether religious, atheistic, satanic, totalitarian, slave societies or others. Intellectual, scientific, artistic, musical, or similar BSTs are more tolerant and relaxed, but they still have specific lifestyles and agendas.

The only agenda of the Park is for us to review the

just finished earthly life, recover from traumas, evaluate karma, and reconnect to our Higher Self. The goal is to eventually prepare for the next conscious reincarnation by formulating clear intentions of what is to be accomplished. As I will describe later, some highly developed souls who have finished their earthly education might decide to leave the Earth Life System altogether and proceed further with their development in other physical or nonphysical systems.

There are lots of movements between the individual Belief System Territories or "BST islands." If we use our planet as a reference point, we can talk about movements downwards, upwards, or lateral. Obviously, we are not talking about physical movements in space, but the vibrational movements of spiritual beings. For example, someone becomes bored with a situation and moves into another spiritual island. Others might decide to change to another group for a variety of other reasons. They usually will move laterally into a different group on a similar vibrational level. For example, a Catholic decides to become a protestant; or a Hindu might try to be a Muslim for a while; or a Buddhist joins the Shinto BST.

Other souls might reincarnate quickly back to Earth, because they remember goodies like sex, booze, and fried chicken. Occasionally, some of the souls discover their true nature on their own and move upwards into spiritual areas like the Park. Or someone can help souls residing in the BSTs to move into the higher and more conscious areas of spirituality. That was the case with my mother.

In July 2009, I observed my mother for the first time in a BST village environment very similar to where I grew up. She was sitting on a bench with other ladies and all of them looked young and very healthy. They were enjoying their conversation. Then the group went together to a nearby church. After a while I heard the melody of Silent Night. A month later in another visit there, I surprisingly found my mom with my mother-in-law who used to live in a neighboring village in Slovakia. Even though the Catholic BST is tremendously huge, it was not difficult to find her when I focused on her and not on the environment. She recognized me, so I quickly left because I did not want to be detected by the priests who would not like my presence. But when I showed up later with a rescue vehicle and crew, the priest was waiting in front of the church. He reluctantly agreed that he would call my mom and mother-in-law since that way I would cause much less disturbance. They two came out and the priest was doing everything possible to speed up our departure. During the trip to the Park, it became obvious that both were happy with the change of venue even though they had been in the Catholic "heaven" they had been dreaming about for most of their earthly lives.

I need to say here that most of the people on Earth have no idea what they would do in heaven, even if all there would be of pure gold. Ask yourself what you would be doing there and how long that activity would be enjoyable. Because heavens are simply Belief System Territories, I suggest that you consider the possibility that there is far more out there than any heaven you might try to imagine from this side.

Chapter 22
KUNDALINI MACHINE

"The higher we soar, the smaller we appear to those who cannot fly." (Friedrich Nietzsche)

During the Lifeline program, I again did some browsing in the Park. I enjoyed the peaceful environment with the lakes and surrounding woods and hills created for those who like solitude. I visited the gathering place, which some like to call Hyde Park, where I saw my Plautus fragment giving a speech about the boundaries of the Earth Life System and how one can eventually cross them. It was also very interesting to encounter animals there. I met our very affectionate dog, Teddy, who died years back and our cat, who never had any name.

But by far the most interesting thing that happened was when busy Morphon had some time to talk to me. His body form had very unusual skin, light brown like white coffee; he had curly hair and a roundish face. When I asked him what his race was, he answered:

"Universal. This is how you will all look on the Earth in a thousand years."

"Why do you have the name "Morphon?" Do you know something about the morphogenetic field by any chance?" I continued in my curiosity.

"Of course, it is my hobby. That is why I changed my name. But that would be a discussion for another time. All you need to know now is that the morphogenetic field is everywhere. It is The Mind of God. You can imagine it as a field with the grass you need when you want to play baseball. Without the field, you would not be able to play. But let me show you what I have designed. You have to see it now!" and, proudly without hesitation, he led me to a device there and immediately proceeded with explanations:

"The main device we have here is The Kundalini Machine."

He continued:

"After people from Earth recover from their previous traumas and finish their education, they come here to our landing platform, and we get them ready to suddenly rise by using our kundalini pipe. It is the most effective way to shoot them up into higher realms, possibly all the way up to the Earth Life System boundaries, depending on their development. When their upward movement stops, they connect to their Higher Selves and then they are ready to return to Earth by way of a conscious incarnation. But, also in that moment of their connection, some of them decide to go back to the Park because they want to learn more and eventually reach a higher level of development."

I saw another pipe next to the platform. It was coming down and passing up alongside, but not going through the platform or even connected to it. I asked Morphon about it.

"Some people, while still in a physical body on the Earth, can ascend here on their own during their meditations or prayers, and we just observe them. But their connections to their Higher Selves are only short term and they do not stay here very long. A full connection to your Higher Self is possible only after shedding your physical body."

"Oh, that is what happened to me! I apparently passed through that side pipe when I had my kundalini experience!" I thought to myself.

When I later shared this experience in the highly spiritual Lifeline group, it was strong coffee even for some of my classmates who tried gently to mock me. Apparently, they thought I just made it up. I have never made up anything, I was and am a responsible reporter. One of the participants playfully said:

"This Lifeline should be remembered as the Kundalini Machine Lifeline!"

I did not protest. I liked it and decided to include the story in this book. Some participants apparently understood the very important principle of our looking for connections to our

Higher Selves. The happenings from the parallel no-time spiritual environment had been transformed and interpreted by my brain into an entertaining story for our earthly understanding. Do you remember one of the best science fiction movies ever made, "Contact" with Jody Foster based on the book by Carl Sagan? Did they not actually build something like a Kundalini Machine for her?

Chapter 23
LOOSH AND GARDENER

"And the Lord God planted a garden eastward in Eden, and there he put the man whom he had formed." (Genesis 2:9)

I also had other personally surprising experiences happening to me during the Lifeline program. One of them began on the first evening, thanks again to the magic of the place. After getting into an altered state, I ventured into a vast area full of heavy machinery on the ground, ports with ships, and runways with planes and even launching pads with spaceships. The personnel moving around in the area looked organized, as if for a military venue. All the activities seemed to be going on around huge warehouses which spread out far in all directions.

"What is going on here? What is in those warehouses?" I asked my guides.

"These are warehouses for storing the Loosh. If you want, you can stop by and pick some up to take with you as a gift for the higher beings helping you when you move to higher vibrations."

"But why is there so much already here? Is it good or bad Loosh?" I questioned further.

"Well, you people on Earth are producing so much that you are actually over-looshed. But a lot of it is no good, so there is a huge overstock of bad Loosh near your planet. You should produce less of the bad Loosh and more of the good Loosh."

With that, the imagery I saw suddenly disappeared.

Obviously, the next time in meditation I tried to learn more about the Loosh. When I sent my inquiry to the Universe, I heard:

"What about the Loosh? For the time being, you already know more than enough about the Loosh. You will learn more when you grow more. Your time for that shall come later!"

"Could you please, at least, tell me whom I am talking to?"

"Yes, I am Gardener." And that was the end of the conversation.

That is how I communicated with Gardener for the first time. After the interaction I was speculating about who he really might be. We all on our planet want to continue living in a beautiful garden just as the Bible says in the quote from Genesis at the beginning of this chapter.

I encountered Gardener the next time in September 2009. I was asking my guides if they knew how the loop of consciousness and the Loosh were organized and who needed the Loosh. They had different opinions and some of them were even unsure about what to say. They called Gardener who told me:

"You do not need to know at this level of your development who needs the Loosh. But do not worry, it is taken care of, it is produced, purified and then used. That is all you need to know right now. However, you shall learn much more when the proper time comes."

During my later travels beyond the Earth Life System, I met several other highly developed beings and learned a lot from them. But it was Gardener, despite the very laconic beginning of our relationship, who was the main coordinator always directing those beings toward me when I needed them. He always made sure that they gave me complete and satisfactory answers to my questions and that they fulfilled my wishes whatever they may have been. But as you shall see, Dear Reader, as the story continues, Gardener always knew when to step in at the most critical stages of my education and development.

Chapter 24
ATLANTIS SURPRISE

"We shall require a substantially new manner of thinking if mankind is to survive." (Albert Einstein)

During another exercise in Lifeline, we had the intention to visit the Belief System Territories. After I reached an altered state, my ISH advised me to consider visiting Atlantis. According to her, I had lived multiple and interesting lives there. I took her advice.

Upon reaching Focus Level 25 and the BST, I saw a huge seaport with various ships approaching it. Their bowsprits had prolonged shapes of dragons, snakes, lizards, and other reptiles. Access to the port was possible through wide channel. The gate to the port was under a huge semi-arch with short golden rays all over the top. I could see a hillside with a big round tower on the top behind the port in the distance. I was also observing slow flying elliptical objects which were the size of our cars. Some of them were even bigger, like buses. Later, I started to call these things flying potatoes. But what was very strange to me, I did not see any people. I tried to get closer, but I could not because of some invisible barrier. The majestic scenery continued. I wished it would last forever. My physical eyes were full of tears.

Three days later, we had an exercise with the intention to recover fragments of ourselves from the Belief System Territories. I decided to return to Atlantis and try to penetrate the barrier. I conferred with my ISH and guides and asked them if I could get into Atlantis. Their response was obvious, that I could do anything with my mind, but they wanted me to find the way myself. I went to the Recovery Center in the Park to pick up the rescue vehicle I would usually use for retrievals from Focus 23.

Morphon was reluctant to agree to my plan:

"Normally, we only do limited activities in BSTs while respecting the principle of no engagement," he reminded me. I persuaded him that I needed to use the vehicle in the channel. After I landed on the same spot in front of the port and hit the barrier again, I decided to take quick and resolute action. Inspired by a scene from the Polish movie "Sexmission," I cursed in Slovak:

"Whorish barrier, open up immediately!"

Suddenly, I could see people everywhere and my vehicle could slowly sail into the port through the channel. I stepped out of the vehicle and followed the urge to walk up the hill. I stopped in front of a small odd-looking building with a crescent on the door. I knocked. A man opened the door and invited me inside. He was a priest that I knew.

"Hi Munit," I greeted him.

"Hi Plautus, I have not seen you for a long time. I know why you have come." He knew my name too.

"Good to see you again Munit. Why has no one greeted me?"

"They cannot see you; I can see you only because I am a priest and I know how," answered Munit.

Then he led me to a window and from there I could see a plaza full of people. And I saw myself. I was a merchant. Apparently, I was also a money changer arguing with other merchants and people all around my table. I knew that was part of me; I did not like it and I wanted to take that man away with me. But Munit told me that if I did that, I could not come to his town anymore. I heard from my physical headphones that the exercise would soon be over. I sucked the merchant into myself, and everything disappeared.

I was sitting in my rescue vehicle on the water. And there was no more Atlantis to be seen, nothing. All around me was nothing but water.

Throughout my life, I have often had a dream in which I was being chased by a mob as I was running up the stairs inside a high tower turning into a smaller and smaller space. Usually, this dream woke me up before I reached the top of the tower.

But in October 2009, I was able to open a small door at the top of the tower and get on the roof. The next day I asked about this dream in meditation and received this answer:

"Your dream about being chased is from Atlantis. You had five reincarnations in Atlantis, and in the last life, you were chased by a mob. You were The Priest of the Moon, but of a lower rank. The Atlanteans knew about an upcoming catastrophe, and they were blaming the priests for it. During the escape from Atlantis, the higher priests sent you to pick up the records of the temple. After you did that, you ran upstairs to the roof of the temple where a vimana was waiting for you. You got inside as a last person from the temple and the vimana flew away. Unfortunately, you retrieved only part of the records. The high priests punished you by abandoning you on a small uninhabited Greek island. As they pushed you from the vimana, you overheard them planning to fly to what is today called Mexico. You starved to death on that island."

I obviously wanted to know what happened to Atlantis itself. An opportunity to learn about the catastrophe came during the "Manifestation and Creation Squared" program when we were contacting our Total Selves through the powerful Human Plus Free Access Channel utilizing the Hemi Sync frequencies of Focus 11. After I asked how Atlantis was destroyed, I was told it had been caused by a powerful earthquake triggered by underground facilities on the island. According to the message, there was a big tension between military and the priesthood. The military tried to increase their power by gaining new lands on the coast. This was opposed by the high priests. The generals either forced most of the priests off the island or killed them. Then, they tried to raise the island up with injections of explosives into the magma underneath, but the process got entirely out of control and the whole island sank.

Chapter 25
MISTER Q

"Solitude is fine, but you need someone to tell you that solitude is fine." *(Honoré de Balzac)*

About a month after Lifeline, I had a dream of going with Alenka to a magic show. She already had her ticket. When I was going to buy mine from a clerk who was sitting very high up in a vertical booth, I had to stretch my hand way up to get it. When I checked my ticket, I realized that we would not be sitting together.

Later in a meditation during a visit to the Park, I learned that Alenka got her ticket first, because she knew exactly where she wanted to go when she died. My ticket was much more expensive; I had to work hard for it and reach high to get it. But I was also told that not many people would be able to get such a ticket to the Other Side, only those who were educated and prepared.

Then, in the same meditation, suddenly a tremendous force grabbed me and with unimaginable speed shot me high up and I found myself in the middle of nowhere. Nothing was around me, just darkness and complete silence.

"What or who took me out here and why?" I desperately wanted to know.

"Mister Q. Yes, the one you know from Star Trek."

"Why did you take me here, Mister Q?"

"You need to know that there is nothing to be afraid of. All you must do to go back is to use your mind, to command yourself. Your thought is your weapon here! And now I leave you alone here! Remember, you are in the nothing, you are in your pure essence."

And Mister Q left. I stayed there for a while enjoying myself in the nothing; just myself, and God, and everything in a pure joy of bliss such as I have never experienced before.

Obviously, I became very curious about Mr. Q. I had

already learned that everything we create with our minds exists as a spiritual form. Therefore, the zillions of fans who identified with him apparently had solidified his form and made it quite dense. At least that was my thought about how he had been created. But my guides told me that Mister Q had already existed a long time before he appeared in the minds of the Star Trek creators. He had inspired me to do a lot of rescue work, initiated my contacts with higher levels of vibrations, and was preparing me for my expanded role in the Earth Life System.

When I next met him, I asked him about his giving me help while I was sleeping.

"We are not only working in sleep with you. We sometimes must inspire you through your wise Slovak friend on the other side of the ocean. You are not paying attention to our signals all the time, so we are asking him to give you little inspirational kicks. Think about how many times you have acted upon his discussions with you, such as when you decided to leave for the United States or to begin to study spirituality. Even though he is a skeptic, he is wise and inspirational. You are open minded, determined, and consistent. Also, you do not need to worry about him. When he crosses to the Other Side, he will find his way. He is not going to get lost; we shall help him," elaborated Mister Q.

I had several other interesting interactions with Mister Q. In September, I asked him about our Moon, and he told me:

"The Moon indeed is artificial and hollow. Many extraterrestrial and spiritual races who are interested in the Earth are using it. It took us a lot of effort to position her where she is today. She is the fourth one you have had. The first one flew away into space, the second one crashed into the Earth, and the third one melted. This one is finally very stable, and she is always going to be there, regardless of whatever catastrophe might happen to your planet. You are too precious not to be monitored."

Chapter 26
EDUCATION

"Live as if you were to die tomorrow. Learn as if you were to live forever." *(Mahatma Gandhi)*

In October 2009, I took part in another Monroe Institute program, Exploration 27. It is dedicated to further study of the Park, the variety of its functions, its connection to the planet and the Earth core significance for humanity. The facilitators for the program were Paul Elder and Dr. Joe Gallenberger. Joe had also created another wonderful program, MC Squared, which is dedicated to psychokinetic and confidence building practices.

During Exploration 27, we visited different areas of the Park several times. Our individual visits were supported by the whole group energy which was focused on and magnified by a crystal placed in our group minds called "TMI-There." Each participant also built a virtual "Special Place" of their own. Special places were located somewhere in the Park in Focus 27. I chose as my Special Place the spiritual copy of a small shack on the Big Island of Hawaii which I had seen halfway between my favorite Kohala beaches and the cozy town of Waimea (Kamuela). I put a table inside the shack where I would meet and confer with my guides. I continue to use it.

The souls of people coming to the Park for recovery and education are generally directed into three different areas of the reception center. The areas there are for First Timers who have just experienced their first incarnation on our planet, for Repeaters who are in the overwhelming majority, and for Last Timers who believe they have learned what they wanted to know and want to prepare for departure from the Earth Life System.

Many in the reception center, especially the Repeaters, still vibrate in their earthly connections; some of them even carry their crutches or canes with them. Others like those who died of cancer are sometimes blaming themselves. One older lady I saw believed that her cancer was caused by her promiscuous life when young and that God had punished her. Dear Reader, God is not punishing anybody! Such a belief is the biggest bogus idea created by those who control a variety of religions on the planet. God is The Ultimate Creator inspiring us through unlimited Love.

Indeed, the Park is the best place for all troubled souls to learn to understand the important principles of our divine nature. Many people coming to the Park from the Belief System Territories are expressing their disappointments that they did not meet God there as they were imagining Him. But, at the same time, some of them say that they have gotten tired of the demagoguery repeated by numerous priests, bishops, ministers, preachers, Rabbis, imams, ayatollahs, lamas, and other gurus.

From countless conversations with people who decided to work in the Park and help to educate the souls, I have learned that the Soul can connect through a Kundalini Machine or other similar ways to its Higher Self. Very developed souls can connect to their Ultimate Higher Selves any time they feel they are ready. Some of them might make their decisions after recovery, others after understanding the principles of their quest. Still others are asking for help in the detailed planning for their upcoming reincarnations.

The Park has an enormous variety of educational centers. A few of these are for the study of the frequency and development of reincarnations, the study of different fields of consciousness, and how the Mind of God is spread throughout the Universe. Park residents can also study how the consciousness of animals and plants is related to human consciousness. Part of the educational process is the reading of the Akashic records for a Soul. It is done very methodically, respecting the development of an individual.

In one of the halls, I observed an African American

gentleman who had just received the Akashic record about his slave life in the 17th century. He was shaking his head in disbelief looking at it. Then he started a discussion with several others who still had the African American forms of their spiritual bodies. They all decided to go to one of the satellite halls to hear a lecture on the topic. Apparently, they still had difficulty in understanding how one human being could enslave another one. They could not move on until they fully grasped what the purpose of such inhumane treatment was for each one of them.

Chapter 27
GUARDIANS

"The earth does not belong to us. We belong to the Earth."
(Chief Seattle)

In September 2009 on my way to the Park, I received the impression of a long continuous sheet of paper about six inches wide and three feet long. Then after that, I saw about a dozen discs of the size of commercial compact discs, but they were bent into the shape of shallow bowls or plates. When I reached Focus 21, I had a tremendously powerful feeling about home. Naturally, when I got to my Special Place, I asked my guides for an explanation. Here is what I received:
"That long sheet is the contract you signed when you entered the Earth Life System. It is not necessary for you to know now exactly what is in it. We just wanted to remind you about its existence and that you should be aware that you have signed it. And the discs contain everything you need to know to become a Guardian."
Wow! I am unable to communicate further.
"Yes, you are on your way to be a Guardian. Only when you become a Guardian can you go to your true home. That is why you had that strong feeling about home. You will then be able to do things like we do. You will be able to cross back and forth at will through the boundaries between the Earth Life System and the rest of the Universe. But watch out! There are also those who don't want you to become a Guardian. You are often under their attacks and that is why you sometimes have violent dreams. But we are protecting you. Do not worry, they cannot destroy you or influence you unless you allow it."
When I tried to inquire more, the guides suggested that I call Mister Q. I did, and I asked him a lot of questions. I wanted him to explain to me who the Guardians were, if some of them might be in the Park, and, if so, where their

building was located.

"We Guardians are higher intelligences who move around The Earth Life System on our own ships. I have one for me, too." said Mister Q and added:

"We gather and conduct our meetings and other business on the ships while respecting the will of the Ultimate Creator. He wants us to intervene as little as possible. By the way, your Park was built by the Lemurians who knew in their time that a huge catastrophe was coming on your planet. Thus, they created a gathering place for the mass migration of souls after a mass dying off on the Earth itself. However, the main purpose of the Park remains the same. It is to educate people to prevent yet another destruction of the planet."

"Are we in crisis now; is something bad going to happen to us?" I am trying to get as much information as I can.

"There are too many people living on The Earth and most of them really don't care. You have almost approached the point of no return. But we always believe in you and try to prevent a catastrophe. We can move freely between galaxies, but we have our assignments. I spend a lot of my efforts here. You are an interesting and unique species. Other planets in other systems have different life forms and the consciousness on them is also organized differently and incarnates in diverse ways. Your Park is quite a unique place."

Mister Q also told me, that the merging of the human races on our planet is now advancing faster than ever before. I thought about Morphon and his light coffee colored skin. When I asked, he said that Guardians sometimes incarnate.

"How about Jesus, is He also a Guardian?"

"No, Jesus is much more than a Guardian, He is The Overseer. He is above everybody," answered Mister Q.

Then, when I asked about any grand plan for Earth that the Guardians might have, he gave me a little lecture. He said the Guardians would like to remove the existing blockage between the physical and nonphysical realm in the minds of people on Earth. This would allow everyone to freely leave their body and have access to the information and tools of the spiritual realm.

"They would not have to work as hard as you do now, Menev. We know that most of the people are deniers; they would believe in a spiritual world only if they could see it directly without the barrier. But we cannot do that yet. People will have to change first. They need to practice much less greed, hate and selfishness and feel much more love and compassion. I can find only four and half million of those like you who are willing to change. We need at least five hundred million to reverse the current trend."

Chapter 28
RA AND HADIEN

"Earth provides enough to satisfy every man's needs, but not every man's greed." *(Mahatma Gandhi)*

Sometime later I received yet another even more powerful message about our often-greedy nature, which many of us let go too far without putting any brakes on it. The following story made me think that the opposite of love might not be hate or fear, as we usually think, but greed. It happened in an exercise at Exploration 27, when we started to shoot our consciousness into Focus Levels 34 and 35.

To accomplish that, we used the technique of a spiritual slingshot developed by Dr. Franceen King, who is the facilitator for the programs Starlines and Starlines II. Franceen had discovered the vibrational levels of Focus Levels 34 and 35 after Robert Monroe had already passed away. The slingshot uses the combined spiritual energy assembled in the Earth Core in Focus 27 and the group energy generated by the multiplied energy of the crystal at TMI-There in the Park. The vibrational levels of Focus 34 and 35 are beyond the boundaries of the Earth Life System.

I prepared several questions I wanted to ask in those exciting new levels, and I hoped to meet Mister Q again. After I successfully recognized the distinct buzzing of space in Focus 34 and 35, another being appeared instead. I started to call him Ra. His form was about eighteen to twenty-one feet tall, and the best description would be that he looked like a character from the famous 1994 Roland Emmerich movie "Stargate." He had some device in his hand which looked like a walking cane, but it must have been a brain scanner. He apparently chose his form from the "Stargate" movie to be able to relate to me easily. I felt incredible humility as I waited to see what was going to happen. My physical body was breathing heavily, and I was crying.

"Why are you feeling so humble, Little One? You don't have to be. When you grow up, after graduation you shall be one of us. You shall be a Guardian and you will be part of our gathering around your planet. Don't be a pussy!" Ra challenged me.

"What is the gathering about, Ra?"

"We came here to save The Earth because you all screwed up!"

"What do you mean, Ra? Why have we screwed up?"

"You became too greedy, that's why!"

"Lord Ra, can you give me some important sign or message to take back with me to Earth from this trip?" I remembered the assignment from the class.

"Here is your sign, your omen, Earthling!" said Ra.

He suddenly was holding a big clear bag full of golden coins. He turned it upside down and emptied it. The golden coins changed first to dust and then to nothing.

"You see, the subject of your obsession changed to dust. In true reality, money means nothing."

Ra then advised me to remember my respectful but decent humble feelings from our meeting, as this would help me to detect and recognize any other higher beings when I desired to meet them.

During the sharing of our experiences in class, a fellow participant Shays said that he had also met an alien being who was showing him some gold. Another participant met a Being who refused to give him any sign. That Being insisted that his presence in the high spiritual realm and their meeting must be a validation strong enough for him not to have doubts about what is the true reality and what is just an illusion.

Another highly developed spiritual being whom I met during an Exploration 27 exercise, and from whom I learned a lot, was Hadien. Hadien, like Ra, apparently scanned my mind and created a pyramidal form of himself based on my memory of a classic science fiction book by the French writer

Jean Hougron, *The Sign of the Dog (Le Signe du Chien)*.

When I met Hadien for the first time in Focus 35, he looked like a twenty-foot-tall pyramid. Later he used a smaller form to better relate to me. He had small but very lively eyes placed in the front wall about one third down from the top. His bottom wall had zillions of small roots immersed in a steaming liquid in a large pan in which he was sitting. Hadien explained to me that he and other beings like Mister Q and Ra have their homes also on physical planets. When they are around us, they lower their spiritual vibrations, but not enough for us to see them in our physical environment. Hadien asked me what he could do for me, and I said:

"Ra told me that we Earthlings have screwed up. Can you show me perhaps another world where everything is in peace and harmony, unlike on our Earth?"

"Yes, my pilot can take you to Silvana; it is not far from here."

Hadien pointed to a round ship nearby. I could see the lights of an apparent planet body in the distance. He took me onto a huge busy platform full of landing and departing small round ships with cute insect-like humanoid creatures who apparently were piloting them. Hadien pointed to a ship with the name Ariana, and I stepped into it.

After an initial tremendous burst of speed, the pilot Mandi slowed the ship down to my understanding of time. As we were cruising above Silvana, he gave me an overview of the planet. At first, I could see the island of Mirnebier, then the main continent. He said with a laugh:

"You can call it Pangea if you want. The whole planet has only two and a half million inhabitants and Mirnebier is a retreat for approximately one hundred thousand vacationers."

"What do they do, how do they make their living?" I asked with curiosity.

"They are processing the Loosh. They are sorting out and organizing the Loosh coming here from all corners of the

Galaxy. High quality Loosh is sent to higher vibrational levels, where and to whom exactly we do not know. Silvana citizens travel by using an interchange of bodies. They drop a physical body at one place and pick up another one at their destination. However, they must do their work in their physical bodies. And their bodies look very much like yours. You have to graduate first from another physical planetary system if you want to incarnate into Silvana and become a citizen there."

"Interesting. I wonder if I could come here after I eventually graduate from the Earth and would be able to leave the Earth Life System. I would really like to know more about the Loosh, and this would be a wonderful opportunity to figure it out," I thought to myself.

But it was time to return. At that time, I had no idea that I had already spent several lifetimes at Silvana. I learned that much later in my spiritual journey. Experiences from living and working at Silvana were fueling my interest in Loosh in this lifetime on the Earth.

Chapter 29
DREAMS

"They haven't made the hatchet that can cut down a dream."
(Poster in a former Nursing Home in Lubec, Maine)

Throughout my life, I was often trying to find explanations of my numerous dreams. I expected, as probably many of you have, to find explanations of dreams in several various kinds of encyclopedias and other books. It was almost never satisfactory. I wrote in the chapter "Atlantis Surprise" that I had asked about the meaning of my dream of being chased by going into an altered state. I unintentionally learned by experience that it was a very simple, but effective method. Not surprisingly, who can know more about your dreams than you yourself?

Dreams are not only the results of randomly created connections of the synapses in our brains, even though they often can be just that. I learned at this stage that they were messages to you from your Higher Self. They can also be from beings who have an interest in your development. These beings are helping you when you are sleeping, and your consciousness is traveling outside of your body.

Dreams are distorted during the hypnagogic state when you are waking up and returning to your body. That is why they are often seemingly very bizarre and weird. By connecting to their originators, you can discover their true meaning. That is exactly what I started to do, and now I am learning tremendously from my dreams. Many interpretations of my dreams which I have received through an altered state have produced marvelous revelations.

For example, in August 2009, I had a very vivid dream about the TV news reporting vortexes rising out of the different places worldwide. I was told in meditation that each of those vortexes represented the current group efforts of different spiritual movements. People worldwide were waking up, rising and unifying their intentions of reaching a higher state of themselves and society through connections to their Higher Selves. One of these groups was students of at Monroe Institute. But there were many others in different countries, various spiritual movements, and other cultures. Participation in a spiritual group empowers an individual in pursuing her or his specific intentions and goals for communicating in an altered state.

I had another interesting dream in October. I was living with a young woman, and after lovemaking, we fell asleep. When I woke up in the dream, I saw a big fly about two inches long sitting inside of a frame about six to seven inches long on the wall of my bedroom. The big fly suddenly moved and swallowed a regular smaller fly sitting nearby in the frame. Then the merged flies changed into a red shining object in the shape of a flashlight. The flashlight dissolved and disappeared. Then the frame broke into four pieces, and they fell on the floor. Several days later, I asked for an explanation while I was in an altered state. The answer was: "It was again about human greed. What happened when the big fly swallowed the small one? They both disappeared and not even the frame was left intact."

In August 2010, I had a dream about starting my participation in another Monroe program. We were sitting and waiting for the teachers and introducing ourselves. Suddenly one guy left his body, then flew up and around like a dragonfly and afterwards returned to his body.

We watched him in awe. He said he came to learn how to do that more efficiently and pick up bigger speed. I later found him standing in the hallway. He said his name was Adrian. I said I would also like to be able to fly like that and asked him to show me the trick. He said that I had to push my forehead with my thumb in the place of my third eye and that would connect me to the God Sun. I tried the trick and immediately saw in front of my eyes a small computer board.

"That is how we do it in our dimension," said Adrian.

When I later inquired in meditation with one of my star friends about the dream, he told me:

"You really do not have a board in front of your head. It was just an interpretation of your mind. But, of course, you do have a vibrational interface in your third eye which is enabling you to communicate with the spiritual world."

Chapter 30
LUCID DREAMS

"Dreams are often most profound when they seem the craziest." (Sigmund Freud)

Another alternative way to learn about the spiritual world and your connection to it is through lucid dreaming. A lucid dream is simply defined as a dream where you become aware that you are dreaming while in it. Hopefully, you can gain control of your dream. You are trying not to wake up and bring your consciousness back to the physical world. The goal is to prolong your experience.

As many spiritual explorers can explain, there is a clear distinction between an out of body state and lucid dreaming. I will leave all those explanations to them. But for me, lucid dreaming is yet another rather more difficult way to execute one's intentions when going into an altered state. I came to the clear conclusion that using Hemi Sync and the Monroe Protocol worked best for me. As my guides once asked me, why would you drive a Yugo when you have a Rolls Royce or Lamborghini?

I was back in Slovakia in a computer center building in one of my dreams. I was walking down the hallway and looking through a window into the mainframe computer room. Then I walked into the dining room. But soon I thought:

"I must go back to my office and start to do something, otherwise they might fire me."

But when I came to the office which used to be mine, someone else's stuff was everywhere. It was clear that they had apparently hired someone else for my position. I was wondering what they were going to do with me. I realized that a lot had changed since I left, and it would be impossible for me to get my old job back. I was walking in the hallway again and then it suddenly happened:

"This is really stupid; I am living in America. I must be dreaming!"

That knowing lasted only a few seconds and even though I knew I was in a dream and tried to hold it, I woke up.

I was driving a car in another dream in a mountain country. I stopped and asked two men for directions to get to a town. While they were explaining to me how to get there, someone stole my car behind my back. Then I was looking around to find a car that I could steal, because I was in a hurry to continue. But I realized that my thinking was very weird, because I would never be able to steal a car and then I knew that I was dreaming. I tried to convert my lucid dream into an out of body experience. When I felt my body vibrating, I tried to sit up and walk away from my body. Unfortunately, I was interrupted by loud music coming from somewhere outside and I woke up.

I started to dream about the destruction of a city in another dream. At first it looked like Bratislava, then it changed to Washington. Buildings were collapsing into each other, but I was always able to escape. Then I got into a car and guided it safely out of town with my mind. But then I decided to go back to town to see if my family was safe. While wandering the streets, I saw group of men lynching an older bearded man who vehemently protested. But they hanged him anyway. When he was hanging from the neck, he was yelling:

"I told you that I did not do anything, so you see now that you cannot hang me!"

The absurdity of the situation caused me to realize that I was lucidly dreaming. A bus was approaching with high speed directly in my direction, so I told myself:

"I am in a lucid dream, and I can jump over the bus to avoid an accident!" and I did.

Then, I intentionally flew over the crowd of people and woke up.

Later in April 2013, before going to sleep, I set up the

intention to have a lucid dream. In the dream, I was in a spaceship with other crew members flying from Earth to an orbital station. But I knew that we were going to crash, and I did not want to die. After a while, I left the ship and flew in my body on my own looking for the place of the anticipated crash. Then I realized that I was dreaming and that my physical body was lying back home in my bedroom. Some small ships were trying to come after me, but I could easily outmaneuver them. After playing with them for a while, I decided to wake up and I did.

Chapter 31
OUTINGS

"In order to experience everyday spirituality, we need to remember that we are spiritual beings spending some time in a human body." (Barbara De Angelis)

My efforts to reach the conscious out of body states described earlier in the book were being pushed more and more into the back of my mind as my main spiritual experiences started to become more and more revealing and exciting. As the guides recommended, I started to understand out of body states as byproducts of my spiritual journey. Nevertheless, they kept happening spontaneously and some of them were quite interesting.

On one morning in February 2010, after an unsuccessful meditation, I fell back asleep while I was still in a hypnogogic state. I found myself driving a car somewhere. I realized my brakes were not working, so I tried to back up. But the car simply passed through the other cars like they were just air. I got out of the car and started to walk through narrow streets of town where I was. I had never seen it before, but it looked like an old European or South American town. People were walking by and talking in a language I did not recognize. I cursed and tried to go back, but my car was nowhere to be found. Suddenly, I realized:
"I am out of body!"
I heard music, so I decided to follow the sound down some stairs into a club which was full of people. I tried to touch them. Sometimes my hand went through them and sometimes it did not. But they reacted and looked at me. I walked back up to the street and the same was happening there; my hands just slid through the body of a man sitting on a bench.
"I am out of body, and I can control the situation," I thought to myself.
I decided to go out of the town. I was walking through

incredibly rich green grass like I had never seen before. I was enjoying ripping up handfuls of grass and feeling how real it was in the palm of my hand. I walked uphill and came to the end of the plateau on which the town was located. I looked back and saw that the town was sitting in a big bowl.

"I am out of body, and I can fly," I said.

I flew and landed next to a small pond in a town. Then the ground under me started to move and I realized I was on a small platform which was being lifted by a mechanical arm. Then the arm turned around and it was lowering the platform with me on it into a plaza full of screaming and chanting people. I suspected that I was supposed to be sacrificed in a ritual ceremony. I said to myself:

"Hey, I am out of body, I can fly."

I flew off the platform and landed in a nearby tower where I met two young men. I asked them if they were also out of body. One of them said yes, but the other one said:

"No, I am from the town, and I work here in the tower."

I asked him what the name of the town was and whether we were on the Earth. He looked at me and told me with apparent surprise:

"Our planet is 2 N 09, and our town is called Backbone."

The other guy suddenly said:

"I have to go back to my body," and instantly the same thing happened to me.

On my birthday morning in June 2010, I dreamed that two of my deceased friends were playing table tennis in my room. I am a competitive player myself, despite my senior citizen status. I play a lot of matches at official tournaments of the United States Association of Table Tennis. It is not unusual for me to dream about the game. In the dream I said to my friends:

"Let's continue. Can I also play with you?"

"Don't be stupid, Jozef, don't you see that we are dead?" answered one of them.

"But I see you clearly and completely normally. That means

you are either really in my house, or I am out of my body," I insisted.

Then, I walked up to one of them, hugged him and said: "See, I feel you absolutely normally."

Suddenly, he started to rapidly change his form and showed me several different forms in just a few seconds. I said: "Wait! If you can do those tricks, I want you to look like President Clinton."

He did so, and I let him leave. Then, I opened the door and there were dozens of children screaming and running around outside. I felt a strong jolt as I snapped back into my body.

I found my body flying under the ceiling in another dream in November 2011. It seemed to me that I could go very fast through the ceiling, but at first, I intended to just push my hand through it. I pushed the palm of my hand slowly up and the ceiling receded as though it were very soft, almost like fabric. I played with it for a while and then woke up.

During another morning dream in the same month, I started to levitate above my home street in the Southwest of Washington D.C. I was wondering if the people around me saw me, but nobody reacted. Then I started to fly in a horizontal position like a missile down the street and back. I was screaming at the people:

"Hey, do you see me flying?" but everyone either turned their heads away or they did not look at me at all.

Despite the completely euphoric feeling I had, I wanted to know why no one saw me and asked my guides in the ensuing meditation:

"Why did the people not react; why did they not see me?"

"Remember, you were in a higher dimension. You can see from a higher dimension into a lower dimension, but not the other way around. You saw them, but they could not see you."

"But why were they turning their heads away so that it seemed to me that they did not want to look at me?"

"They felt something in the air, and they had a natural fear of that. Remember, when you woke up in the night and went to the bathroom and you had the feeling that someone was in your apartment? That is the same feeling they were having on the street."

I had a very similar out of body experience in the morning of September 2012. I flew high above the Danube River all the way from Bratislava to the Black Sea in a horizontal position and was enjoying full control over my speed.

Two months later, I had a bit of an unpleasant experience. I found myself in my dream in front of the house where I was born. My older brother was admiring a huge truck parked in front of the house. It was just like the one he always wanted to have. I immediately recognized that I was dreaming. My body started to vibrate at a high frequency. I commanded it to rise, and it did. I was about three feet above the bed and looking upward. I felt someone catching my legs and even trying to touch me in my crotch. I started to scream: "Go away, leave me alone!" and that ended the experience. I snapped back into my body and woke up.

In a January 2013 dream, someone carried me on his back while traveling in a higher dimension. Then he, I and a third person discussed inter-dimensional travel. Afterwards the man said that it was my turn. The third person sat on my back, and I just commanded myself to fly away with him. I felt very powerful when flying and I knew I was out of my body. After a beautiful flight, I woke up feeling amazingly strong vibrations in my whole body.

Two months later I had a flying experience in a dream again. This time I flew with Juanzetta, whom I had met in 2010, high above the ground while holding her hand.

Another spontaneous out of body experience happened in April 2014. After only one hour of sleep early in the morning, I got out of the bed because I knew someone was in my apartment. The front door was wide open and off

its hinges. A man was staring at me from the door and he asked me if I had a plug in my apartment. When I asked him why he needed it, he answered:
"Because I need to steal something."
Then, suddenly the whole scenery changed, and I found myself on the streets of a town that looked like Bratislava. Everything was so real that I could not believe it. Two men were trying to attack me, and I tried to scream, but the streets were empty. A nearby car was apparently moving by itself because the man sitting in it looked like he was dead. When I tried to stop the car, the man woke up and tried to steer it. I saw two young women walking into an apartment building and I followed them trying to talk to them. I was hitting the stairway railing screaming:
"This is real. Where am I? I want to go back to my body! This is more real than where I live when I am in my body. I want to go home!"
But I could not. Someone stepped out of a car. He was screaming and running toward me with a camcorder:
"Let's film that freak!"
Women quickly ran into their apartments, obviously scared of me. I tried to scream back:
"I am not a freak!" but I could not.
It was very difficult. I only realized that I was trying to scream with my physical lips and voice when I woke up in my physical body. I immediately got out of the bed to close the front door. But no one was there, all was peaceful and quiet, and the door was closed. Only the computer screen was on, even though I always switch it off when I go to sleep.

Spontaneous out of body experiences are very illustrative of how spiritual intentions and expectations work. Out of body travels seldom happen when you wish for them. But they often surprise you when you least expect them.

Chapter 32
MENEV THE GREAT

"I saw the angel in the marble and carved until I set him free." (Michelangelo)

My real desire to continue my spiritual development by using the tools of the Monroe Institute was now centered on my participation in the program Starlines. I was very eager to further my conversations with my star friends, as I had started to call them. I had already met Mister Q, Ra, Hadien, and Gardener and was looking forward to meeting a female friend named Ruala. In January 2010 my guides had shown her to me, reasoning that I needed a feminine guide who supposedly could teach me the principles of Cosmic Love.

I eagerly signed up for the Starlines, but the program in late January was cancelled due to a heavy snowfall in the foothills of the Blue Ridge Mountains where the institute is located. Today, I have no doubt that the snowstorm was the work of divine intervention. If I had attended Starlines in January, I would never have met my Juanzetta, who is the driving force behind this book. We met later that year at the Starlines program in July.

However, prior to that, I really wanted to go to the Monroe Institute as soon as possible. I attended a program called Manifestation and Creation Squared, to which I would never have gone otherwise. I knew it was about psychokinesis, which was outside of my focus. How glad I was to take it! That program gave me definite proof of the supremacy of mind over matter and dissolved any remaining doubts I had about the reality of the Other Side.

Its creator, Dr. Joe Gallenberger, together with healer and energy specialist, Patty Ray Avalon, led us through a series of exercises focused primarily on the building of self-confidence and the unleashing of the hidden powers of our minds. The buildup of our own individual mind powers, as well as the group energy of the participants, steadily grew by every hour of every day of the program.

We easily beat the statistical numbers of probability when rolling dice, we accelerated the growth of wheat seeds, and we lighted round fluorescent bulbs with our bare hands. I was struggling to light a bulb with my partner Walter and our bulb was merely blinking. Patty Ray passed by; she tapped the bulb with her fingers. The bulb shone in an instant.

But the top activity of the program was spoon bending, which had brought many participants to the program. We were standing in a circle concentrating on our built-up group energy, and we were holding spoons or forks of heavy silverware with both of our hands, ready to bend them. A muscular Russian fellow Alex was counting while holding his fork up and waving and saying:
"One, two, three, bend!"
I looked around me. Only three participants, beside me, were unable to do it. The end of Alex's fork was hanging down like it was made from modeling clay. I was disappointed but determined, and immediately had to remind myself not to be a chicken. Alex counted again, and all the remaining spoons or forks bent easily, including mine. The feeling was ecstatic, incredible. I spent the rest of the day talking to spoons and forks and bending them.

Everybody used their individual ways of bending; the main point was that they had been created by a mind, so a mind could influence them again. Nothing in a spoon or fork is static, all particles inside of them are in constant motion and the movement of the particles can be affected by a mind.

All of that was very persuasive, and I bet most of my classmates were very happy. But for me, the most important experience came on the last day of the program. Here is what happened when I got into an altered state:
"Welcome, Menev. Now you shall become Menev the Great!"

"Why is that?" was all I was able to say.
"Because now you will know that you are an unlimited timeless being!"
My consciousness started to inflate and had the form of a giant balloon without boundaries to be seen.
"Now all of The Universe will be in every cell of your body."
Zillions of balloons of varied sizes, from space, from the air around me, from the Earth below, from water and from fires, were all sucked with incredible speed into my body. My consciousness stayed in the giant balloon, and I knew it was the ball of time. Earlier, we had created the wheel of time in Lifeline to try to understand the circular essence of time, but my wheel at that time completely collapsed. Later, I developed an understanding of time to be a ball in which you can travel not only on the surface, but across the ball from one point to another. Now my ball of time started to spin with incredible speed:
"You see Menev, there is only Now, no beginning and no end. There is only spinning and there can only be a change of direction and pulsation."
And the ball started to change size and pulsate. One moment, it was tinier than an atom and next, larger than the whole Universe. It sometimes suddenly stopped and then spun in a different direction. Then, the godly instructions continued:
"If you understand what we just told you, Menev, you also have to disperse. We are Menev, you are Menev. Menev is everywhere. When you disperse, then you can take any form and any shape of consciousness you desire. You do it just like the desert wind when it raises dust and shapes it into various forms. You can be Menev jumping joyfully over the Alps in Rhaeto Romansh, Switzerland, you can be an octopus in the ocean, or you can have any shape you can imagine. Remember, a mind is the most powerful force in the Universe."
      And then, my physical heart started to beat loudly and wildly in my chest, "Ta-dum, ta-dum, ta-dum…" to the end

of the exercise, which I welcomed because I was completely exhausted. That is what my participation in MC Squared was about, the understanding of our divine, unlimited, and timeless essence.

Yes, we are spiritually what we want to be without limitations. Our limitations on this planet are only determined by our earthly vehicles, our physical bodies. We exist only in the present! And, this knowing, which we can gain only through personal experience, is our ultimate spiritual security.

Chapter 33
WEDDING

"What lies behind us, and what lies before us are tiny matters compared to what lies within us." *(Ralph Waldo Emerson)*

In April 2010, I traveled with Alenka, my girlfriend at the time, to the beautiful green Hawaiian island of Kauai. She was a military widow, and we were able to take advantage of military recreational facilities around the world for our numerous travels every year. We decided to spend two weeks at the Kaulike housing at Barking Sands next to the Pacific Missile Range Facility. We found it to be a beautiful secluded, peaceful, and healing place. It was especially good because Alenka was already battling cancer.

The facility had a protected natural nesting area for shearwaters. Every night we enjoyed walking nearby and watching them majestically slide into their nests on the ground. When they called to each other they sounded like toddlers calling for attention. Every night, there were also hundreds of small yellow lights everywhere, in the air, on the beach, and around the trees. Spiritual people usually call them orbs. I had seen and photographed them before, but I had never seen so many anywhere else. Even Alenka, who was a skeptic and the devout Roman Catholic, was amazed and curious about what they were and what was happening.

The waves and currents on the beach at Barking Sands were high and strong and dangerous, and we would drive around beautiful Kauai looking for some nice quiet places for swimming. We were also looking for local attractions. I took a helicopter ride above the waterfall known from the "Jurassic Park" movie.

But mainly, I really wanted to see the statue of the Hindu elephant God Ganesha in the Hindu temple on the eastern side of the island. I had read about the statue in the book *Serpent of Light: Beyond 2012* written by Drunvalo Melchizedek. I just felt that I had to see it; why I had no idea. I found, admired, and greeted the little statue of Lord Ganesha in front of the temple, which was closed.

During our stay, I tried to meditate in my room. While in an altered state, I kept calling on the spirits of the Kahunas known as Hawaiian shamans. But for the whole week, I did not have any significant experiences. Finally, shortly before the end of our stay during a morning meditation, something happened that completely took my breath away.

When I got into an altered state, first the Hindu God Ganesha appeared; then my Internal Self Helper (ISH), Kamaláska, appeared in a long white wedding gown. I looked at my human form and I was completely naked.

"Why is that My Lord?" was all I could say in awe.

"You are going to have a cosmic wedding. For that you do not need to be limited by any clothes. That is why you came here to Kauai. Did you see all those orbs?" asked Ganesha.

"Yes, I did, and I photographed them. Who are they?"

"They came here for your wedding. They are all your reincarnations, your friends and friends of the friends."

"Are you Ganesha or Ganesh?" I was just trying to buy time. I was a bit reluctant, even though I was going to marry my ISH. We men are usually reluctant before a wedding.

"Both," answered elephant God.

"Are you a Hindu God?"

"Yes, I am, and I am not only a Hindu God."

Then Ganesha raised both of his upper hands, picked me up with his right lower hand and ISH with his lower left hand and asked me:

"Do you want to be married to her and do you understand and accept your new responsibilities? Do you understand that as the husband of your ISH you have to finish your task on the Earth?"

"Yes, I do."

Then Ganesha turned his elephant head to ISH:
"Do you forgive him that he did not always understand you? Do you accept him now, and do you want to marry him?"
"Yes, I do," said Kamaláska.
"Now, I proclaim you to be spiritual husband and wife, and you can merge."
We hugged and started to spin and hundreds of the orbs were also sucked into our vortex. Then it was all over, everything disappeared, and I returned to the physical.

ISH appeared to me one more time before we left Kauai. She said she was pregnant with a girl and her name would be Maturity.
"That child is your spiritual maturity," she added.
"You can call her when you need to talk to her."
And I did. I called Maturity immediately after returning to Washington. She appeared to be six or seven years old, because time as we know it on the Earth does not exist in the spiritual realm. Time does not matter; it does not exist there.
"Daddy, I love you and I know you love me. You must love everybody. Remember Daddy, if I had not been born, you would not have grown into who you are becoming now."
I knew I did not have enough Love inside of me yet, and that I needed to be reminded to be loving and accepting of every new day and of everybody. I expressed these feelings to her.
"That is a good sign of maturity, Daddy, that you know that you do not have enough Love yet and that you have to build up and cherish Love in every aspect of your life. That is how your Love can grow and spread around you and affect everybody you know and meet."

Chapter 34
INTRUDER

"May the forces of evil become confused on the way to your house." (George Carlin)

As the storyline goes, it is 2010 and I am now married to my Internal Self Helper. This fact has given me new and tremendous internal self-confidence and power. I eagerly and impatiently wanted to go to Starlines. However, after finishing the writing of the previous chapter in May 2014, something happened which caused me to interrupt the natural flow of the story. I had to write it down immediately and insert it right here. For that reason, some of the terms I use in this chapter will be described in detail much later in the book.

I had a dream about participating at a meeting in a spacious room full of people. Everybody had a red book which was supposed to be the topic of the meeting. Two men in fancy striped suits were walking around and checking the situation and atmosphere. They were obviously in charge. Some woman was giving me a red book, too.

The mood in the room was celebratory because the book described a study that was an immense success. The men in suits started to talk about the development of mental tools capable of infiltrating human brains to control them. That was the purpose of the study. I could see that all the participants were already under the influence of those tools, except for the two men in striped suits. I found this disgusting and wanted to leave.

I looked outside through the window and saw a wildly screaming man trying to dig into the soil with his bare hands like an animal in an apparent effort to hide underground. I ran out of the building. No one was following me, but I knew that cameras were everywhere. I saw another man furiously cutting the bushes with a large machete without any coordination.

Then I discovered that the building was on a large plateau and the only way to go down was through elevators in the middle of it. The elevators were heavily guarded by men in military fatigues. I knew I could not go there, so I ran into the bushes aware of the cameras following me every step. I was thinking that they can either kill me, make me crazy like the man digging in a soil, or reduce me to a wild creature like the man cutting the bushes. I woke up and was lying there thinking that my dream was like a movie about a hero trying to destroy a place which had such a despicable purpose.

A few days later, I went to sleep shortly after midnight. About ten or fifteen minutes later, I was awakened by a very loud tremendous explosion. Immediately after that, I heard voices. I was sure the voices were either in some of the neighboring apartments or right below on the street. I opened the door to the balcony and, with a shocking surprise, saw nothing. Nobody was outside, and everything was quiet. I could not understand this because I could also smell gunpowder everywhere in my apartment. I was walking around somewhat reluctant to go to bed again since I had the feeling that someone was there with me. Finally, I did go to sleep again, but soon I was dreaming about wrestling with someone right there in my bed. I was screaming:
"Get out of me, get out of me...!"
The wrestling was very real, very physical. I felt that someone was trying to subdue me to either take something out of my body, or force something into my body, or both. Sometimes when I am going through a hypnagogic state, I can hear myself screaming with difficulty. You probably have done this when you are trying to talk and wake up at the same time.

After I woke up, I went into the bathroom and saw that the left side of my head was red and irritated, as if someone had tried to push me or drag me or slap me. It took me awhile to go to sleep again. It was ninety degrees

Fahrenheit in my bedroom, because the air conditioning was not yet running in the building. Nonetheless, I had to pull a thick blanket all over my body because I was shaking from cold. I stayed like that throughout the rest of the night. In the morning, I saw that my sheet was turned completely sideways, and it was far more wrinkled than usual.

For the next few days, I was questioning the people in security, in the office, in maintenance and other tenants about the loud explosion. Nobody had heard anything.

I was eager to know what all of that meant and tried to connect with Gardener twice in an altered state, but I was not successful. Then I had another dream. I was walking under a bridge somewhere when I met someone looking exactly as if I would see myself in the mirror. I said: "Jozef, why are you doing this to me? We are usually united and only one!"

We were standing very close to each other like a manager arguing with the umpire at a baseball game. The other Jozef said nothing, and just calmly walked away.

Now I really needed to know what all these things meant. I was able to find Gardener near Alpha Squared Station in Focus 42 that evening during meditation. He was waiting for me, and we started to communicate. I thanked him for coming and asked him to explain the incident with the explosion.

"An unfriendly entity not only crossed the membrane from another dimension, but with the explosion also created a hole in the membrane to be able to temporarily enter your world in one of his extra-dimensional identities. Obviously, the people in your building could not hear it or smell the gunpowder, because they vibrate on much lower frequency than you do," said Gardener.

"Who was he and what did he want?" I asked.

"It was a Reptilian king. It is better to say one of the kings because they have many. When they reach a higher level in their hierarchy, they can call themselves kings. Likewise, there are many Reptilian kingdoms. This king wanted to replace a part of your earthly mind with part of his mind, so that he could radically change the course of your development and stop your work. Didn't you feel that you were wrestling with a reptile in your bed?"

"Yes, I did. I felt like Crocodile Dundee!" and only then did I realize and remember that I was being grabbed by four limbs instead of two.

"He had lowered his vibrations almost to your level. He kept just a small difference which enabled him not to be seen by you when you woke up. But he also created a cold spot around him, and you started to shake from the cold. He left when you fought him off."

"Can you also explain my dream to me, Your Majesty?" I asked.

"Well, you secretly visited the Reptilians' school where they teach how to manipulate and control human beings on your planet. Many Reptilians incarnate into human bodies, usually into rich and influential families through which they are trying to control planetary political and economic structures. These entities have lost their connections to the Ultimate Creator. You must be careful now when they know about you and your visit to their school because they might attack not only your mind, but, through their planetary servants, they can also harm your physical body. But I am confident that we can protect you. Meeting your doppelganger in a dream was just a reminder to contact me. It was also a warning that the Reptilians might be aware not only of your presence in their realm, but also of your ability to be multi-dimensional."

It was obvious to me now that there were not only beings who were helping me, but also those who did not want this book to be published. And now back to Starlines.

Chapter 35
BEYOND THE EARTH

"Experience is evidence." (James Redfield in Celestine Prophecy)

During the last week of July 2010, I was finally back at the Monroe Institute for the program Starlines, because I had fulfilled the requirement of graduating from Gateway, Lifeline and Exploration 27. Both Starlines and Starlines II are the jewels of the Monroe lineup of programs. They were created by Dr. Franceen King after she received instructions from her internal guidance. This was after Robert Monroe departed from our physical world in 1995.

Franceen's internal guidance asked her to develop ways for participants to be able to travel in an altered state to the galactic core as representatives of the consciousness of our planet. She also received the secret of the slingshot technique from her guidance. This technique enables a superfast transfer of consciousness throughout the space and time spectrum of very high vibrational frequencies.

At Starlines, we would go to the Focus Levels of 34, 35, 42 and 49. Lee Stone assisted Franceen at this program. Franceen gave us all the necessary background information related to and needed for all that we were intended to do during our space travels. We had a lot of lectures and discussions about it. I was very eager to look for answers to the questions I had brought with me.

I wanted to understand the I-There, the Bonded I-There Clusters, and the Infinite Sea of Bonded I-There Clusters mysteriously described in Robert Monroe's books. I also wanted to fly to the Great Emitter aperture and see what the Stargate was and what might be behind it.

The magic of TMI brought the first marvelous experiences with the very first resetting exercise. Immediately after getting into an altered state, I felt that my physical, emotional and mental bodies were being balanced, and I was being told that I needed to be perfectly balanced for the higher vibrational levels. I felt wonderful and I was told that it had been done by the Guardians. They were now talking to me:

"You see, Menev, when we put you in balance with everything, then the Universe is within you, and you are everywhere in the Universe. The Galactic Core is right in front of your nose!"

"Then what should I do when I feel like I just want to surrender and enjoy my journey to the stars?" I asked.

"Well, surrendering is not enough; it can only move you to the front of the Stargate. You will need much more to pass through the Stargate. But remember, you must grow into it! You have merely finished The Monroe Kindergarten! Then they showed me my ISH, my spiritual wife, in beautiful white clothes: "You see, she is waiting for you, and she has unconditional Love for you. She is waiting for you, and she wants to cross new boundaries with you and maybe she can even help you to pass through the Stargate."

"What should I do now?"

"You should show her your unconditional Love. At the beginning, you could just bring her a flower! And then, things might start to happen!"

In the next exercise, we applied the slingshot technique to reach vibrations beyond the Earth Life System, which Franceen defined as Focus Levels 34 and 35. I would describe the solitude of such a state of mind as quieter than quiet. I was sending out the question:

"Is anyone there?"

Mister Q arrived on the back of a huge black cricket.

"What are you up to?" he asked me.

"I want to know about the Stargate, but I do not know how to begin."

"Don't be so humble. Look at yourself, you are very small compared to me. You want to tell people that they are unlimited beings and, yet you now choose such a small form? Did you forget that you are Menev the Great who knows how things work around here? First enlarge your form; just do it!" I did and became as tall as Mister Q was, twenty feet tall.

"That is better. You want to take a ride with me? My cricket is big enough for both of us, and if he is not, I will just make him longer."

I jumped on.

"As you can see, we are right above your Earth Life System, and up above us you can see a number of our observation spots. We like to come closer to your frontiers to talk when someone like you shows up."

In the next exercise, I asked for somebody new. The Being who showed up was Starman, and he looked just like Jeff Bridges did in the movie with the same title. He suggested that he could help me in a unique way:

"I was living on your planet, and I have incarnated into some human bodies. Many other spiritual beings don't do that; they are mostly very curious, yet careful and hesitant to incarnate. However, we can communicate with humans and other life forms from your planet by scanning your minds when you shift out of your physical bodies. It is quite convenient for us to communicate with you that way when we are observing you and your planet."

In another exercise, we also researched the vibrational level of Focus 33, which I found to be very interesting. When I was looking back towards the earth, I could see zillions of different alien consciousness vehicles forming a ring around the planet. Many of them looked like jellyfish or giant bacteria, but they were also constantly changing their shape. Very occasionally, some of them moved toward the planet and disappeared from the ring, apparently trying to incarnate. But most of them looked reluctant to do so. Occasionally, some of them also flew in a different direction, going upwards and leaving the ring and the Earth life System.

During a sharing of our experiences, one of my

classmates described being at a party with aliens. Another classmate was touched by some alien beings during his experience.

Chapter 36
VOYAGER AND ALPHA SQUARED

"Things are not physical or spiritual. We are, always. We sometimes have physical experiences." (F.H. "Skip" Atwater)

On the second day of Starlines, with Franceen's guidance, we created the tools necessary for our class to work effectively together by empowering our group consciousness.

We focused our minds on the inter-dimensional spacecraft, Voyager 8, which had already been utilized by other Starlines groups in programs before. We found Voyager in the now familiar vibrational space of Focus 34 and 35. It was obviously in the planetary system of our Sun, and it would always be there waiting for us. Later Ra told me that he usually saw Voyager 8 hovering in orbit in the space halfway between Earth and Mars. It had a huge logo of TMI on its side. Inside, I saw a generator room with chairs in the circle around the bottom of the ship which was made of glass. The Generator room had a large crystal in the middle that was waiting to be charged by our intentions which would then power the ship. Voyager 8 also had small personal pods for use in our individual venturing outside.

Each participant had personal quarters on the ship which we could design according to our personal needs and preferences. A young man from Colombia, Alejandro, had visited a very similar ship before coming to Starlines when, in a meditative precognition state, he had apparently moved a little bit ahead in time.

Our repeated and continued presence at the Voyager vibrational level finally enabled me to start to understand the concept of consciousness originally defined by Robert Monroe as I-There. When I was in I-There mode, I was fully aware of being out of my temporary physical existence on planet Earth. I was also fully aware of numerous connections to Earth representing my incarnated lives there. At the same time, I was fully aware of pointers leading to other aspects of me residing in other star systems and other dimensions. This knowledge remains with me even today.

After Lee reminded us that gratitude amplifies receiving, we started our first trips outside of or within Voyager 8. I opted for using my personal pod and decided to just fly around our planetary system. There was no sense of time at the vibrational level I was in. And space was no obstacle either, I could be anywhere in an instant. Also, information was flowing into my mind instantly. Usually, it was not even necessary to know where it came from.

I found many non-physical beings present in our solar system, but also physical biological life underneath the surface of Mars and Jupiter's moon Europa. These included some Martians who had been forced to abandon their physical bodies and had to learn to live in different dimensions. I saw that just as our planet was being watched from the stations on the Moon, also the Sun was being observed by advanced beings from the system of Aldebaran. They had built observation stations on the planet of Mercury. I tried to absorb all the information, but I also eagerly wanted to move on to the stars.

After several exercises in our solar system, we were ready to venture out of it. But, before we could do that, we needed to learn to move our consciousness into the vibrational level of Focus 42. As a group, we were looking for a large non-physical spiritual station called Alpha Squared. Again, the station had already been used by other explorers from TMI programs. I found it far away but still in our Local Bubble. There was a large platform for the landings and departures of the numerous ships of spiritual explorers who constantly created a buzzing cacophony around it.

Inside the station, there was a large, impressive lobby

and numerous rooms with specifically designed tools for explorers. One of the bigger rooms was The Memory Room, which, besides other devices also had some communication tools for connecting to the Akashic Library. I wanted to go there, but first I decided to see my personal quarters. My ISH wife was there; she praised me for the continuation of my exploration, wished me good luck and then left.

When I was finally sitting in my armchair, suddenly someone opened the door from outside, peeked in and left. Wow! It was Juanzetta, one of my classmates! What did that mean??? By now, I had been to several programs, but I had never had the desire to get involved with one of my classmates. It was not even on the list of my intentions when going to the Monroe Institute. Now, however, I was not only physically aroused, I was also deeply exhausted, yet awaiting and excited. I needed to quickly go back to the physical.

Chapter 37
HADIEN THE FRIEND

"One loyal friend is worth ten thousand relatives."
(Euripides)

After settling comfortably into the higher vibrational levels, I decided to use my newly gained abilities for some travels deep into the vast Universe. I asked Hadien to take me to various places on separate occasions during our exercises. I also used these opportunities for the numerous questions I wanted to ask.

Hadien was always very friendly and usually asked me to use the same pyramidal form as his for my spiritual body. Then, we enjoyed our additional connection through the liquid in which our numerous roots on the bottoms of our pyramids were immersed. But first, he wanted to give me some interesting information about what he characterized as the local area of our Milky Way.

We were heading to Sirius, Arcturus, Orion, and the Pleiades in our first trip. According to Hadien, Arcturus was an old star which could be very helpful for spiritual travelers. When we were approaching the Pleiades, I asked him if he knew where the beings called Annunaki had come from to our Solar system:

"The beings you call Annunaki on your planet are a very old physical civilization who built their societies around Betelgeuse in the Orion constellation. But, when their mother star became too hot, many of them moved to the Pleiades. Then later, some of them even moved to the Sirius neighborhood. They used the movement of a giant planet some of you call Nibiru or Planet X, with its eccentric orbit around your Sun, for coming close to the Earth. Now, they stand ready if a catastrophe should happen on the Earth. They are prepared to save and support the surviving people and animals, renew terraforming, and preserve the continuation of the livability of your planet and humanity."

Then Hadien asked me if I would like to see more planets. I remembered the newly discovered Gliese 581 g, so I suggested her. He moved the ship and soon I could see a red dwarf star. He took me closer to the planet, so I would have a good overview. The side of the planet facing the star looked like the Sahara Desert, but with big, tall bare mountains; the other side looked like the Antarctic, with icy mountains. Between these two very different halves of the planet was a green belt. Apparently, the planet was always facing its sun with the same side, like our Moon is facing our planet. Hadien told me that the inhabitants live in the green belt and their venturing into either the cold or hot part is very limited. But he told me that they were very happy, living there in true mutual Love.

"How can they have real Love and be so happy in such a difficult physical environment?" I asked.

"They do not pretend, so no lies or mutual deceptions are necessary. They are always telling the truth and they do not know what greed is," answered my friend.

On another opportunity, I curiously asked why Hadien was always waiting for me and was eager to help when I expressed the intention to see him. He answered:

"I want to help you because biological life is very rare and precious throughout the physical universe. And I am glad that you chose to communicate with me. There are a lot of us spiritual beings for each one of you temporary spiritual travelers from the biological planets. It is always great for me to learn about physical entities. What can I do for you this time?"

"Tell me how I look in my spiritual form?"

"You look as you choose to. But most of the time while you are here, you are not thinking about it. Your form naturally corresponds to the environment or to the beings you are communicating with. Right now, you look like me, you have a pyramidal shape. But you are little smaller than I am, because you are showing me some respect. And that is not really necessary for you to do."

"But how do I know then who the spiritual forms truly are?" I continued.

"Simply ask them; just tell them to show you their essence. Many of them will not want to show you who they truly are, just as people on the Earth like to pretend that they are different than they seem to be."

Suddenly I had a tricky idea:

"Can you show me your essence, Hadien?"

And even though he was reluctant to do it, in a flash of two or three seconds, I saw a big gray head shaped like a drop of water upside down, a very small box-like almost square body, and very tiny but long hands that looked like hoses. He seemed to be a little embarrassed and suggested another topic.

During another exercise, I learned about pulsars from Hadien.

"They create, maintain and stimulate the morphogenetic field net which is a matrix for spreading the Mind of God in the physical Universe. They are like knots in the matrix of the Universe. After pulsars are created by natural processes, sometimes they are moved into the knots of the matrix to keep the proper alignment of the physical universe," said Hadien.

"Who is moving them?"

"Some say super-intelligences, yet others say God. I can tell you only what I know. I also must learn from beings more developed than I am. If the pulsars positions in the matrix happen to change, super-intelligences move them back into proper alignment. The conclusion of many of the scientists on the Earth that consciousness is not involved in the expanding of the physical universe after what they call the Big Bang is an illusion. Pulsars are parts of the complex warning system about the proper or improper balance of the physical universe. They are also used for navigation. The basic consciousness structure is perfectly organized according to the principles of sacred geometry, even though the physical structure of the Universe looks to be very random. God and the Creators have a lot of work to do to organize the physical universes differently all the time. It is a never-ending process of creation. God is not only pouring newly manifested physical matter into the Universe, but also black matter and black energy."

He then wanted to show me how to do an advanced type of traveling by using black holes. As he said, black holes are gateways into different galaxies which can even be in different clusters or even in different universes or dimensions.

"But you have to pass through nothing," he said and mysteriously smiled.

"To go through a black hole, you use pulsars for the navigation. Those who don't know how to get through black holes are warned by pulsars not to try as they could be annihilated."

He took me into a big ship that looked like a giant vortex and explained that we would move through a black hole with tremendous spinning. During the spinning, we were passing through a large tube with incredible colors. Then, we had dived into nothingness, no stars, no light. He let me enjoy the nothingness, only the two of us in the ship, no light, and no sound outside whatsoever, just complete darkness.

Afterwards, we spun back into the manifested universe through a different black hole. I recognized that we came out somewhere else, like into another universe or at least another cluster or galaxy. I asked him where we were. He said we were in the Virgo Super-cluster. I have no idea how in that black nothingness he had found the proper black hole for our return. Then, he became visibly emotional and rather sentimental. He said that he would like to check on his family since he had been away from them for a long time. Hadien put me on another similar big ship and said:

"Do not worry; my friend shall take you home."

The new ship passed through a black hole again by spinning into the nothing and back into the manifested universe. But Hadien's friend piloting the craft was not happy about me and said:

"If you guys knew how much energy these excursions of yours cost us, you would probably think twice about traveling out of your galaxies!"

With that he stopped talking to me completely until he let me out of the ship. You can imagine how impatiently I was waiting for my friend Hadien to come back into our Milky Way. Later, I saw him again many times and continued to learn so much from him.

Chapter 38
RA THE COP

"Be kinder than necessary because everyone you meet is fighting some battle." (J.M. Barrie)

While Hadien was visiting his family, I decided to see where Ra could take me for a change. I wanted to try to travel with him even though I knew that his approach could be quite different. I also already understood that when we reach the high vibrations, and we properly call the Higher Beings; they will usually show up. Ra showed up indeed and said:

"Hey, I know that you guys are always in a hurry because you have those funny exercises, so let's quickly do what you want. Oh, look at him, boy! He's learned a lot! He looks like me!"

And I looked at myself and saw that I was shaped like him, like the tall and cruel Ra from the movie "Stargate."

"I see that you are not a pussy anymore! Hurry up! I have to crush a rebellion at the planet of Vida, so you will really see some cosmic action of the Enforcer of the order!" insisted Ra with obvious pleasure.

I tried to tell him that I did not know when I would need to go back to the physical, but he said it had been taken care of. He quickly took me to his intergalactic tetrahedron ship.

After passing through a black hole and back into the physical universe, we approached a line of maybe ten or twelve stars. Ra anchored the ship in space, told me that we were in the Constellation of Spear, called someone inside the ship and told him to wait for me. Then, we transferred into a smaller craft. He said he had programmed everything, so I could return to the intergalactic ship any time. I would just push the button on a little pocket device he gave me. Then we were quickly approaching the planetary system where Vida was located. I could see that she had two Suns and that she had a pale bluish color. I could see greenish water and brownish land but in the opposite ratio of that on Earth. There was more land there and the seas looked like giant lakes.

"We are going to land," Ra interrupted my observations. "Remember, we are now in another dimension. Your physical body is at your Monroe Institute, so you cannot materialize here and even if you could, I would not let you. You shall see some action, so watch carefully!"

Our craft was slowly approaching a medieval type of town protected by walls around it.

"Look at them, these lawless gangsters are attacking the capital city and the government does not know what to do. We have to keep order!" insisted Ra.

When we got closer, I could see men with spears riding giant grasshopper-like insects who were attacking similarly looking defenders who were spread outside the walls of town on their own giant grasshoppers. Both sides also had several even bigger insects that looked like praying mantises who were grabbing men off the opposing grasshoppers and ripping them apart. The scene was very chaotic and violent. We landed on a plaza inside the town behind the walls. Dozens of men there immediately fell on their knees and started to worship Ra. But he quickly ran into the building that looked like a hangar and pulled out a big weapon like a mortar. The men opened the gate in the wall and Ra started to spray everybody outside with large flames from the weapon. The grasshoppers, praying mantises and fighters were burned alive. I could not take it anymore and I expressed my disgust to Ra. He was busy with the weapon and did not even look at me, but said:

"I knew it! Go home! You are still a big pussy!"

I jumped into the small craft, pushed the designated button, and returned to the intergalactic ship to go back home. "It is not only on Earth that we would be doing something like that," I thought to myself and became very sad. I realized that we were not the only violent humanoid creatures in the universe. I docked at Alpha Squared early. Juanzetta saw me at the station, and seeing that I was sad, she tried to cheer me up. I returned to the physical breathing very heavily and with a headache.

When I was sharing the story in the group, some participants expressed displeasure, wondering how I could see something like that. Franceen even suggested for me to look for possible conflicts within myself. I respectfully disagreed. I saw what I saw. This was not the first time that I realized that participants at various new age functions want to see and share only rosy stuff. They wish to see angels, rainbows, lights, beautiful colors and so on. Again, I have a different outlook. While we should be trying to look for the good, we must understand that we are the reflection of not only the good spiritual world, but also the bad one. And when we see injustice or violence, we cannot and should not ignore it.

Another participant, Stig from Norway, discovered a way to travel back and forth through a black hole from the vibrational level of Focus 15. After hearing that, I have often used "Stig's shortcut" and I really appreciate it, my friend! During his travel in the same exercise, Stig also saw a planet where primitive beings were viciously fighting. He also saw another planet shortly before the collapse of its civilization where everybody was desperately meditating to prevent catastrophe.

Another extreme experience of participant Bob from the same exercise properly illustrates my point. After he was unhappy with the area of the universe where his trip took him, he simply asked there:
"Why is there so much shit here?"
And the answer came quickly:
"Because there are so many assholes around here!"

Chapter 39
COUNCILS

"Not only does God play dice with the world. He does not let us see what He has rolled." (Stanislaw Lem)

After the experience with Ra, I wanted to have a more pleasant time. I looked for the Cosmic Lady named Ruala. I found her near Sagitarius A, a place relatively close to our galactic black hole where she had parked her intergalactic ship. She asked me where I would like to go. I do not know why, but I asked her for one more trip through a black hole. She discouraged me by asking why I would like to see nothingness again. So instead, we just were observing ships going into and back out of the black hole. I realized that more ships were going in than coming back and I asked Ruala about that:

"Well, those going in are mostly cargo ships and they are carrying the Loosh," she answered.

"Why are they not coming back?" I asked.

"We do not know; they just disappear in the dark. There are many theories about why."

I told her that I knew about the planet of Silvana. She was surprised about my knowing what was going on. She said she knew that there was one planet with Loosh processing plants in each galaxy being administered by that galaxy's Gardener.

The next time when I was in the Memory Room, I wanted to download information about the Loosh. All I got back was a message telling me that I used to work in Gardener's office at Silvana. I wanted to know more, so I tried to call the Cluster Council, but instead seven members of Council of Galactic Guardians showed up.

Gardener was presiding, but he was different from how I usually knew him, he was very official. He said my issue was not important enough to gather the Cluster Council.

He also said that the only reason they let me know about the Loosh was that I had worked for him at Silvana. When I was trying to ask where the Loosh goes, he avoided answering my question. He said he oversaw processing and shipping and that was all I needed to know. The meeting was over.

Obviously, I tried again to ask about the possibility of meeting with the Cluster Council in the Memory room. "They will not come here, you have to use a teleporter," was the surprising answer.

I found a teleporter and stepped into what was like a very small elevator booth for one person and expressed my intention. Shortly, I found myself standing right in the center of a large round room. There were several rows of seats full of maybe fifty or so beings with various forms. Some of them looked like British judges, others were in astronaut suits, and some were in fur coats like from the Ice Age.

"Oh, now we have one of those Earthlings. What is your name Earthling?" a loud voice came from an unidentified place in the room.

"Menev Skjoerg Plautus" I almost stuttered.

"Do you have a question or suggestion for our Council?"

"I have several questions, if I may!"

"Look at him! Go ahead quickly!"

"Is Ra a robot?"

I could not believe what I had just said. I had indeed had a suspicion for a while that Ra could be a consciousness robot, but certainly it was not the question I wanted to ask; it did not fit the situation at all.

"What kind of question is that? We do not know who you are talking about; you must find that out for yourself! Another question?"

"Can I know more about the Super-Loosh?"

Again, I could not believe that I pronounced the word which had come into my mind for the first time right in the moment when I formulated the question. I could see that several council members were clearly irritated.

JOZEF SIMKOVIC   HOW TO KISS THE UNIVERSE

"That is none of your business! Mister Secretary mark it for the investigative committee! Next question, Earthling!"

"Why did God create duality and evil?"

"Finally, we have a question which makes sense! Look pal, all that spiritual talk about unity and oneness is nice, and it is important that you grow that way and recognize the need for that direction. But can you imagine how things would develop if there were only unity and oneness? That is why the Lord God His Majesty created duality and evil, so he could develop and enjoy himself! The worst evil inspires magnificent, good, unlimited hate inspires unconditional Love, and the deepest desire inspires peaceful compassion. And now, go back to your planet. It is up to you to figure out how to spread this message around!"

The Council disappeared, and I found myself crying in my physical body.

Chapter 40
RUALA

"Vocatus Atque, Non Vocatus, Deus Aderit (Called or not called, God will be there)." (Carl Jung)

After I had surprised myself by asking the Cluster Council about the Super-Loosh, obviously I was eager to learn more. Another visit to the Memory Room and an inquiry into the Akashic Library did not bring me any answers. I decided to connect again with the female entity Ruala. In accord with my precognition, Ruala was supposed to teach me about Cosmic Love. I had a feeling that the Super-Loosh probably had a lot to do with Love.

Ruala was again at her station near Sagittarius A. I told her what happened to me at the Cluster Council. She suggested that I might also ask to meet with the Personal Cluster Council. She said that it was not a permanent body, but an ad hoc committee that could always be appointed when someone asked. A Personal Cluster Council would be willing to be more specific in relation to the needs of the requestor.

Then I asked her what she knew about the Super-Loosh. Ruala told me that I first had to understand the Cosmic Love. Then she reminded me that she was supposed to teach me about it and that she had sent me an advance signal to prepare me for the lesson. Cosmic Love, as she explained, is unconditional Love supplied by the Ultimate Creator which is expected to be cherished, magnified, and returned to God from all manifested living beings. Unconditional acceptance of one being by another is supposed to be added to the Loosh. She said there were several theories in the spiritual world about how the Cosmic Love and Super-Loosh were interconnected.

According to the most popular spiritual world theory, the Ultimate Creator, God the Source of All, produces the

Super-Loosh from the Loosh supplied from the physical universe. God allegedly needs very large quantities of high quality Loosh just to get lesser amounts of the Super-Loosh. God creates another local Big Bang and another universe only when a big enough mass of Super-Loosh has been accumulated.

According to what Ruala told me, there are infinite numbers of creations, Big Bangs, and universes. It became clear to me that Super-Loosh must obviously be the substance of godly-like essence because it is composed of only the highest, the most positive and compassionate emotions extracted out of the Loosh that we humans and other biological creatures produce.

"Apparently that is what they do at Silvana, they purify the Loosh for God," I thought to myself.

I was very happy that Ruala was willing to give me information about subjects that were utterly fascinating to me. I expressed my desire to know more about the Stargate.

Meanwhile, we were cruising in distant parts of the Universe and when I looked back, I saw the Andromeda galaxy and the Milky Way galaxy looking just like ordinary binary stars. I could sense the surge of energies which were heading toward our Milky Way and Andromeda like gales of winds.

"Stargate means out of the stars, out of the universes as we know them," said Ruala.

"Where does the Stargate lead?" I eagerly asked.

"It leads into the Unknown and beyond. We in the spiritual world have theories about it. You have already experienced the Nothingness encountered when we speed up time travel by using the black holes gateways. But the Stargate is not a black hole as many on your Earth believe; neither is it a device for creating a wormhole. The Unknown and the Stargate are beyond the Nothingness. We believe that the Unknown beyond the Nothingness is mainly composed of Dark Matter and Dark Energy with no physical manifestation present at all. Only very few spiritual beings have ventured into the Unknown."

"Is it perhaps heading to the Aperture, God, Source, Great Emitter, or however you call it?" I impatiently try to grasp at least a little bit of understanding.

"Some say so. Some say that there is an unlimited sea of pure consciousness without any form whatsoever beyond the Stargate."

"Can I get through the Stargate in my present form?"

"Well, maybe some would tell you it could be possible, but only if you would have enough Cosmic Love."

And I knew I did not have enough yet, but I was determined to begin work on it immediately. With this new knowledge, I felt myself going back "down" into TMI-There in Focus 27.

I suddenly felt that I had something small in the palm of my hand. Somehow, I knew it had to be a piece of the Super-Loosh. I opened my hand and saw that I was holding a red pulsating heart about half inch big. "That is the souvenir Franceen suggested we might ask for during our exercise," I thought to myself. But I had not asked for it; someone had given it to me without my asking. Perhaps, the Ultimate Creator had done so. There must also be another earthly name for the Super-Loosh. That name apparently is the Super-Love.

Chapter 41
GUESTS

"All of reality, as we know it, exists because we intend it to. I suspect that if we didn't intend it to be, then it wouldn't." *(Joe McMoneagle in, Mind Trek p. 136)*

I was always feeling incredible support from the group during Starlines. This support was not surprising because everybody had already participated in at least Gateway Voyage, Lifeline or Guidelines and Exploration 27. Some of us had participated in even more programs at The Monroe Institute.

We also expressed the notion to do something extraordinary together. Some of us had taken numerous pictures of the orbs that gather around the large crystal on the grounds of TMI. One of us, the lady from Holland, suggested that we could use our unified energies and try to call the extraterrestrial beings to visit with us right there on the beautiful meadow in the foothills of the Blue Ridge Mountains.

Tuesday evening, we stood around the crystal holding hands and quietly sending our intention to the sky. Each one of us expressed our intentions in her or his very polite unique, inviting, friendly, appreciative, and humble way. We received good feelings; but we could not see anything extraordinary except for the magnified number of orbs flowing around and caught by our cameras.

The next evening, while trying again, several of us, one by one, recited invitations for the ET's. These invitations were in the several different languages represented in our group that week. By doing this, everyone could focus on the intention at the same time. This second night, even more orbs were present. Dozens and dozens of them swarmed around the crystal and around the trees. When we looked up at the sky, scattered clouds formed an almost perfect circle with the middle right above us.

With this much progress, we were very determined to magnify our effort the next day, which was the last evening of our program. Alejandro had consulted with his shamanic teacher in Colombia over the phone. The shaman supported our effort and gave Alejandro a formalized evocation which Alejandro recited in Spanish.

The orbs just went completely crazy: they were everywhere. We knew we were visited. Some of us were yelling when seeing large round light objects moving around with lightning speed. I concentrated on taking pictures. On one of the pictures, in the left upper corner, there is a clear silhouette of a saucer shaped object. Stig had two very similar pictures. The visitors with the orbs did not land or show themselves in any other way, but we were, nonetheless, elated with the obvious success of our endeavor.

At that time, I did not expect any follow up to this story. But later, I had a very powerful and vivid dream on Selge Beach in Turkey in September 2010. Several shinning-colored discs, like small compact discs, flew in rapid succession through my third eye area. I woke up screaming: "What is going on?!"

The next day in the morning, I had a successful meditation about that dream and received this message:

"The discs were sent by those who visited you at Starlines. They were specifically sent through your third eye interface to confirm that the visit at TMI was very real indeed. The discs were just carriers of information coming into your mind for your use in the future. These informational discs needed much less energy than the real ships at Monroe which came quite close to all of you there. Inter-dimensional beings do not make visitations into the lower physical vibrational areas very often because they require a lot of energy for manifestation, but your efforts were very genuine, and they wanted to honor them."

Chapter 42
MIDNIGHT, THE STARS AND YOU

"Love starts when we push aside our ego and make room for someone else." *(Rudolf Steiner)*

This chapter is dedicated to my beloved Juanzetta. During Starlines, when I saw her for the first time, she was sitting across the room on the carpeted floor while I was enjoying a seat on my favorite sofa. We were quite indifferent to each other during the first days of the program. I was not very pleased by her comment while I was sharing my opinion about the movie "The Imaginarium of Doctor Parnassus" with the group. Apparently, I misunderstood her reaction. However, after she peeked into my quarters at the Alpha Squared Station during an exercise on Tuesday, the next day something happened that started a wonderful relationship which is blossoming more and more every day.

Before my first trip with Hadien, I came to the Alpha Squared Station and took the elevator from the platform to my quarters. When the door closed, Juanzetta was in that elevator, too! Without any waiting, our spiritual forms changed to spinning vortexes and melted together into one vortex. An incredible ecstatic orgasmic feeling overcame not only my spiritual, but also my physical body. It was better than "real" lovemaking on the Earth and I just wished that it would last forever. When I met physical Juanzetta in the carpet room afterwards, she told me:
"I saw you in the elevator at Alpha Squared."
"I saw you too!"
I answered, shocked, and both of us just stared at each other in awe. It took us a while to exchange information about what had happened in the elevator. Juanzetta's experience was not different than mine.

I was with her again that Wednesday during our exercise into the Earth core. I held her around the waist while we were both enjoying the beautiful colorful energies flowing all around us there in the belly of our Mother Gaia. Then, during the traditional closing circle of the program on Thursday evening, while posing for group photos, it was obvious that Juanzetta and I had to stand next to each other. Our hands, at some moment, somehow also naturally found each other.

Later that evening, after the exciting interaction with our extraterrestrial guests on the meadow of TMI which I described in the previous chapter, everybody left to go into the building except for Juanzetta and me. Suddenly it was Midnight, the Stars and the two of us. And our lips found each other. As she told me later, while she was thinking, "I want this man to kiss me," at the same moment, I bent to her and did.

Our growing closeness was feeding on that kiss over and over the next eleven months we spent on the phone between Washington D.C. and Birmingham, Alabama, until we could meet in person again and fall into each other's arms.

I immediately googled her after I got home from Starlines and found out what a wonderful human being I had just met. Dr. Juanzetta Shew Flowers has dedicated her life to studying, practicing and teaching nursing and is a member of the Alabama Nursing Hall of Fame and the Alabama Health Care Hall of Fame. She is also a very knowledgeable and devoted lover of animals and nature.

During my life, much more than most men do, I have admired ladies. From my many spiritual experiences, I know that we shall not move significantly towards a new quality of civilization without raising the feminine aspect and achieving a true genuine balance between the sexes on the whole planet. In Juanzetta, I have finally found a female from whom I can learn every day how to flow in that direction. When I called her the same day after returning home, we were on the phone for three hours. And even today after more than seven years later, our conversations are just as interesting and exciting as they were when the flames were first lighted.

Then, interesting things started to happen to me as had similarly occurred when I have first started my spiritual journey. I could hear Juanzetta calling my name when I was in a hypnagogic state, or in my meditation I felt that she was sending her Love to me. She also sent me her spiritual healing dolphin, Sydney, to help me with some of my physical discomforts and slight illnesses.

I saw her in one of my dreams in her bathroom getting ready for bed. She was dressed in a beautiful satin gown. I was standing in the bathroom door with ice skates on my feet (I am a good ice skater) staring at her, smelling her perfume. The scene was very surreal, and I knew it was a lucid dream. I realized in it that I was in a house I had never been to before, but I was unable to take control of the lucid dream.

In another dream two days later, I came to her office and grabbed her around the shoulders from the back. She turned her face toward me, and we kissed like in the meadow at TMI. I felt an immediate physical arousal. I would rather not describe the other spicy erotic dreams I had with her several times.

But, because these strong spiritual urges were coming and coming, I wanted to know who she was and asked my guides. They gave me this message:
"You and Juanzetta have been entwining spiritual beings for thousands of years. You were together very often because both of you are very strong and developed individuals. And now you have the opportunity to tie the knot with her again."

Chapter 43
CONTEMPLATING STARGATE

"The greatest illusion is that mankind has limitations."
(Robert Monroe)

I was quite occupied by thoughts, dreams, and meditations about Juanzetta after returning from Starlines, and was now starting to prepare myself for the upcoming Starlines II in October. I had secured the last available place before leaving Starlines. My intention for the program was clear - to resolve the mystery of the Stargate.

But before I could analyze further what I had learned, I had to resolve a vivid nightmare dream which happened to me in August. I was somewhere in an apartment trying to go to sleep while I was already dreaming. But I could not sleep because I felt a very strong demonic presence all around me. I could not see any specific entities, but I just wanted them to go away. I was screaming and waving my hands trying to chase them away. I was not afraid of them, but I wanted them to disappear. Obviously, I was screaming from the dream when I was waking up. It had been very, very scary. It made me think about the Amazonian shamans helping people to deal with demons while under the influence of ayahuasca, known as the "soul wine."

Two days later, I decided to connect with Ruala and talk with her about the Stargate. At first, I asked her about the dream and whether it had any connection to my efforts.
"Obviously you tried in your dream to pass through the Stargate, because in a dream you can indeed gather enough Cosmic Love to accomplish that. However, you apparently did not accumulate enough, and you were also reluctant and unsure of how to proceed. You were attacked by the powerful demons who like to hang out around the Stargate."
"What do they want from me?" I asked.
"They want to scare you; they do not want you to know the

Truth! You should learn how you can pass through the Stargate in your meditations. Gratitude and Love can be your accelerators. You should also improve your slingshot technique before you attempt the crossing. And do not forget about your Super-Loosh heart."

She then reminded me to take diligent care of my precious gift because it represents the concept of unlimited Love.

I learned later about the power of my Super-Loosh heart when I used it in Voyager 8 during the group's charging of the crystal of intention. The crystal started to pulsate in the rhythm of a heartbeat and the feeling of the magnified power of intention became tremendous.

"What does the Stargate look like, Cosmic Lady?"

"It depends on how it has been manifested for you. By the way, there is not just one Stargate, there are infinite numbers of stargates just as there are infinite numbers of spiritual beings. You just have to look for yours, the one which will let you pass through."

I also used the opportunity to ask Ruala about her essence.

"I am pure Love," she said, and when her form faded, all I could see was a big red pulsating heart about a foot high.

She then said:

"Love has no boundaries and hate has no boundaries. Joy has no boundaries and sadness has no boundaries. You can find unlimited Love and joy, or unlimited hate and sadness in the deep corners of the Milky Way galaxy and the Andromeda galaxy. But you can also find unlimited Love and joy or unlimited hate and sadness on the tip of your own finger. A balance between observing, involvement, and acceptance is a very necessary condition for learning how to Love."

Chapter 44
MICROWORLD

"The Universe is the periodical manifestation of this unknown Absolute Essence." (Helena Blavatsky)

My understanding of the enormous vastness of the Universe also made me think about all that exists in the opposite direction. If things can be as big as we can imagine, they also must be as small as we can imagine. Hadien once told me:

"Look, anything can always become bigger and bigger. Likewise, anything can always become smaller and smaller. There are no limitations in the growing and there are no limitations in the shrinking. There is no limit in the speed. There is only vibration and spinning. There is spinning into bigger and spinning into smaller. Spinning into shrinking can go well beyond the quantum unit. There is simply no smallest unit, no smallest anything. However, there is a stillness, and you must figure out what that is."

Afterwards, I started to feel that the keys to understanding the relationships between the manifested universes and mind or consciousness are not only deep in unlimited space but also inside the elementary microcosmic particles and beyond.

In October during meditation, I started to detect something like a fog sparsely distributed beginning on the vibrational level of Focus 21. When I reached the level of Focus 27, it was all around me and around everything. After an inquiry, I received the message that the foggy substance could be shadows which are created when consciousness starts to manifest. But, also in reverse, they are manifested when matter and energy are dispersing into consciousness. According to the message, the shadows contain particles which Earth physicists call bosons and gluons. A so-called strong force pushes the flow of intention from consciousness into matter; a weak force pushes the Loosh into the opposite direction from the matter into consciousness.

I wanted to know more and two days later I decided to call Starman into my personal rocket.

"You do not need your rocket; we can just fly and talk," said Starman. I stepped out as he suggested.

"Please Starman, do you know how the strong and weak forces work? If not, maybe you can suggest someone else who could help me."

"Anyone can know this if they are properly interested. And you are. The forces are like an interface between matter and consciousness. The strong force which creates matter is produced in the generators of manifestation. It is powered by intention. We are talking here about a change from something which has no units and cannot be quantified into units. Consciousness has no units. We can say it is like a fluid or gas, but without quantification. The weak force is produced in the generators of release and is powered by experience. With the weak force, you go from something which has units and can be quantified into something not having units and which cannot be quantified. Both types of generators are present everywhere in all the universes."

Wow, now I really had a lot to think about when preparing to go for the top Monroe program, Starlines II in October 2010.

Chapter 45
MULTI-EYES

"Everything has beauty, but not everyone sees it."
(Confucius)

The Starlines II program, again under the guidance of Dr. Franceen King with the support of co-facilitator Lee Stone and 22 participants, began in October 2010. We had people from all over the country, but also from Japan, Germany, Spain and Canada. One of our classmates was the Monroe facilitator Patty Ray Avalon. Four of the participants were taking the program for the second time and one for the third time.

I was sure I could count on help from the group, because anybody coming to a top course at TMI obviously has a lot of courage, dedication, and determination. Therefore, immediately in the first reset exercise, I asked my guides what I was supposed to do in such wonderful company:

"You will continue your communication with the beings you already met before at Starlines and other programs. But you can also learn about the beings living in particles."

"How can any be so small?"

"Size as seen with your eyes does not matter at all."

"What am I going to do with such small beings?"

"You can ask them questions like you ask us. Sometimes you may get answers. A question sometimes brings an answer, but it always creates another question. That is why you are here. We also have given you multi-eyes now. When we give you another pair of eyes, it means you can be in another Universe."

"If I would have ten pairs of eyes, could I then be in ten different universes at the same time?"

"Yes, but you are not that far yet!"

"Sometimes people are telling me that I seem to be

channeling somebody. Can I know who that being is, or who those beings are?"

"You are channeling yourself. And you have a lot of work to do!"

Only later during the program did I fully understand what had just happened. The new multi-eyes enabled me to build completely new ways of communicating. I was developing a new understanding of downloading, exchanging, and analyzing the batches of information. Robert Monroe called those batches ROTE, related organized thought energy. But I shall have more about ROTE later.

Chapter 46
DECEIVER

"You know, old friend, the appetite for power is the result of an incapacity for love." *(Gabriel Garcia Marquez)*

As I discussed before, we can encounter not only our guides and friendly entities in the spiritual world, but we can also meet entities who are looking for vulnerable souls. All kinds of attacks were happening to me throughout my spiritual journey. An interesting event also happened at Starlines II. During the meditation exercise, I was not focused enough because I had not set up clear intentions. When I slingshot myself into Focus 34 and 35, suddenly an entity in a Japanese samurai costume appeared.

"Why do you have that costume on and who are you?"
I asked with almost immediate suspicion.

"My name is Kokoro. I relate to you because I like you, I have martial arts experience and I want to lift your kokoro. (Kokoro is the fighting spirit or heart in Japanese martial arts. (My ex-wife Sasha used to call me "My Kokoro" when she felt down and needed to elevate her sad mood.)) I thought you might like my name."

"Really! What can I do for you?"
I was still not impressed, and I did not like his somewhat suspicious way of introducing himself.

"Well, you are now at the stage of your development when you need new tools and I can show them to you," insisted Kokoro.

"Why do you worry about me and, anyway, where are you from Kokoro???"

"I am from your future after your graduation from Earth and after your planet becomes uninhabitable from an upcoming catastrophe. We will have an exciting new assignment for you. We need experienced souls such as you are. The assignment is going to be close by, in Andromeda."

The exercise was over, but I had a lot to think about. I knew from my previous meditations that I would eventually stay around to help confused souls after the catastrophe on the Earth. I wanted to know what Kokoro's intentions were, so I called him again in the next meditation and asked him about my alleged Andromeda mission.

"Well, Menev, that is going to be your new I-There cluster!"

"When do I start and what am I going to do there?" I asked, seemingly curious.

"We got permission from the Cluster Council to take you to Andromeda around the year 2500 of your earthly calendar. We have a new biological planet there where terraforming, and evolution has just started to produce creatures you would probably call mammals on your planet. We need you to be part of the speeding up process of that evolution because you have had a lot of experiences. You can have a chain of plentiful and very exciting reincarnations there. Other spiritual beings would appreciate and take such an offer immediately!"

"Let me think about it, Kokoro, I will tell you the next time we meet. I love my current planet very much and I want to help her as much as I can."

I already knew that I was supposed to be on or at least around The Earth in the year 2500. As I wrote earlier, my average reincarnation cycle here is 130 years and, I have ten reincarnations to go according to the current plan. But I also have already learned that nothing is written in stone and my spiritual plans can change.

All this was very suspicious, so I asked my trusted friend Hadien for advice. Not surprisingly, he told me that Kokoro was apparently a Reptilian trying to deceive me. I was sure I was not going to allow anything like that to happen. One of the amazing tools we learned to use at Starlines II was the Portal Room which had screens where we could see another space and another time. Later we developed the ability to project our consciousness into such an environment by using a screen showing it.

I focused my intention on one of those screens wanting to see what Kokoro was doing. When the foggy picture cleared, I saw a big field where Reptilian creatures were whipping humanoids who were digging in the ground. The Reptilians looked like Calybos from the classic movie "Clash of the Titans." The humanoids had round ashy white faces with curly hair on their heads. It was obvious to me that I saw slave laborers and their masters. And I saw my guy, so I teleported to the scene:

"Hey Kokoro, how are you doing?"

I challenged my deceiver. He turned his face toward me in shock and suddenly he was in his samurai costume. But he could not control the situation; he flashed back and forth from his reptilian to a samurai form. And he knew he was caught.

"Hey buddy, you were bullshitting me, weren't you? You know what? Fuck you!"

I was morbidly enjoying his surprise. But Kokoro was gaining strength and confidence; he was getting bigger and cockier. I was feeding him with hate and that was just what he wanted. I suddenly knew what I needed to do:

"But I love you Kokoro, you are my brother!"

He shrank to the size of a rabbit in his shock, and screaming, he was running away as fast as he could. He reminded me of the baby alien from the movie "Alien." Then I pursued my idea further:

"I love you all!"

I screamed so all the Reptilians could hear me. They all shrank into rabbit sizes and ran away. The white-faced humanoids insecurely looked around, then they tossed their tools on the ground and ran into the nearby forest.

When I shared my story about Kokoro in the group, I again received a rather doubtful reaction. It was even suggested that the story might have been triggered by the darker side of my personality. I knew I needed to discuss it on the Other Side, and I choose my trusted friend Hadien for that.

"Do not worry about it Menev, you are a reporter, and you need to tell the truth. You know that you are a very happy human being. You do not carry any guilt or fear with you anymore. There is real love and wishful love. Wishful love can be full of fake talk about love, light and positivity. But sometimes people can use these expressions as a tool to compensate for their residual guilt for whatever they did that they regret. They are practicing wishful love to feel better about themselves. No wonder that skeptics often say that those who claim to know the Other Side only see there whatever they want, whatever they wish for. Just continue your reporting, Menev."

The next time I went back to the Portal Room, I still wanted to know about one of my possible lives in the year 2500 which Kokoro mentioned. I sent my intention to another screen. The picture cleared, and I saw an old man in a village dragging a cart with two wheels. It was in a mountainous area, and it looked like Afghanistan. I teleported, but this time I was just flying overhead and observing the scene. Several young boys were running toward the old man. He sat down, and I knew he was a future me.

"Hey Grandpa, tell us one of your fairy tales!"

"Which one?"

"About America!"

"All right, boys! According to the old legend, far away over the big waters there was a rich land where people lived in such high dwellings that they called them skyscrapers."

I was sad, I felt that I had to go back, but I waved to myself on the ground. The old man stared into the sky apparently aware of me flying above.

Chapter 47
LOVE AND STARGATE

*"If I have the gift of prophecy and can fathom all mysteries
and all knowledge, and if I have faith that can move
mountains but do not have love, I am nothing." (1
Corinthians 13:2)*

Several wonderful things happened to me during
Starlines II. At the beginning of one of our next exercises, I
saw our group for the first time. We were sucked into a
vortex, then into the energy cord connecting us to Earth core,
and then to TMI-There in Focus 27. We repeatedly
oscillated, moving in the cord between the core and TMI-
There accumulating tremendous energy in preparation for the
slingshot. Finally, after applying the slingshot, the energy
cord spat us out directly into our chairs on Voyager 8 in
Focus Levels 34 and 35. I immediately fell in love with this
wonderful method of support from the group. Even now, I
continue to use the energy of my friends in this way when I
am using the slingshot.

Starlines II participation brought my ability to
perceive and exchange information with my guides and star
friends up to a significantly higher qualitative and
quantitative level. My previous perceiving could be described
by comparing it to the data flow of a dial-up computer
network. Then suddenly, I started receiving so much
information that I could not write everything down in my
diary quickly enough during the breaks between exercises.

I had gone from dial-up to broadband. A fellow
participant, Birgit from Germany, advised me not to wait to
start to write things down after the exercise, but to begin
immediately after the communication was over and the
descent to the physical has just begun. That way I was able to
record several major experiences every day. All of it was
enabled by my new understanding and embracing of the

universal Love flowing to us from the Ultimate Creator.

Even though I was still using my standard procedure described earlier as the Monroe Protocol, I became aware of some very supportive changes. I realized that I did not actually need the security repository box, because I stopped carrying the limitations of guilt and fear with me. All I carried was pure Love. I did not need the protection balloon, because I was not afraid of any negative influences since my Love could overcome them.

I was opening my heart to the Love of the universe, and I was releasing my Love to the universe. Love is timeless and boundless, and I carried it across all the time frames of the past, present, and future. I was testing my Love at the next meeting with Ruala:

"I am bringing to you, My Lady, boundless gratitude and unlimited Love and I know you have the same Love for me. I know when I am speaking with you that I am also speaking through you to the Lord Jesus Overseer and with the Ultimate Creator, and that we are all One."

She wore a long gown which was repeatedly changing colors from the innocence of white to the red of Love. And I knew that I had reached innocence and I did not need to beg; I just wanted to reach out and know the Truth.

"Tell me, My Lady, if I want to pass through the Stargate, do I have to use a Light Body?"

"Yes Menev, the True Light Body, not the illusion many people see and believe they are in. It is the way of The Truth; it is the channel through which Melchizedek and Jesus descended and ascended back. Indeed, only through Love can one become an Ascended Master."

"When I want to enter a Light Body through Love, I need to disperse myself into subatomic particles, correct? How can I do that?'

"Love shall do it for you, Menev. You must acknowledge and practice the power of Love repeatedly and then you can disperse into particles."

Crying overcame me again. I started using the following affirmations during the exercises:
"I am leaving the physical, but before that, I am sending my Love to everyone on the planet, then to all those who are stuck in Focus 23, and all those who are temporarily residing in the Belief System Territories, and I am offering them my help. I Love all those already in the Park and beyond."

Then I met Ruala again and with her help, I called Gardener, expressing my gratitude to him, and asking him to tell me more about Love.

"You can read over and over the first letter of your St. Paul to the Corinthians; it says a lot. But, I can also add a little bit. I can tell you what Love is not. True Love is not monkey love, it is not blind, and it does not expect anything in return. Love is flowing like a breeze on the beach and Love connects like a kiss or hug. Love simply is. You go think some more about Love. Then, you can come back, and I can help you to peek beyond the Stargate!" said Gardener.

But I impatiently and eagerly asked him to take me to the aperture of the Stargate just for a moment, ensuring him that I had nothing else with me but Love. We flew toward a big ring about twenty feet in diameter. He positioned me close to it and asked:

"Can you feel the breeze coming out?" I did. Then he moved me again:

"Can you feel the breeze going in?" I did.

"That is the flow of Love that goes both ways between us and the Ultimate Creator."

I peeked inside and saw white silhouettes holding hands in a circle while enjoying the breeze. They looked like angels but did not have wings; they were dancing and happily laughing. And I had my second cry of the day.

The next day I asked for a meeting with Gardener again:

"Do you think, Your Majesty, that I could now go through the Stargate?"

"Well, it depends very much on what you have brought me,"

to test me asked Gardener.

"Only unlimited Love, My Lord," and I reached out to him with the hand holding my precious pulsating Super-Loosh heart.

"I can help you with the Stargate, but are you sure you want to do it?"

My energy body started to shiver a little as precognition was getting me ready for a surprise. But being myself, I for sure did not want to give up after getting all the way here, so I said firmly:

"Yes, yes, and yes, Your Majesty, I want to know what is out there!"

We moved to the large aperture I had seen before.

"I highly recommend that you not stay there for too long," said Gardener.

Then the hands of his form grabbed my hands and he rotated me quickly several times over his head. My form changed into a ball about five feet in diameter and he tossed me powerfully right into the middle of the aperture.

"Stargate slingshot," I thought to myself.

Then I flew for about five seconds into a pipe which turned sharply to the left. It spat me out into complete darkness filled with constant buzzing.

"Hey, is anybody here?"

Nothing, no answer. I waited for a while, and nothing was changing. Then, I remembered what Gardener said and directed myself back to him. He smiled at me and asked:

"How was it?"

"What was that Your Majesty, where was I?"

"That is the other end of your Stargate, Little One."

"What does it mean?" I did not understand.

"Nothing, nada, zip, non-existence, spiritual suicide. Do you want to go back, Menev?"

"No, no thank you. But why was it like that? I questioned further.

"I have tried going in there several times," said Gardener.

"But like you, I had also been warned. Despite what you just experienced, many spiritual travelers apparently stay there for too long and they do not come back. We believe that they dissolve into the Nothingness."

I felt exhausted like I had left a lot of my emotions behind in the Stargate. And I remembered that Robert Monroe often reminded TMI participants that, when returning to the physical, they should leave their emotions behind in the spiritual realm. Robert was obviously indirectly reminding us to release the Loosh we might have created while still living in our physical bodies.

Chapter 48
PAUL OF TARSUS

"There are heavenly bodies and earthly bodies, but the glory of the heavenly is of one kind, and the glory of the earthly is of another." (1 Corinthians 15:40)

My relationship with Saint Paul had begun in September 2009 shortly after Lifeline when I had received my first impression about him. In a previous life, I had first met him while I was a Roman soldier and had listened to him preaching in Antioch. Almost a year later in 2010, I asked Ruala for advice on how I could start communicating with him. She told me I could reach him in the Earth Life System, because he administered numerous Christian heavens in the Belief System Territories. But he also freely crossed over into higher dimensions, mainly to communicate with Jesus the Overseer.

In September 2010, I traveled with Alenka for a vacation to southern Turkey in the resort area of Selge Beach near Antalya. I had planned to rent a car and drive along the coast to see The Cave Church of Saint Peter where, as a Roman soldier I had seen Paul preaching. The church was in antique Antioch outside the modern city of Antakya close to the Syrian border. Alas, I had to cancel my plans under unfortunate circumstances. A local company in the resort had rented me an old car which apparently badly needed an overhaul. They had set me up for disaster. I had to pay for the overhaul under threat from the police who were obviously cooperating with the rental company. I was afraid that I might land in jail in Turkey, so I chose to pay and not risk any more troubles. I went to bed completely exhausted from the situation.

In the morning when waking up in a hypnagogic state, I saw someone entering our room through a large balcony window. The next day in meditation I received the following message:

"Your room and your current environment were visited by Timothy, who was sent by Paul. Paul knows about your effort to come to meet him in the church in Antioch and what happened to you, so he has sent Timothy to help you find an alternative way."

The next day in meditation I called on Timothy. He started our conversation with some quotes from the Bible passage in which Jesus was declared by God to be the High Priest of The Order of Melchizedek. As Hebrews 6:16 says: "who has become so, not by the law expressed in the commandment concerning physical descent, but by the power of a life that cannot be destroyed."

Then Timothy explained to me that Melchizedek incarnated long before Jesus (he called him Jeshua), but he mistakenly concentrated only on the Jewish people. Jeshua used an analogous way of incarnating as Melchizedek had done. That is why the Bible calls Jesus the High Priest of the Order of Melchizedek. In his human body, Jesus understood that his message belonged to all of humanity. I was wondering why I was being reminded of all that. But before leaving Turkey, Timothy gave me one more explanation:

"When you came to Turkey Menev, you had too many physical plans and you simply forgot about the power of Now. You can talk to me anywhere and everywhere all the time, in the Now! I am dispersed like you are, so binding meditation and communication to a physical place is not necessary. That is why your intention to meet Paul was highly appreciated by him and was good enough to trigger his action to send me to help you."

I had continued with occasional conversations with Timothy until Starlines II. But I wanted to meet Saint Paul himself. When I learned to use the Portal Room, I proceeded to one of the screens and teleported into Antioch's cave church with the intention to meet Paul. He was kind enough to show up; we sat, and he told me:

"You have brought a lot of Love with you throughout the ages, Menev. I remember you from this church, you were the tall Gentile standing in the back when I was preaching. I knew looking at you that we would meet again. It seems to me that you have a question."

"What really happened on the road to Damascus, why did you change from being Saul?"

I asked the question which had been intriguing me for a long while.

"Well, I started to hate myself for persecuting all those people who were following Jeshua. I thought to myself, that if he really were so powerful, even though he was already dead, he could show up. I called him, and he showed up indeed! You know the rest, I simply had to follow him."

"How is my friend Barnabas? Why was I born on June 11, his feast day?" I asked another question.

"You were big friends. He liked you very much even though you were a Gentile. To celebrate your friendship, you decided to leave the womb of your mother on his feast day in your current reincarnation. And June 11, 1948, when you were born in your current life, is also the day when the peace treaty for creating the modern Israel was signed."

I nodded my head in surprise, but I still wanted to ask the big question:

"How many Christian heavens do you administer, Paul?"

"Seven and many times seven more. Look Menev, I know what you want to ask me. You call them differently, something like Belief System Territories. But ask yourself; is it not better for all those souls to be somewhere where they can at least be temporarily happy, where they hoped to go throughout all their earthly lives? Would you rather have them be stuck? I would never try to prevent their leaving, but some lower priests and sometimes bishops do try to do that. All souls have to find the path to the true teachings of Jeshua on their own; no one at our level should force them, and we never will."

I did not want to bother Saint Paul again, so the next time I meditated, I asked for Timothy. I wanted to know more about the possibility of reincarnating from the Belief System territories. He explained:

"Many inhabitants of the areas you call the Belief System Territories reincarnate back into the same area on the Earth where they lived their last life. They are predisposed to return to their physical religious lives repeatedly until they find out who they truly are. But we do not influence them to do that, they just usually announce that they have decided to go back on their own. But, I also have to tell you that many inhabitants quietly disappear from our territories, and we do not know whether they went back to Earth or to the higher vibrations closer to God."

On the last day of Starlines II, together with Timothy, I visited the Spa at the Alpha X Station on Focus Level 49, where our newly acquired tool of a Subatomic Particle Accelerator enabled us to bathe with other light bodies. Light bodies were flowing, merging, dividing again, dispersing into fluid, and forming again. I asked Timothy to tell me more about who Jesus was.

"Jeshua is the Highest Light Body. He is the Ultimate Pure Love and Ultimate Truth. If you want to get closer to Him, you must frequently come to this garden and bathe in pure Love. Repeat it very often!"

Chapter 49
SOUL TRADERS

"It is easier to follow than take responsibility; that is why we have religions." *(James van Praagh on Coast to Coast)*

Even after Paul and Timothy had given me their take on the significance of the Belief System Territories, I still wanted to know more. And, after all those communications with star friends, I also needed to change my focus for a while into more earthly matters.

I started to meditate again using the Lifeline exercise, because it was designed to set up intentions related to issues of the Earth Life System. Thinking about what St. Paul had told me, I wanted to know more about the possible connections between the Belief System Territories and their heavens and Focus 23 with its purgatories and limbos. In November 2010, I asked my guides in the Park and they told me:

"Some of the Belief System Territories leaders very often visit Focus 23, or lower astral plane if you will, and they are reinforcing the unpleasant feelings of the souls stuck there. Stuck souls remember their different religious affiliations from their incarnations and the law of attraction applies and is highly used there. That way the BST leaders can very easily take such souls vertically up into their domains."

"But this does not seem right. Why would they do that?"

"What are you yourself doing, Menev, when you are bringing souls from Focus 23 up here into your Park? You are doing the same, aren't you? One way or the other, these processes are stages of spiritual evolution. The souls stuck in limbo, even when they have a religious or other belief, are not strong enough to be able to get into the Belief System Territories. If nobody helps them to go up, they simply become part of the earthly realm, recycling back and forth between the lower astral plane and physical life."

I still did not like the described activities of the BST leaders and asked for more explanations:

"Menev, everything is part of the divine order and has divine purpose. How would you like to help a caterpillar when her purpose is to feed a bird? Or how would you like to help an antelope when she has to feed the lion?"

"But we are talking about human souls here!" I protested.

"They, too, are part of the divine process and they need to develop. And the best way to develop is through self-discovery. Do not worry, Menev, they can find their place without you. You cannot save the entire world!"

"Was I also residing in Focus 23 and the BSTs?"

"Of course, you were, many times. Without that, you probably would not be here with us."

"Can I still end up there?"

"It is a very remote possibility for you, but any Soul can drop very low if he or she should make a big mistake. You don't have to worry about that. But remember, when you are helping others, you should not, and you cannot disrupt the divine process of spiritual evolution."

I decided to see what was going on in Focus 23 on my own and went there with a strong intention in February of 2011. I immediately detected the presence of "Soul traders" dealing with stuck souls. The traders were offering deals of all possible kinds to the confused souls. It was kind of disgusting, so I went again to the Park to discuss the issue with my guides. I asked them:

"Who are these Soul traders?"

"Well, Menev, you know very well that the souls in Focus 23 are disoriented and lost. The traders are coming from all possible civilizations and alien races from everywhere in the Universe."

"What do they want?"

"The traders are looking for and targeting souls who can help them pursue their specific interests in your planet. They do it in three diverse ways. They can use part of their own consciousness to merge with targeted souls and reincarnate with them. Then, while they are partly on the Earth in such souls, they still maintain connections with the main part of their consciousness here on the Other Side. They can also simply manipulate or, as you would say, program souls for their own interests before they reincarnate, or as you like to say, before they recycle. And finally, sometimes they just take souls away. We do not know where they go, but they apparently are bringing them back into the physical world later after they have been manipulated."

"Do they go only into Focus 23 to do their dirty business?" I asked.

"Where would you go Menev if you were they? The souls here in the Park are basically free and under protection; likewise, the souls in the BSTs are protected by their administrators. But surprisingly, the traders are still trying to work even here in the Park. They are looking for those who are not yet strong enough to decide to stay permanently in the Park. The traders often cooperate with the BST leaders who are also looking in the Park for undecided souls. Vulnerable beings often let these traders manipulate them and they willingly return with their captors back to the Belief System Territories. Fortunately, that is only a small part of the trader's business, because a lot of these souls in the Earth Life System are still hanging around in Focus 23."

"When they are taking souls away, are we talking about abductions?"

"No, only sleepers in Focus 22 are abducted. During the abductions, higher intelligences are checking on their subjects to see if they follow what they were programmed to do. With abductions, we are talking about people living on the Earth. Their souls are still connected to their physical bodies. The souls in Focus 23 have separated from their physical bodies."

"Does it mean that we are hybrids?"

"All people on Earth are hybrids, Menev. Injections for

development are always coming to the planet from the outside."

"Aren't we slaves then?"

"No, not at all. Here is the game; you want to move yourself as close to your creators as you can. After all, you are part of them, and they are part of you. And you Menev, you are already very safe because you know. Knowledge gives you freedom Menev."

Chapter 50
MORE RETRIEVALS

"Sometimes limbo is a tolerable place to be stuck." (William Boyd in Any Human Heart)

When I was navigating around in Focus 23, the lower astral plane of the Earth Life System, I naturally came across some of my former co-workers who had recently died and were still in a state of uncertainty as to what to do. One of them was Phil. When I was observing him for a while, I realized that he was moving around curiously on his own. After I contacted him and asked him about why he did not take a direction to go somewhere for good, he said:

"I have to figure it out on my own, Joe. They are too many people here and everyone is telling me different stuff. I met my parents and some friends. They asked me to stay with them and they were also inviting me into different churches. I understand what you are saying, Joe, that you are just visiting here. I am not surprised to see you here, you always had a curious nature, Joe. I also visited these places often when I was in my coma, so I knew before I died how it would be to be here. Despite that, I still need more time to figure it out. But I can tell you that I am very happy that I do not have to write those bank checks anymore. That drove me nuts."

It seemed to me that he probably had tried to venture from Focus 23 into the BSTs, but he was not yet sure if they were the right places for him to settle in eventually. But just two days after our meeting, Phil surprisingly showed up in my way even though I had a completely different intention for my meditation. He went directly to the point:

"Joe, I've had enough of these people here, what would you suggest that I do? I feel like you know. What you were telling me last time was making a lot of sense."

"Then if you want, Phil, you can go with me. I am going to a place we call the Park, where everything is very much different from here. Look, the most important thing for you to know is who you really are, and you can learn all of that in the Park. Do you want to try a trick? You were not always an African American gentleman as you were on Earth. Just think about it and you can be any other race. Try it."

  And he did. As I was looking at his form, he was Asian, then Caucasian and then black again. He obviously liked the game because he did it several times. Then he said he would go with me because he trusted me. I explained to him that the guides in the Park would also help him to overcome the trauma from his stroke. I took him to Morphon. He wanted to talk more, but I had to go. I just reminded him not to be afraid to use the newly discovered power of his mind whenever he needed it.

  Retrieval and rescue attempts are not always successful. They can often fail. In January 2011, I found one of my deceased colleagues from the Slovak Service of Voice of America on a lower astral plane sitting on the railroad track next to a river. The conversation happened in Slovak and here is the translation:

"What are you doing here, Jožo? Nobody else is here yet, I am sitting here all alone all the time," said Vladimír in his typical former earthly, hyper and cocky style.

"You are here alone, Vlado, because you wanted it that way. Your whole life on Earth was like that, all the time just about yourself. If you do not want to continue like this, you can go with me, and I can show you a lot more. I can come back if you want, but now I have to go," I answered.

"Wait, wait, why are you here? Did you die too?" Vladimír tried to keep me there.

"No, but I know how to visit you here. I am still alive on the Earth. I can explain everything to you later."

I was leaving, but it was clear that Vladimír was pissed off.

  I told myself to at least try to help him, so I went to the Recovery Center in the Park. Morphon gave me an automatic rescue vehicle. When I asked him what an automatic rescue vehicle was, he said:

"You can fully engage your prospect in conversation to keep him busy when going through the BST areas that might be attractive to him. This vehicle will automatically and safely come back to the Park with both of you without interruption."

When I came back to Vladimír, he was still visibly irritated.

"Again you, Jožo, what do you want?"

"Vlado, you have created your environment here based on your life on the Earth, where you often liked to be alone and depressed, as you know," I was trying to start a sensible conversation again.

"How do you know that smart ass, and why are you sticking your nose into my business?"

"Because I love you Vlado and I want to help you. You are much more then you think. But you must discover it by yourself. I can take you to a place where others can help you!"

"You are not going to drag me into any church; you were always talking God and I don't need him. I just want everybody to leave me alone. By the way, why didn't you visit me in the nuthouse? When I was there, I was often visiting this place and it was always better here than there. Here nobody bothered me."

"I am sorry, Vlado, but I am studying the ways of how to get to the Other Side from the Earth while I am still alive. You should go with me; you cannot be stuck here forever! Here you do not even have all those gallons of wine you were drinking!"

The signal from the Hemi Sync reminded me to return soon to the physical.

"Are you going with me or not Vlado? I have to go now!"

"Just fuck off then!" Vladimír closed the conversation.

In January 2011, another former colleague of mine from the Slovak Service appeared in my dream where he complained about me to our boss. We used to have a very cordial working relationship by respecting each other, but sometimes it could get rocky. He demanded from our boss in the dream that he should oversee me, because otherwise, he would not be able to do his reporter's work. Several hours later in meditation, I met him in Focus 23. He was running toward me, smiling from ear to ear, and much slimmer and younger than when he had died:

"Jožko, I am so glad to see you here!"

"Why did you enter my dream and, not only that, why were you complaining to our boss?" I tried to calm him down and make him explain.

"I am so sorry Jožko, but I knew you would react because you would want an explanation. You know, as we Slovaks say, the purpose is justifying the means."

"OK then, how are you doing, how is it here?"

"It is so cool around here; you can sniff around any beautiful female you want."

Then he changed the tone, leaned to me and whispered into my ear:

"But you cannot have sex with them, I tried many times, everything just goes through them. And, to tell you the truth, I am also missing my work a lot. I would like to go quickly back to Earth, but I do not know how to do it. Can you advise me?"

After I explained to him about the Park and the possibility of a quick conscious and planned reincarnation back to Earth, he very willingly and enthusiastically jumped into the rescue vehicle. He said:

"I trusted you on the Earth and I trust you now."

I performed a very interesting retrieval in April 2011. While I was browsing the spiritual space of Focus 42 in a somewhat isolated and empty area, I ran into the spiritual form of George Carlin.

"What the fuck are you doing here?" he asked me immediately.

"And what the fuck are you doing here?" I likewise tried to

be polite, and added:

"You do not belong here; you should be somewhere else."

He quickly understood my further explanation and followed me to the Park and Morphon. Later in meditation I asked Hadien how something like that could happen. He said:

"Very free and independent developed individuals can sometimes end up far away in very high isolated spiritual areas. That is what happened to your guy when he died. He suddenly grew big wings of spiritual freedom and flew uncontrollably as far away as he could from an environment which irritated him so much."

Chapter 51
SOLDIER

"And now these three remain: faith, hope and love. But the greatest of these is love." (1 Corinthians 13:13)

Throughout all the wonderful experiences I have described so far, I still could not give up the hope that I would be able to recover my stolen diary. Early on when I discussed what happened in Stockholm with my American Indian friend Gene Taylor, he suggested that I should first forgive the thief. At that time, it was very difficult for me to even consider such an option.

I could not imagine how I would be able to describe my stories without the help of my beloved and precious written recordings. The hidden desire that I would be able to recover my treasure was still with me, even during Starlines II. I really needed advice. On the last day of the program, I called for Gardener, humbly expressed my Love, and apologized that I was asking for him so often.

"Do not worry about calling me often, Menev. I can use my multi-teleporter and be in many locations at the same time."

"How many?" was all I could mutter, being again surprised.

"As many as I need, thousands, hundreds of thousands. There are many just like you throughout the galaxy that I want and need to handle. How can I help you now?"

"Your Majesty, do you think that I could possibly recover my stolen diary? I am sure if I could get it back it would contribute to increased production of the Loosh."

"Well, there are two possibilities. Probably, the better one would be to send that thief as much Love as often as you can to soften his heart. He might receive your Love and decide to send the diary to you or call you to negotiate. A more difficult option would be to find him during your spiritual travels. But you would have to look for him, not for the location, not for Stockholm. It is extremely rare to succeed this way."

"Your Majesty let me ask you, I bet you know where my diary is!"

I was not giving up easily.

"Sure, I do, but I cannot tell you. I would break not only the laws of the Galaxy, but the laws of the entire Universe. I worked hard for my position. You certainly wouldn't want me to lose my beloved job, would you, Little One? I could be demoted by the Intergalactic Council. You have to figure it out on your own."

And the conversation was over.

At the last sharing session of the program, I was asking my fellow participants to somehow send Love from our group to the thief with the intention to soften his heart as Gardener had suggested and maybe encourage him to send me my diary. The Stockholm thief had everything, my address, phone number and e-mails in the stolen backpack. But I did not find the support in the group I had naively expected, probably because my appeal had likely sounded very pathetic.

About one month later, when I had a completely different intention, in Focus 23, I surprisingly and unexpectedly ran into the soldier who had followed me into this life and had stolen my diary. It was a shocking surprise also because, for a young guy, there was a high probability he was still alive on the Earth. I understood that I was facing a big fragment of him, who was staying behind in limbo while a separate part of his consciousness continued to live in his body on the Earth. He looked at me with hatred and suspicion in his face and asked:

"Who are you and what do you want?"

"You know me very well; we have met several times and you have always hated me as you hate me now. You killed me in our past life together, and in this one you stole the property which was so important and dear to me. But I am here to tell you that I love you very much and want to help you," answered I.

"How can you help me? All around me is misery. I am miserable and everybody around is miserable. We all are like that, and you are trying to tell me that you are different?"

"There is no different, there is only the same. We all are brothers and sisters. And I shall prove to you that there is help available. You would just need to go with me."

I really felt sorry for this being. It seemed to me that his whole spiritual essence was dark and probably had been stuck for the eons in the mud of Focus 23. His fragment that had reincarnated and was wandering somewhere in Sweden apparently was not much different. I tried to explain to him that part of him was living on the Earth, and with my help he should try to connect with his physical body in Sweden. "You are him and he is you, so both of you should change," I explained.

"How can I help him and why do you love me? Why don't you hate me if I did so many terrible things to you so many times?" he insisted again.

I had to explain more to him:

"I love you because I see your misery and I feel for you. I see that you hurt me because that was your nature, and you were driven to do it by evil forces. I am not judgmental about you anymore; I also do not want anything from you anymore. You can even tell your part in Sweden that he can keep my diary and all that was in the backpack. But, mainly, you should tell your part in Sweden that you love him and send him all my Love. You can do it by entering his dreams and filling them with Love. If you are unable to do it all now, I suggest that you go with me now to the Park. You can learn there not only how to love and why to love, but also everything about yourself."

He finally decided to follow me. After I got him to the recovery center, we waved goodbye to each other.

Chapter 52
FIVE RESOLUTIONS

*"The best and most beautiful things in the world cannot be seen or even touched. They must be felt with the heart."
(Helen Keller)*

My growing up by recognizing the power of Love led me to the participation in yet another Monroe program which was held in February 2011. Heartline was created and is facilitated by Penny Holmes. The program is dedicated to researching the emotions. It is based on the recognition of the significance of the heart, not only by numerous cultures on our planet, but also by modern science.

According to Joseph Chilton Pierce in a lecture held at Heartline, the heart is one of the first two organs to develop after conception. It develops even more quickly than the brain. Most of the meditations in Heartline are in Focus Level 18, which was discovered as a heart space and a spiritual place that is very sensitive and responsive to emotions.

One of my guides gave me a little lecture in one of the first exercises:

"After a person is conceived, the Finger of God touches it. Everyone is touched in the same way. Your species on the planet was created with the intention to love one another. And all of you had the same chance to do that when you were conceived. But you people twisted it and love on your planet became a matter of individual choice. Some people choose to love, others do not. Love is universal, and it is the most powerful force in the Universe. By making it a matter of choice, you disrespected the intention of God. It seems now that there are more of those who choose not to love than those who choose to do so. And, thus, as a species, you are heading nowhere."

In one of the other exercises, another guide

emphasized to me that time and space are just illusions. As such, they can be overcome by a focused intention exercised by the power of the mind. The technique he showed me used the so-called singularity transfer point through which consciousness from our time and space can immediately move to another time and any other space.

I was very surprised that when I asked my Internal Self Helper, Kamaláska, how to get back to the Stargate, she just took me there immediately. She explained that even though I had needed to go there with Gardener the first time, now I could repeat the experience without him whenever I wanted. So now, right there in front of the aperture of the Stargate, I could finally ask the burning question that had been with me for a while.

"How did I come into my spiritual existence? Did I separate from the Source through here?"

"You already understand that when you reach the Ultimate Graduation, you will come to the front of the Stargate to contemplate your spiritual expiration," said Kamaláska and continued:

"Likewise, you came into existence here from behind the Stargate through the Ultimate Conception."

"When did it happen?" I asked.

"It happened in the Now because there is no time and no space. Your Ultimate Conception happened in no time and no space. You separated from your Ultimate Creator, and you shall remain separated until you are able to reach your Ultimate Graduation. And if you accomplish that, it will be up to you to decide if you want to merge again with your Ultimate Creator. It is your choice, and only your choice. It is The Ultimate Choice."

"How many I-There Clusters do I have to go through?"

"As many as necessary and as many as you desire."

"Can it be an infinite process?" I asked further.

"Yes, indeed. Look, His Majesty Gardener is an Ultimate Graduate. He chose not to go back to the Source, to the

Ultimate Creator, so he could continue to work for God in your manifested Universe."

I was thinking of how much work still lay ahead for me, and I understood that I needed much more Love to be able to finish it. I asked ISH how I could get more Love. She said: "All you have to do, Menev, is to look inside the Stargate and ask for Love!"

I did, and a strong yellow stream of light started to flow into my heart. And, then my heart spoke to me by expressing five resolutions which were born at that moment:

"I will not hate anybody anymore!"
"I will not judge anybody anymore!"
"I will not push down anybody anymore!"
"I will lift everybody I know and meet!"
"I will love everybody I know and meet!"

Even though I had thought earlier that my crying while at the Monroe Institute was over, it was not. A stream of tears was running down my physical cheeks up until my complete return to the physical in C1.

Chapter 53
HEARTGATE

"Keep love in your heart. A life without it is like a sunless garden when the flowers are dead." (Oscar Wilde)

After Heartline, I intended to continue in my emotional research on the connection between the heart and the flow of Love from the Ultimate Creator and back to him.

On the very first day of the program in February of 2011, an amazing thing happened. I am describing the story as it happened, even though my previous biological knowledge could raise some questions. As a Central European, I have always believed, apparently based on our textbooks and numerous movies showing sword fights, that our heart muscle is more on the left side then in the middle of the chest where it is located. I also thought it was little bit lower, almost like under the left lung. However, I learned about its rightful place in the middle of the chest from Juanzetta.

That day, when I tried to meditate at high noon by focusing on my heart chakra, my second body heart tried to pull itself into the place where I previously thought it had been. I had to exert a lot of effort to reach the proper alignment. But when I did, a magical thing happened.

When I was approaching the heart space of Focus 18, my heart chakra started to have sporadic geyser-like spurts. The spurts started to form a vortex as if something had accumulated in my chest and needed to get out. The vortex was getting bigger and bigger. After I stabilized myself in Focus 18, the chakra's vortex reached the size about three feet in diameter and well beyond the limits of my physical body. The vortex become stable; it was almost flat, like a giant mushroom, and it was slowly doing a majestic rotation. There was a clear distinct small cone at the bottom with its pin inserted directly into my heart.

"What has happened here?" I asked eagerly.

"Well, Menev, you have just discovered and opened your Heartgate," the answer came from the Universe.

"What is the Heartgate?"

"Your experience at the Stargate when you received the large dose of Love directly from God empowered you to be able to initialize your Heartgate. It is going to stay in your heart securing a flow of Love both into your heart and away from your heart. You have just created a Loop of Love which is now flowing directly through your heart. The driving force of the loop is the Love sent directly by the Ultimate Creator."

"What am I supposed to do now?"

"Absorb and spread, collect and release, and enjoy!"

"I understand how to enjoy, because I am already enjoying what is happening, but what about the rest?"

"Menev, do you remember how during Starlines II the receiving of downloads changed from dial up to broadband? Very similarly, up to now you were receiving the Love from God through dial up; now because you have opened your Heartgate, you are on the broad band. Absorb the Love sent by God into your heart and spread it all around your physical environment. Then collect your emotional experiences and the experiences of people around you and release them all the way 'up' to God. Remember that the Loosh contains all the emotions, including hate. The spiritual Love sent by God is intended to motivate and create more Love in your C1 physical environment. But as you know, many times Love can be twisted and create a lot of hate due to the greedy desires of you people on the Earth. Keep your Heartgate open and cherish it all the time."

Chapter 54
ROTE

"Curiosity is the most important thing you own." *(James Cameron)*

Related organized thought energy, ROTE, as defined by Robert Monroe is basically a ball of information which is exchanged by spiritual beings when they interact. All the information contained in it is completely parallel in the non-time environment of the spiritual world. But when someone wants to bring it into the physical C1 environment, it needs to be transformed into serial sequences because that is how we operate here on this planet. I call such a process the unwinding of a ROTE. When I had asked my guides during Heartline for an explanation about the ROTE, I received this answer:
"The principle of the ROTE, Menev, is very simple. A ROTE is simply a ball like any other; you can turn it in your hands, shape it and interpret and use it in any way you desire. From an earthly point of view, when you receive a ROTE, you can even withdraw the first information last from the ball and the last information first."
But there was a lot more to it. I had a series of dreams shortly after coming home from Heartline. I was in a room with other people in the first dream while a higher being was explaining how to do effective downloading. All I remember from the dream was that the downloading often must be processed twice about the same issue. In the second dream, I was aware that a lot of information was flowing into my brain through my third eye. In the third dream, I saw a lot of images on a screen, but I had no idea how to handle them.

Not knowing what all of that meant, I used my Heartgate for the first time and took my Super-Loosh heart with me because I was curious as to who would show up in a high vibrational space of Focus Levels 34 and 35. Starman did, so I asked him if he had called me and what all those dreams meant. He said:

"Sure, I called you. There is a lot of work you must do. You are at the beginning of the beginning."

"Am I supposed to know all those processes you showed me in my dreams or were those just leaks of some kind, and I should not know about them?" I asked.

"Leave leaks for those who are not as determined as you are, Menev. You are not only going to be witnessing changes to come, but you shall also be an active participant in them. You will need a lot of additional information. You have to understand all processes very well."

"Why do I have to download twice about the same issue?"

"You always have to do follow up. Sometimes you are unable to fully understand a ROTE after the initial unwinding. A ROTE can be very complicated, and some information can be scrambled in the third eye interface. After you have brought information from a ROTE with you into the physical, then you can compile additional questions and do follow up in your next meditation. You also have to keep your buffers clean because they can accumulate useless garbage which limits their capacity for storing what you really need."

"What kind of garbage are we talking about here?" I wanted to know.

"Influences trying to distract you that are sent from those who do not want you to succeed. They are trying to fill your brain with sludge. On the other hand, we also do not need the doubts you try to send us often. They also take some important capacities of the buffers away."

"And what about the screen?" I asked.

"That is the Screen of Manifestation we created for you. When you are bringing a ROTE back and you are having trouble unwinding it, place it on the screen and you shall see its meaning."

"Can I see you now on the screen because I just want to

check it out?" I immediately asked Starman.

He reluctantly agreed, and again I could enjoy Starman's somewhat clumsy walk on my new screen as he looked like a young Jeff Bridges in the movie. There was no doubt I would use the screen very often in the future. Then I asked another rather speculative question:

"Can I eventually receive the information contained in a ROTE directly when I am in the physical plane if I place it on the screen you gave me to use?"

"No Menev, you can't. You cannot get a ROTE into the physical environment of C1, you must go to an altered state for it. Only then can you bring back the information you transferred from the parallel into the serial form. When you are in physical form, you can receive information from us only in short and quick bites, as remote viewers do."

However, two months later, I learned from Gardener that I was unknowingly producing my own ROTEs and they were being tossed in the opposite direction. At that time, I was having a lot of dreams about playing table tennis and organizing tournaments and I was just asking him what they meant. He told me:

"We are playing cosmic ping pong with you on a cosmic table and the ball is a ROTE. As we are placing all the information and instructions for you into our ROTE, so you are sending back to us your experiences from the physical world. Also, when you are tossing your ROTE to us when you are in the spiritual realm, you are also sending the Loosh we need."

Now, I understood that experiences as serial information had to be transformed into a parallel form when I was approaching the no-time spiritual environment.

"And, just as you can organize tournaments for others, so can you also show others how they can also play cosmic ping pong with us," added Gardener.

Chapter 55
CHALLENGE

George Noory: "Do you know why the heck we are here?"
Jonas Elrod: "Even if it might sound blasphemous for some,
to evolve and grow to be like God!" (Conversation on Coast
to Coast in December 2011)

In March 2011, early in the morning, someone touched my hand and shook me, but no one was in the room when I woke up. The next day I had a dream in which I placed an empty frame on an empty wall. Both dreams inspired me to look for their meaning. I added some questions that I had been pondering in my head for a while, set up my intentions and went into meditation. My new Heartgate was pulsating in the rhythm of my heart when I arrived at the Alpha Squared Station on Focus 49. I knew that someone was waiting for me in the Memory Room. It was Gardener.

"I am so humbled, Your Majesty, that you came to see me. You know that I have questions and would be very grateful for your answers. What did my dream about the empty frame on the empty wall mean?" I asked eagerly.

"It was to remind you that you are not using your new tool, your Screen of Manifestation," answered Gardener.

I apologized and asked how it was supposed to work.

"The Screen of Manifestation is a tool of your brain. It connects a screen from your memory to a desired time and space using the Singularity Transfer Point. You can use the transfer point both for gathering information and for directing your consciousness whenever and wherever you want."

"Do you know, Your Majesty, who touched my hand two days ago?"

"I did, to try to get you to this conversation."

"I am so humbled and thankful, but why do I deserve your attention, Your Majesty?"

"You earned it Menev, but now you have to move on. You should not waste your C1 time anymore, you know what you have to do."

I did not know where Gardener was heading and what to expect, so I gathered my courage together quickly and asked him:

"You obviously are giving me some instructions or orders about something I have to do according to your wishes, Your Majesty! Can you tell me whether these orders are coming directly from God? Is God directing and controlling our lives in the physical C1 environment, and is God planning everything for us?"

Gardener seemed to pause for a while. Then he said:

"We all are God, Menev. I am God, you are God, Juanzetta is a Goddess, and we all are Almighty beyond the physical. We are directing your life in our realm, and you are directing your life in C1. The more you come here, the more you know and the more you can influence your somewhat limited physical life on the planet. But remember, we cannot turn your head, move your legs or lift your hand. Only your brain can do that. That is why we talk so much about interfaces and transfer points. Also, remember that even though you are currently trapped in your physical body, you are still Menev the Great."

"Why this meeting, Your Majesty?" I did not feel completely comfortable.

"You should not even ask that question, Menev."

And the conversation was over.

Even though I was very curious about what Gardener had in mind and why he was obviously pushing me to do something and reminding me not to waste any time, the struggles of everyday life in C1 pushed the issue into the back of my mind.

About two months later, I again had some troubling dreams. In the first one, I was at a religious gathering. I went up some stairs, but when I got up there, men dressed in suits pushed me to the wall. I could not go anywhere, felt cornered and wanted to scream.

I climbed on a high mountainside in another dream and was very afraid to look down. I crawled into a tube which was winding into a mountain. But when I was inside, I was forced to climb up the tube against a stream of water, and the end of the tube was not in sight. Obviously, the dreams were expressing fears I had in my mind, so I went into meditation.

After getting into Focus 42, I immediately saw some huge building-sized vertical discs slowly rotating. I asked for the presence of higher beings and Starman showed up. I asked him about my dreams. Unlike Gardener, Starman was very straightforward:

"All of your dreams about being stuck and unable to proceed where you want to go represent your fears that you might die without finishing your mission on earth. And you know very well that we are talking about your book here. Of course, you can unexpectedly die like anybody else. But you have developed unreasonable fears about your health which have started to restrict your liberties. You would not be the first one to take his knowledge into his grave without sharing it with others. Do not worry, if you do not fulfill your mission as planned and you do not contribute to the expansion of human consciousness as we desire, you would still get a great deal of personal compensation in the case that your early departure would happen."

"What do you mean by that, Starman?'

"Those big discs you saw rotating in space contain everything you can access very quickly when you get here permanently. Instead of just touching the universal knowledge as you do now, you shall have access to it in a very deep and very wide way. Remember, we here in your Higher Self always want good for you. One way or the other, you should stop worrying about whether you will finish your mission or not!"

I realized for the first time that it was not only my desire and dream to write my story for the benefit of everybody, but I was being directed to do it by higher beings!

Chapter 56
SPIRITUAL DEVICES

"Aut viam inveniam - I will either find a way or make one."
(Hannibal)

I was still occasionally having desires to play with intentional classical out of body experiences even after I graduated from Starlines II. When I was discussing the issue with Starman, he was wondering why I needed to go from being fluent in very high vibrational areas into lower vibrations such as out of body experiences. He playfully suggested a technique in which I was supposed to raise my spiritual vibrations beyond my Higher Self and then quickly drop into my physical body and align them with the physical vibrations. I tried to create a spiritual vibrator for that purpose while visiting the Alpha Squared Station, but quickly reminded myself of what Starman said. Our spiritual friends will always help us even when our wishes are weird. I felt like I should explain to Starman that sometimes you can be little bit tired of traveling to distant exotic places and you simply want to have a beer in your local pub. That would be the equivalent of having an OBE as part of local entertainment. But then I forgot about it because I went back to my real spiritual work.

About two weeks after the discussion with Starman, I found something very interesting in the generator room of Voyager 8 in Focus Levels 34 and 35. One of my friends probably put it there to inspire my curiosity. The device looked like a traffic cone. I went into space and found Hadien who invited me into his ship. I described the device and asked him what it was. Said he:
"It is a resonator."
"What is it for? How can I use it, I want to know, please!"
"It can align you with the Universal Harmonic Frequency of the Universe. But first you must get rid of all your

unnecessary earthly baggage when you are here. You are very free, but for that you must be ultimately free," explained Hadien.

I asked him what that meant, and he said:

"You have to completely conquer the fear and worrying about yourself, your family, your friends, about everyone on the planet and the planet itself. Physical harms and the destructions are happening all over the Universe, and they are integral parts of the manifestation of God and the physical experience. Because you cannot do anything about them, you must accept them. You must be able to observe yourself and everything without intention, judgment, or conclusion. Observe all that exists in this way. Then you can use the resonator and align with the Universal Harmonic Frequency of the Universe."

I was starting to be a little confused about what spiritual devices to use for what purposes. I had already learned about the buffers and interfaces used for the exchanges of information between the physical environment and the spiritual world, and about vibrators and resonators. I had also heard about the Calibrator and the Screen of Explanation, but I had not tried to discern their exact purpose any further. Now I wanted to try one interesting experiment.

I was wondering if I could use the Screen of Manifestation for seeing myself manifested in my body on Earth. I set up my intentions from Alpha Squared and zoomed first to our planet, then the United States and found the apartment building where I was living in Washington D.C. The screen zoomed and focused on my balcony and the bedroom window, and there I was, lying in my bed in black sweatpants and a white shirt with headphones on and my eyes covered with blindfolds.

From that experience, I learned that it is not necessary to explicitly know how to operate such spiritual devices. Meditation is driven by intention, which is the most crucial tool for spiritual discoveries. The devices are used by the implicit effort of your unconscious mind and the guides and friends who are always there for you. They put the devices in motion when your intention is clear and genuine.

Chapter 57
TRANQUILITY OF TIME

"Then I saw her face, now I'm a believer; not a trace of doubt in my mind; I'm in love, I'm a believer!" (Monkees, 1966)

Meantime I had been getting ready for the next exciting adventure. Juanzetta and I had signed up for another Monroe program, Timeline, which was scheduled to begin on my birthday in June 2011. I would finally meet with her in person after eleven months of almost daily conversations over the phone.

She was arriving at Dulles International Airport. To make sure I would recognize her, I was holding the sign, Dr. Flowers, while waiting, pretending to be a limo driver. When I finally saw her pretty face and green bedroom eyes again, I was sold. We were excited that on the eve of my birthday, we could finally enrich our spiritual symphony with the symphony of our eager yet curious and scared bodies. But that is another story.

The Timeline program had been developed and facilitated by Lee Stone. Besides his work at the Monroe Institute, he had been working with the past life regressions of his clients since 1976. He also has a lot of his excellent artwork hanging in a variety of places at the institute. As an artist, he also restores old houses. As he explained, his understanding of time has roots in his own Egyptian reincarnation when his body was overtaken by a high priest, and he had to spend a lifetime in a nonphysical realm. Our group with him had only eight participants, five men and three ladies, so we received a lot of personal attention.

The magic of the place occurred immediately during our first exercise of resonant tuning when dozens of little flying fairies wearing gowns of all possible light colors imaginable flew into my CHEC unit. All of them had

Juanzetta's smiling face.

During the first break in the exercise, they sat down on both sides of my bed and then they flew all over the unit again. I tried to communicate with them, but they stretched out their teeny tiny hands from the sleeves of their gowns, put their even tinier fingers on their lips quieting me with ssh…ssh…ssh…! Then one by one they started to kiss me on various parts of my face and all over my body.

During the second break, they disappeared. They came back for the last part of the next exercise. This time they had the faces of all the women I had met in my earthly life. While flying, they started to slide their gowns all over my body which was tickling me, and my resonant tuning changed to chuckling:

Chi…chi…chi…!

I really welcomed the end of the exercise when they finally disappeared.

The Timeline program was mostly facilitated in Focus Level 15 where the perception of time as we know it on Earth disappears. Robert Monroe simply called such a state of mind the State of No Time. That is the place in which I met my first guide, Flying Grizzly, so I decided to call him. After expressing my appreciation of him, I asked him a question:

"Tell me my dear Grizzly, how do I recognize that I am in Focus Level 15 or any other level for that matter?"

"You started to understand the power of your mind when you created me. Remember that? If you need to contemplate it, return to that moment of creation. You not only just recognize; you command where you want to be. By the way, try to loosen your connection to Hemi Sync a little bit and remember the Singularity Transfer Point that you discovered while in Focus 15. It always goes with you, and you can be in any Focus Level, any time, or any space in the blink of an eye! And, when you eventually get tired in your quest, you can always come to this Sea of Tranquility of Time that you call Focus 15. You can experience your Godly Essence as a Timeless Being here. Then if you need help, just call on me and I will help you to calm down."

In the next exercise when I got to Focus 15, I immediately felt pressure on my chest as if someone had put something heavy on it. I called Grizzly and he explained:
"I placed the gold brick on your heart, so you will not rush anywhere this time, just this one time, this one exercise. You do not need to go anywhere now; you do not need to go to see your star friends. Just experience your essence now, which is right here. And open your heart."
Incredible peace came over me. My Heartgate was pulsating and absorbing the stream of unconditional Love. Slowly flowing in the stream were flashing signs "Love is all that exists." I could have stayed like that forever and tears filled my physical eyes. At the end of the exercise, the last thing showing up in the stream of Love was Juanzetta's face.

Chapter 58
CHILDHOOD REVISITED

"All grown-ups were once children... but only a few of them remember it." (Antoine de Saint Exupéry in Little Prince)

Lee wanted to prepare us for more exciting adventures in various times in the past and the future. He led us into a series of exercises involving our childhoods in our current incarnations on this planet. We needed to go to the roots of our lives here to be ready for a more sophisticated playing with time. These exercises reminded me a little bit of the emotional cleansing from the Gateway Voyage. After explaining a variety of different theories and the perceptions of time, Lee also gave us several useful tools and recommendations.

An incredible thing happened to me in the first free flow exercise. I relived my whole childhood again in the blink of an eye because I received everything in just one ROTE. Now it was up to me to describe the most interesting observations and interventions after unwinding this ROTE of my childhood on our planet.

I saw myself at five- or six-years old crying in my bed night after night because I had learned that everybody, myself included, had to die. I was having cramps in my belly for a long time until finally one of the doctors was able to help me. I was growing up in a very poor family. We often were hungry or had very little to eat. I did not have a coat for the harsh Slovak winters. I started to intervene. I called on my guides and guardian angels and asked them to tell that little boy that he would live a long happy life; that he would make the right choices and that he would be even happier later in his life after he had found his life's mission. I was asking my guides and guardian angels to watch over him and protect the boy throughout his life.

I was also seeing myself as a small boy trying to

make myself a toy car. These days when I try to tell my granddaughter with her hundreds of toys and gadgets that I never had any toys, she gives me a very funny look, obviously not believing me. I guess she is sure I am just kidding. I took a piece of wooden board and cut a piece of it with a saw. Then I took a wooden stick and, with big effort, cut four wheels. Next, I took pliers (we never had a hammer) and drove four nails through the new wheels that I had cut from the stick. I tried it on the ground, and it rolled. I knew I could not to show it to anyone, they would laugh, but I had my first toy and was happy. I was also a little sad. I intervened and told that boy that he would be an engineer as an adult working with sophisticated equipment and that he would have several real cars in his life.

Next, I was maybe eight years old and walking back home from the other side of the village carrying milk in a small cannikin. Suddenly right in front of the church, a man jumped down from his bike and without saying anything slapped me. I did not know why, maybe I was just walking on the wrong side of the road, maybe he just hated me. I felt tremendous injustice and throughout all my life I have wanted revenge, I wanted payback. I was always imagining beating him up. Now, I intervened, advising the boy to go home and tell his dad what happened. I saw the man in a court being given a fine to pay and a warning that if he did something like that again, he would go to jail. I finally forgave that man.

Then I saw myself ten or eleven years old with my best friend playing in a tractor cart full of wheat. We were wrestling and suddenly impulsively, we were pulling down each other's boxers and we were discovering our first erections in this innocent play. I intervened and told that little horny boy that those things are not just for playing, that they are supposed to be the tools of love. I promised him that he would learn how to respect and admire the other gender and that he would learn to use those things properly as he would fall in love several times in his life. Absorbing and unwinding the ROTE had helped me to rediscover and embrace that child in me again.

Chapter 59
PAST AND DYING

"When your time comes to die, be not like those whose hearts are filled with fear of death; so that when their time comes, they weep and pray for a little more time to live their lives over again in a different way. Sing your death song and die like a hero going home!"
(From the teachings of Chief Tecumseh)

After initial preparations, we were ready to venture into various times in the past. Because I had seen myself intervening in my childhood, I wanted to do the same for my mom and dad. I went again into the tranquil time space of Focus 15. Soon I saw my young ten to twelve-year-old mother walking geese to the pasture. She would rather be playing with other girls, but she had no choice. My grandmother sent her because they were poor and there were another four younger needy siblings at home. I intervened and told my mom that she would marry when she grew up and she, too, would have five kids and be very proud of them.

Then I saw my dad trying to crawl out of a muddy pond. His father had angrily pitched him there because my dad had thrown a stone at a Gypsy walking by. He had missed and instead had broken a window at one of the houses in the village. My grandfather was furious. I intervened and told my dad that he would become a smart man who would read and know a lot and that people would like to listen to the stories he learned from literature.

The next time, I decided to see Skjoerg the Shaman doing something else besides just preparing berserkers for war. I found him in an environment like the one I described in an earlier chapter. He had small wooden pots with steam coming out of them on a wooden table. Soldiers were bringing a man with foam coming out of his mouth and whose body was shaking all over. Skjoerg was moving his hands around the man's upper body chakras. He seemed to pull something out of the man's chest and threw it away. The man stopped shaking and completely calmed down after the shaman gave him a drink from one of the pots on the table.

Then the soldiers brought a woman with unnaturally pale skin who was staring as if she were not there at all. Skjoerg ripped the upper part of her clothing off, put his hands under her breasts and pushed himself against her. Then he slid both hands down to her pelvic area and moved them to the sides again as if throwing something away. All the time he was murmuring weirdly, but steadily and in cycles. The woman started to move her body on her own and it looked like she just came to her senses. Skjoerg gave her a drink from another pot.

Finally, they brought a little girl who was having constant hiccups. The shaman put both of his hands on the top of her head for a while and then moved them in small circles. The girl's hiccups stopped completely. Then, Skjoerg suddenly looked up, saw me floating above him, and asked: "Who are you?"

"I am you, Skjoerg, from your future," I answered.

"What are you doing here, are you coming to give me advice?"

"No, actually I want to learn from you Skjoerg!"

The villagers and soldiers were looking at him in surprised awe. They did not see me; for them, nobody was there and Skjoerg was talking to the gods.

After these exercises, we started to use the technique of dropping from the tranquil space of no-time into different local times in the past.

In the first drop, I was in the second half of the 13th century. I was a young woman bringing rice in wooden bowls for workers who were building ships for a planned Kublai Khan invasion of Japan. One of the workers was my boyfriend. I was pregnant, and we could not marry, since he had to be working all the time because they were in a big hurry. In another drop later, we had a little house and four children. We were married, he went fishing and I planted the rice. In the last drop, I was dying on the Eastern Coast of China. Grandchildren and kids were all around me. I did not mind dying because I had been lucky and had lived a simple and good life.

In another exercise, I dropped into the ocean. I was a dolphin calf in the same pod where my dad from this life was my dolphin cousin, also a calf. Our dolphin moms were teaching us how to hunt for fish in shallow waters. We often missed, and the older dolphins were telling us we needed to get the fish to the shallowest water possible and very quickly.

In the second drop, they were teaching us to jump and swim on our backs. We were taught to pick up big speed and then suddenly change directions and go straight up. In the third drop, we were with a group of dolphins on an educational trip. The leader of the group took us to an underwater structure shaped like giant stairs. She telepathically talked to us about an old legend explaining why dolphins live in the sea. According to the legend, inside the structure were the skeletons of people. Catastrophes on the surface of the Earth had occurred again and again for millions of years. The dolphins decided to adapt and live in the water. She said they understood that the surface was and always would be dangerous for them.

In the third drop, my dolphin cousin, my earthly dad from this life, and I were suddenly separated from the group, and we went to investigate the structure on our own. We had often swum there before trying to find the opening. This time we did find it and swam inside. We were seeing benches, vases, statues, and skeletons of people. When we were swimming out of the structure, we were attacked by orcas. My cousin (my dad) was killed, and I barely escaped.

In the fourth drop, I was an old dolphin and I felt that I was going to die. I had mastered all the necessary dolphin skills. But I wanted to create; I wanted to become human. I knew that my cousin (my dad) wanted to do the same and that we would meet again on the Earth, on the surface as humans.

Death is not the end; it is just a graduation and a new beginning. Investigating possible scenarios from the past and future is a very interesting activity in Timeline. In one of the drops investigating deaths from the past, I was a young wooly mammoth hunter. I was running impatiently toward a huge animal with a spear in my hand. But I slipped, and the mammoth stepped on me several times with full power. My guts gushed out of my belly and blood was running out of my mouth. I learned a big lesson and I reminded myself to be more careful in future reincarnations.

In another difficult death, I was trapped in a mine somewhere in the land of today's Czech Republic. The tunnel I was in was not much taller than five feet and the way back to the surface was hopelessly blocked. The whole space behind me was no longer than twenty feet. I had only one bottle of water. I have given up on digging myself out with my pickaxe and was exhausted. My wife and seven children were waiting at home. I was having doubts about going to heaven and was in total despair. Not knowing where I would go after I died just multiplied my misery. I was scratching the wall in a last desperate effort and was losing my consciousness. Three family members who had died before me were pulling my Soul out through the hundreds of feet of soil above my body. At the end of the exercise my right hand, arm and shoulder were hurting me, as Juanzetta later said, "Due to the picking."

Next time, we were targeting an easy death we had in the past. I was again Menev the Healer but was old and had a weak body. They had taken me to the house where I was born. It had a very simple room with just a wooden bed. I was old with a very long moustache. I was starting calmly to shut down the physiological processes in my body. I knew how to do it; I was the healer. Villagers were bringing flowers, some of them had small crosses and they were singing because I had asked for that. My spiritual teacher from the Other Side was waiting for me. I saw more and more of him as I saw less and less of the people around me. We flew directly into the Park for my preparation for the next reincarnation.

Chapter 60
GARDENER THE TEACHER

"It is the supreme art of the teacher to awaken joy in creative expression and knowledge." (Albert Einstein)

Throughout my spiritual journey, I have often wondered why I was able to receive so much groundbreaking information from higher beings. I reasoned that these abilities of mine had somehow been developed in my previous lives. I constantly feel very blessed, humble, appreciative, and thankful.

Another issue that puzzles me is that all this amazing information must be stored somewhere, not just in my brain. Since I had experienced the easy almost enjoyable death in my most important Menev reincarnation, it made me want to learn more about his life. I wanted to know why this reincarnation was the most important for my spiritual development.

I had a very interesting dream in November 2010. I was traveling somewhere by train. The train I was on stopped in a station and another train was waiting for me on the other track. I took my big suitcase and put it on my new train. Then I left to get something to eat, but the train departed with my suitcase. I was desperate and did not know what to do. I finally decided to ask the station manager for help. In a meditation on this experience, I learned this:

"Your suitcase contained everything you know, and the train took it to the Other Side. But you had to stay on the Earth because you still have your physical body. You will always be able to find your suitcase on the Other Side because it is under the direct protection of Gardener. This is important because the suitcase contains not only your knowledge about the Earth Life System, but also about the Galaxy, the Universe and everything. Don't worry, there are many trains going back to the spiritual world all the time."

I had another dream about this issue in April 2011. It was a reoccurring dream that I had before. It was very long, and I knew all the time in the dream exactly what was going to happen next. I asked Hadien about the purpose of such a dream and he told me:

"We gave you proof that you could pull out the same information repeatedly from the Akashic Library. The library contains everything that has happened, including the creations of thought forms, dreams, and meditations. The Akashic Library is part of the Mind of God."

In the Timeline, when we had the exercise of going to the Akashic Library, I had asked my ISH to go with me to help me find what I wanted. We pulled out the book "Menev the Healer." I saw in it the small square house on the side of the mountain where I was born as Menev. I saw myself going to the school down in the valley and saw my schoolmates and little Hilda, with whom I would fall in love later in life. I saw myself already as a young man healing people's injuries with plants and leaves. And I learned the secret I wanted to know. I had regular visitations from a Light Being who was my teacher and mentor. I could see him materializing before me without my making any special preparations or going into an altered state. It was always happening at the same place on the remote grassy edge of the mountain. That being had told me everything about the non-physical realm.

In another Timeline exercise which Lee called Origin of Beliefs, I invited Flying Grizzly, Menev and ISH to Focus 15. I asked them who that light being was that I was frequently meeting on the hill. I must admit I was not surprised when they said it was Gardener. I thanked them and, through the singularity transfer point, went immediately to my Memory Room in Alpha Squared Station where Gardener was already waiting for me.

"Why do I have to believe all that is happening to me, Your Majesty?" I asked him.

"You don't have to only believe because we are not just

trying to make you believe in something, we are giving you knowledge. You know that you must write a book about these experiences of yours. And I'll tell you why. Don't you see that your three most important reincarnations are in a progression in your earthly time? As Plautus you learned to write, work with words, and spread joy and laughter. But you had no idea how to talk to us. As Skjoerg the Shaman, you learned to talk to us, but you had to work very hard for that. As Menev the Healer you were helping people, you were meeting me, and I told you a lot of what you know today. But you did not have the resources to spread your knowledge wider across the planet. You were very local. Now you could finish your progression. After you have finished what we planned for you in this reincarnation, you could decide to be a Graduate. Even if terrible things happen on Earth, you shall still be free to go wherever you want after you die on your current planet."

I started to cry and cried and cried until I was completely exhausted when I fully returned to my body.

Chapter 61
LOVE THROUGHOUT AGES

"Being deeply loved by someone gives you strength, while loving someone deeply gives you Courage." *(Lao Tzu)*

Approximately a half year before going to Timeline, I had several dreams on different topics which had something very important in common. They happened to me while I was having very intensive and profound conversations with Juanzetta without our seeing each other. When I was inquiring about them, I was told by my guides that I should cherish my connection with her because it was very old. When I asked why, they told me:

"You were the commander of a small garrison guarding one of the largest port cities in Atlantis. Your station was on a big rocky hill between two rivers flowing through the town and discharging themselves into the sea."

"What was the main purpose of the garrison?" I asked.

"To observe and absorb the first wave of possible attacks by the Lemurians, but that never happened. You were in love with the same woman you are courting now, and her name today is Juanzetta."

"What happened to us, did we marry?"

"No, she had to leave because she was called inland into the capital city."

"Why, what was she doing? Did she leave by train?" I asked because I was often dreaming about trains at that time.

"She was a famous healer and a publicly admired nurse just as she is now. But the transportation in Atlantis was very different then you have in your country."

When I wanted to ask more, I lost connection and had to go back.

This story stayed in the back of my mind until I decided during Timeline to see what really happened to us in Atlantis. After I went through the singularity transfer point into local Atlantean time, I was able to locate the garrison barracks and I could observe us in local Atlantean time. We sat on the bench outside of the garrison at the edge of the airport which was adjacent to the base. I was in my military uniform with its big shoulder and chest covers. Juanzetta's dress was comprised of a variety of colorful silk-like fabrics in the shape of big leaves. We kissed and hugged. She was telling me that she was worried about the upcoming war, and she was sure she would have to go back to the capital because of it.

"Everybody in the town talks about upcoming war," she said. I told her loudly and a little bit irritated that all that talk was just bullshit and the Lemurians would not attack.

"I overheard at the military headquarters that war mongering is supposed to keep us in fear and under control," I said.

She turned around and pointed to a bush behind the bench where we saw the face of a man who apparently had listened to our conversation. When we looked at him, he ran away. I tried to calm her down saying she should not worry about him.

We went into her house on the hillside. She had a lot of lush vegetation and flowers around the house, half domesticated peacocks, and black cats as big as our ocelots or lynxes were lazily walking up and down. We went inside, and she said:

"Let's make love; maybe it is for the last time."

I had a sad feeling that something bad was going to happen. She pushed a large round button, and a bed came down from the ceiling. We were very gentle at first but then became very wild during our lovemaking, screaming like animals when reaching orgasms. The peacocks outside started to shriek and the cats roared. After the orgasms, we left our bodies and were flying over the town holding hands. We saw other couples doing the same. Shortly after we returned to our bodies, someone hastily knocked on the door. A messenger had brought an order for her to leave immediately. I had to take her to the airport. When she was leaving in a flying potato machine, I knew I would not see her again. At least not in that life.

Another time that I saw us together happened during an exercise in which Lee set up the intention to explore an ancient civilization. I specified my personal intention again just to be an observer. I landed on a very old ancient town plaza paved with large stones. I was an observer from another dimension and the people there did not see me.

I saw big carts filled with stones being pushed and dragged by people. They were building a city. I was in Ur in Sumer. An eight- to nine-foot-tall giant man was directing the workers building the stone walls. He was standing next to the walls and waving something like a magic wand with his hand. He was settling the stones, which were floating in the air, into their proper places. He had to try very hard because he was not always successful and had to use his wand repeatedly on the same stone.

I saw a red light flashing on the ground. When I came closer to it, I saw an opening with steps to the underground and I walked down. I was in a blacksmith shop where smiths were making weapons from a deep brown metal. I walked back up into the plaza and then into one of the towers built on the corners of the plaza. Inside next to a big window, men were preparing wheels with markers carved out of stones. I was seeing a device for observing the stars. There was another giant man directing these workers.

Then, I walked back to the plaza and into a shrine. A procession of women was following a giant female going toward a big stone table in front of the altar. I looked at the giant woman and I knew she was the same spiritual being as today's Juanzetta. There was a big picture on the wall behind the altar. It was a portrait of a huge man with two legs and six arms. He was Lemurian and he was a god for the locals. The women helped the giant woman lie down on the table in the supine position. Another giant man, apparently a high priest was coming out from behind the altar. Standing at the end of the table, he copulated with the woman. I knew the high priest was me and that I was trying to impregnate her because she was the only giant woman still alive. Women were bringing a variety of gifts to the altar during the coitus.

Then I was flying up and leaving the scene, waking up in my physical body. I was back in my room at another Monroe Institute facility, the Roberts Mountain Retreat. My room was connected through a common bathroom to another room, which was Juanzetta's. I was physically aroused from the scene in Sumer and sat down on a small comfortable loveseat which was in my unit. I was trying to cool down by closing my eyes. Suddenly, Juanzetta rushed in from her room and kissed me. It was a clear signal for me and, immediately, we had the most wonderful quickie you can imagine, Dear Reader. The ceremony of ritual lovemaking from the ages had beguiled us. Afterwards, we continued in gentle kissing in wonderment at the strong feelings engendered by such a spiritual connection.

In the last free flow exercise at Timeline, I set up the intention to ask Gardener why I was chosen and why I was urged to write a book about my experiences. I met him in Focus 42 by using the singularity transfer point.

"Why did you choose me for this mission, Your Majesty?"

"I chose you because you are a rare, organized Soul. Many times, before we have tried something similar on your planet but were unable to succeed. Now you have your chance. That is why I promised you would become a Graduate. But even more, to find the unique symbiosis of two souls that you currently have with Juanzetta is even rarer. Now you have your partner to be with you and support you. And, if you do what you are supposed to do, Juanzetta can become a Graduate too. All that is possible because you were able to obtain your Super-Loosh heart. Only a few souls have been able to accomplish that. Not only will that heart keep your bond with your partner in the Loop of Souls very strong, but it shall also enable you to understand the Loop of Creation. Then, when both of you have made your transition, I will be very happy to welcome you home. When you arrive home, you can pick from any of the Infinite Sea of Bonded I-There Clusters for your enjoyment; or, if you choose to do so, you can hold hands and pass through the Stargate and unify with the Ultimate Creator together. Congratulations! I am jealous of you, Jozef (he called me by my current name for the first time ever!). I have been looking for a connection such as you have with your Juanzetta for eons, and I have not found one like that yet."

After returning to the physical, I thought about what happened. I finally understood Robert Monroe's observation about chunks of the Infinite Sea of Bonded I-There Clusters disappearing from time to time. Those are spiritual beings completing their Ultimate Graduation, and who have decided to leave both the material and the spiritual worlds and return to unity with the Ultimate Creator.

Chapter 62
SILVER CORD

"There are only two mistakes one can make along the road to truth; not going all the way, and not starting." (Buddha)

In another one of my dreams, I was somewhere with a group of people who were apparently experimenting with devices unknown to me. I had something that looked like a cartridge in my hands. There was a cabinet sized device with slots for cartridges and a glass container nearby that looked like an antique hourglass. Some people in the room were frantically pointing at the glass container. I put a cartridge in one of the slots and then turned the glass container to a horizontal position. It started to glow, but then it broke in my hands.

When I asked Hadien about it later, he told me that I was in a parallel universe experimenting with an inter-dimensional generator. According to him, the cartridge contained vibrational ratios for activating a generator and the resonator in my hands was supposed to help me to disappear into another dimension. Instead, I got out of sync, the generator overloaded, and I broke the resonator.

I was also often wondering about the importance of silver cords. But another issue I often discussed with Juanzetta was the importance of suppressing the so-called monkey mind in meditation and the ability or inability of reaching the emptiness or blackness of mind.

Earlier when I was younger, I had a suspicion that the emptiness was probably not a goal, just simply a tool. Spiritual teachers often do not explain this properly and the students are disappointed when they have not quieted their monkey mind enough. I suspect that some of the teachers in inferior or less than genuine schools apparently may even use this inability of the students as a means for disciplining and manipulating them. I believe that they are not emphasizing what the real goal of meditation should be.

I decided to put these three issues into one unified intention and ask my friend Hadien about them. When I reached his vibrational space, Hadien invited me into his ship. What struck me immediately was that I saw his flashing silver cord coming from somewhere in the middle of his pyramidal body. I expressed my surprise and Hadien told me: "Yes Menev, we spiritual beings all have silver cords, and they always go into the higher dimensions all the way up to God, The Source of Everything. You people on Earth also have other cords between dimensions that go all the way from the physical body to your Ultimate Higher Self and God. The dimensions are distinct and strictly separate for the developments of souls. You people on Earth can sometimes see the cords clearly when you are out of your bodies because you are in the densest environment and their manifestation is strong. Here in the higher dimensions, we are not obsessed with them so much. We know they are always connecting bodies and they do not have to have a form. I am flashing yours and mine now, so you can see them."

I looked at my pyramidal body and saw both. One was going down towards the Earth and the other one up like Hadien's was.

"What exactly are they for?" I asked.

"It is a double connection. They carry Life Energy and Love from God, and they carry experiences and Loosh back toward the Source."

Then I asked Hadien about the role of emptiness in meditation. Said he:

"You have to see the entire process of meditation in its full complexity. When you meditate or pray, you are opening a channel between you and the higher dimension. You build a pipeline. And why would you build a pipeline if you would just like to keep it empty? The pipeline is built for the flow."

"So why do we often hear about emptiness being a goal in

meditation? It is just the tool, isn't it?"

"Correct. Most people who meditate would end up right there. They build the pipeline, but they are unable to use it fully. They do not know how to create the flow and they are often also afraid of the flow. Unfortunately, they do it like that because they were taught like that. Blind Guru-ism is like an organized religion, Menev. Emptiness and peace of mind are very important, you cannot have the flow without them. But once you have reached the emptiness, your pipeline will be ready for you to fill it all the time."

"And what about resonance, what is its role in the entire process?"

"Resonance enables you to cross dimensions easily and quickly. It creates power impulses which push your consciousness through the pipeline in a very rich and massive flow into the desired dimension. One of the very effective examples of this type of resonance is the kundalini. You know what I am talking about, you have already experienced it. The quest never ends unless you decide to go through the Stargate after reaching the Ultimate Graduation and you have decided not to come back into the manifested dimensions," said Hadien with his pyramidal smile.

Chapter 63
GOING TO SCHOOL

"All you have to do is decide what you are going to do with the time given to you." (Gandalf in Lord of the Rings)

Next, I wanted to know how much we are influenced or programmed when we incarnate on the Earth and what happens to us when we enter a human body. When I met Hadien, he told me:
"There are two kinds of programming if you want to call it that. Your Earth and the environment for your physical bodies were formed by the Creators through a manifestation of the process you can call terraforming. That is the first programming of a viable environment for sentient beings on a planet. Creators are very highly developed Beings; they were created by the Ultimate Creator. For example, one of the Creators on your Earth was Jehovah, described as God in the Jewish scripts or Old Testament of your Bible. Frankly, the Creators could have done a better job on your planet, especially regarding your DNA. But despite that and because of that, your Earth is very diverse and, thus, a very good school for the development of consciousness.

Then, there is individual programming, which is your own plan of what you would like to accomplish while you are on the Earth. That is much more complicated and less predetermined. You set up your intentions before you enter your mother's womb in the human body. You try to follow your intentions, but there are no guaranties of successful fulfillment whatsoever. Yes, Menev, your life can even become like a box of chocolates or the lottery, if you will. In this kind of programming, the Creators would never interfere. Your accomplishments in an earthly life depend on your previous development, and on your specific will and determination."
"Please, tell me Hadien, what is happening when we enter the

human body?"

"Something completely opposite is happening during the entering of the Soul into a human body than what happens in the process of dying. When you are leaving the body, you are becoming free, you are euphoric, and we are waiting for you. You have the freedom to choose how you will continue to live on what you call the Other Side. But, when you are entering a fetus-embryo, you voluntarily go to prison. Then, for a while you are alone, stuck, and there is no way back unless your new body quits. This experience can be horrifying, but you choose to do it, and there is no other way to enter the Earth school for anybody. You are alone until you get out of the body of your mother. Many have already forgotten who they were by the time they see the light of the world when they are born. And, even if after you are born you might remember who you are, you cannot tell anybody because you have no tools to do that. Your new conditioning into the physical world begins immediately, and soon you forget all you had previously known. That forgetting was intentionally created so as not to interfere with the proper conditions for the development of the souls."

In my next meditation, I called Starman wanting to get additional information and to compare what both of my friends were saying. I thought that Hadien had been a little bit gloomy and provided only second-hand information and imagination, apparently because he had never incarnated on the Earth. I asked Starman how we know that we have really entered a human body.

"That is very simple. After you have made your critical decision, you figure out that you cannot leave the body even if you want to do it desperately. You know that you are there and that you are stuck. But I disagree a little bit with Hadien about the so-called horrifying experience. He is your friend; I am your friend, and I am his friend. He has not incarnated on the Earth himself, so he gave you information based on the experience of others. As you know, I have been on Earth several times. For me, being in the body of the mother is always a valuable experience. Yes, you are in prison, and you are stuck. But you can appreciate your spiritual freedom more if you understand what it means to be in prison. I always have a plan, and I use my time in the mother's body to contemplate my plan because I know being there is just temporary. After you get out of her body and you enter the Earth's environment, you must be conditioned to your new life and that is always all right with me," said Starman. I thanked him and looked forward to our next conversation.

Chapter 64
DIVINE STRUCTURE AND EVIL

"From my point of view, God is the light that illuminates darkness, even if it does not dissolve it, and a spark of divine light is within each of us." (Pope Francis)

In my next conversation with Starman, I wanted to know if there was another part of me on the Earth in someone else's body. Said he:

"No, you are a unique individual in this particular time and space. But they are many of you in parallel universes. Remember as Hadien told you, your silver cord goes all the way "up" in dimensional steps to the Ultimate Creator. Yet on any dimensional level, you can have other silver cords leading from your unique Soul to other separate parallel universes. But there is always only one silver cord going from your human body or Soul in a universe to a higher dimensional level. All parts of you are parts of the consciousness structure."

"Can you tell me something about consciousness robots Starman?"

"Yes, many try to create them. But they usually do not last long."

"Why is that?"

"They do not have silver cords, so they are not connected to God. Only the Ultimate Creator can give you a silver cord. That is the main principle of the Divine Structure of Consciousness. The consciousness machines are not fed by the Godly Love which binds all real spiritual beings to the Ultimate Creator. Those machines are usually created by dark forces for manipulation purposes. But when they encounter true Love, they are simply forced to crash and dissolve. That is also the problem with you humans trying to create artificial intelligence. Such systems will work just to a point. They cannot get silver cords and be connected to the

Ultimate Creator unless God would decide to allow it. As far as I know, God is not doing that. The Creators want to keep the Divine Structure of Consciousness in order, too."

Next, I was trying to change the topic; especially since I wanted to know more about how my experience with the Stargate was connected to all that business with the silver cords. Starman said:

"Look Menev, you only have one connection to the Source, to the Ultimate Creator. It is the connection of your Ultimate Higher Self to the Source. You have your Higher Selves on many levels, you can call them Higher-Higher Selves, or you can call them First Higher Self, Second Higher Self and so on all the way up to the Ultimate Higher Self. You have many Higher Selves on different dimensional levels, but you have only one Ultimate Higher Self."

"What happened to me when Gardener threw me into the Stargate?"

"You experienced your Ultimate Higher Self just for the moment, just for the sake of the thrill of the experience you were begging to have."

"Please tell me Starman, can there be crisscrossing in the Divine Structure of Consciousness?"

"Yes. You can even do crisscrossing in your own structure. That is when you see yourself in various times, various places and different I-There Clusters, or in different parallel universes. Also, you can have crisscrossing between different spiritual beings. One example of that might be possession. But remember that each genuine spiritual being has his or her own spiritual tree of structure from the Source all the way down to the levels of biological or similar educational levels of existence. The crisscrossing connections are very temporary, and they are quickly interrupted or dissolved unless there is a tremendous effort to keep them. They are just anomalies in the Divine Structure of Consciousness."

Later, I realized I would have to talk to Gardener. He told me:

"Watch out! Dark and evil forces can be trying to take over you. We protect you because you are important to us. And if you keep your bonds to goodness, compassion, and acceptance, you do not have to worry. As you know, I am responsible for the Loosh, and we desire only the high quality Loosh which is produced by those emotions which you might call positive. While you are involved in them, we shall continue to protect you. As you also know, the high quality Loosh is used in the continuation of creation. God creates more of the physical only when enough of the magnified and multiplied Love has been accumulated. That is God's very important principle."

When I met Gardener the next time, he told me immediately: "I know you are going to ask me more questions. You now want to know about bad Loosh, don't you?"

"Yes indeed, Your Majesty, what is happening to it? There must be a lot of bad Loosh, right?"

"Well, you probably expect me to say that it is for the Devil or Satan. But both are just two of the powerful and dark destructive forces. And there are many more of them. There simply is no opposite of God."

"How many evil beings are out there?" I asked.

"As many as you can count. They feed on the bad Loosh like vultures feed on a dead physical body," answered Gardener.

"Why do they need the bad Loosh?"

"It gives them more fuel for hate, greed and cruelty. They want to disrupt the order, harmony, and sacred geometry of the Universe. They are always trying to slow down the continuation of creation, and sometimes, they can even reverse it."

"But what happens when there is simply too much bad Loosh?" I continued questioning.

"Then God has no other choice than to administer an annihilation. God has to use a lot of the Super-Loosh originally intended for creation if He wants to eliminate or neutralize the bad Loosh."

"What does that mean?"

"Annihilation destroys not only manifested matter, but also both good and bad Loosh and only nothingness is left. It is a void: spiritual processes are in vain; they have been wasted."

I thought to myself that disconnected evil structures are also annihilated and thought it was good. I asked Gardener:

"Do dark entities and devilish forces have cords between themselves?"

"Yes, they maintain their connections through cords; they want to keep the big structures. The bigger the structures they have, the more powerful and influential they are. Some of the examples you might know or have heard described on the Earth are the Devil, Satan, Antichrist or Lucifer. What they do not have are their silver cords from the top of their structure to God. They do not have them because the Ultimate Creator decided to severe them in order not to absorb all the hate they accumulated. Some other existing evil creatures were even able to sever the cords originally given to them by God. They did it under claims of freedom and independence, accusing God of being an oppressor. That is what Lucifer did. They have very deceiving natures. If you would be part of their structure, you would seemingly perceive it like another normal divine structure of a spiritual individual. However, you would be very surprised to reach the top of such a structure and discover you would be unable to reach the Source and see the Stargate. God is letting evil structures operate because they are necessary for environment of duality. And duality is necessary for the education and development of souls."

And that was enough for me to know at that moment, it was too overwhelming. I told Gardener that I loved him, praised his knowledge, and expressed deep gratitude for everything he had told me.

Chapter 65
GRASSHOPPERISTICS

"You become what you think about all day long." (Ralph Waldo Emerson)

In November 2011 in an evening meditation, I tried to call Hadien, but Ra showed up instead in his tetrahedron ship. After he invited me into his ship he told me:
"You seem to be very much interested in cosmic toys, so I sent you the dream about the grasshoppers. But I want to show you what happens when intelligent beings like you earth people start to be obsessed with toys and gadgets. I'll take you now to the grasshopper's planet!"
While the ship moved with tremendous speed toward the galaxy center and wormhole, I had to remind myself what dream he was talking about. It took me a while to remember that several days before I had been dreaming about seeing imitated copulation by mechanical grasshoppers. Soon I recognized the same planet and the town which was under siege where Ra had taken me to see the crushing of the rebellion. A variety of mechanical grasshoppers and praying mantises were slowly walking and jumping all around with their mechanical moves. But there were no live grasshoppers or mantises to be seen.
"What happened here?" I asked with surprise.
"You were with me here the first time ten thousand years ago of their time. Wars and diseases killed all the grasshoppers and praying mantises. Those were the only big significant creatures the people here had. Now they have only stories and legends about them, like you have on the Earth about dinosaurs, although you have a much larger variety of creatures on your planet. After generations and generations, the current people here are trying to recreate grasshoppers and praying mantises by any means possible. At first, they were building them from wood and metals in very primitive

idolatrous ways. Now they have succeeded in recreating some of the grasshopper tissues, but their genetics are still in diapers."

Ra took me to a big hall where there were staged fights with the mechanical grasshoppers and mantises trying to destroy each other like in gladiator battles or cockfights. Outside of the hall, there were speed races with these mechanical creatures.

"It looks like that is all they are concentrating on," said Ra and continued:

"People on this planet are obsessed with their grasshoppers and praying mantises, and all of society on the planet is degenerating and crumbling. The poor people are dying from hunger. All the scientists and researchers are involved in what they call Grasshopperistics."

Ra then took me to another hall where I could see mechanical grasshoppers trying to copulate like those in my dream. Said he:

"They are creating hybrids and some crazy scientists believe that they can really birth grasshoppers again by the interaction of machines and genetically cloned tissues."

"Why were you showing me such crap, Ra?" I asked a little bit irritably on the way back to our Milky Way.

"So that you could see where obsession can take a society. You have your obsession on the Earth, too, and you know what it is," said Ra.

"Money" I replied and thought about what my Dad used to say when I was a little kid:

"Whorish money, one never has enough!"

"That might be correct, but money itself just creates another obsession. Your planet is already in obsession with all your smartphones and other screens and games. People are forgetting to live normal human lives. You are heading into disaster if you don't wake up. Think about it again, Menev!" emphasized Ra as we parted our ways.

Chapter 66
UNDERSTANDING OF DREAMS

"The other night I dreamt I went to the gates of heaven. And St. Peter said, 'Go back to earth. There are no slums up here'." (Mother Teresa)

As it is no doubt obvious, I have long been mesmerized by dreams. In the past, they often scared me until I learned to understand that, in large part, they reflected our past lives. Just think about the history of our planet, Dear Reader, how much of it has been filled with violence and fear for regular human beings. But on the other hand, human progress has been facilitated by our dreams. Likewise, I have received a lot of inspiring messages in them myself and decided to ask someone how dreams work. Starman seemed to be the suitable candidate for that question because of his incarnations on our planet. I invited him to my Memory Room. He had never been there and was pleased by my invitation. He told me:

"There are three distinct categories of people on the Earth when we are talking about the understanding of dreams. The first group, often claiming support by science, believes that dreams are just randomly created synapses in the brain and there is nothing influencing them from outside. According to people from this group, a dream is just rearranged information stored in your brain. These people have completely shut off their perception of the Other Side. When we send information to them, they always consider it to be a wild and weird construction of their own brain. I would say that there are also experts in this group who are trying to explain dreams by traditional ways, such as in all those various kinds of dream interpretation books.

The second group of people believe in a divine origin of dreams, mostly by God or angels or other divine beings who can induce the dreams. While they understand that the dreams come from outside of themselves, they do not consider their active participation in the process possible. They consume messages passively without any further consideration of direct or follow up communication.

Then there is the third yet very small group who understands that dreams are communication messages from those of us in the spiritual world who want you to fully understand and to be involved. While we obviously use a lot of the information stored in your brain, the way we connect the synapses is intentional. The information we are giving you requires the attention and analysis of your left brain and then the follow-up by the right brain. We often send you information that is not in your memory. But such information can only be identified with the effort and clear intention of an individual to understand it. We often emphasize the need to decipher the message by sending a series of similar dreams. I can give you an example of that if you want."

"O.K. Starman, here are two similar dreams I had recently. In the first dream I was working inside a high tower and needed to go down. I called the elevator and tried to hold the door by putting my bag there, but it slipped. Then I put my leg in trying to prevent the door from closing. Before the door could close, another fellow jumped in. The elevator then changed into hanging swings circling around the tower and slowly going down. When we landed, we had to go into a pub full of people, and I did not know how to pick up my bag. An unknown woman picked up her stuff from a big black trash bag and my bag was in there also. I woke up.

In another short follow up dream, I was again trying to get down from a tower and looking for the elevator. I could not find it and had to walk down. I also was looking for a toilet, but when I found it, I could not fit in it because I was too tall. I woke up. What did those dreams mean?"

"Obviously when you were high up in a tower it meant something. A tower in a dream usually means the Higher Self. The elevator in a dream can take you quickly up to or down from your Higher Self. We wanted you to learn that when you are returning down to the physical self from your Higher Self, you might have some difficulties and you need to be careful. You always need to make sure to bring the information contained in a ROTE back to record and analyze it in the physical. And your ROTE was in your bag. The woman represented the help we sent to remind you that we are always watching what is going on. We need you and your stuff, Menev."

"Who was the other guy in the elevator with me, Starman?"

"It could just be someone taking advantage of your opening in the membrane. Almost every dream has a real meaning, Menev," concluded Starman.

Chapter 67
MIRACLE ON HIGHWAY 95

"Miracles are not contrary to nature, but only contrary to what we know about nature." (Saint Augustine)

It happened on Interstate 95 in November 2011 near Dale City, Virginia. My son had just repaired the brakes on my old 1995 Mercury Sable in a shop close to Fredericksburg.

I was returning home to Washington D.C. unaware of how strong and effective they were after the repair. The interstate was full, but traffic was moving quite well in all three lanes at a speed of around fifty miles per hour. I was driving in the far-left lane. Suddenly, the car in front of me braked and stopped. I did not have enough distance to stop safely. I slammed on the brakes and my brain quickly created an image of impending disaster. I expected trashed cars, broken glass, screaming people and blood all over everything. My car veered right toward the middle lane which was full of cars. I turned my steering wheel sharply to the left and slid in a 90-degree angle into the center ditch on the left side of the highway. The car stopped there with the engine running.

I got out and looked up at the traffic which was slower now but moving as if nothing had happened. Only one man ahead on the far-right stopped, looked back, and screamed at me to ask if I was okay. After I said yes, he got back into his car and drove away. My car did not have a scratch on the body; only the bottom dust cover under the front bumper had been partly broken from the impact with the bottom of the ditch. When I had slammed on the brakes, I had been expecting to hit at least four or five cars. I was in complete shock that nothing like that had happened.

I already knew that my guides were not just giving me advice in meditation and messages in my dreams, but now I understood that they were also watching over my well-being in my physical life. They were my true Guardian Angels. I had a very strong feeling that they were involved in my miraculous escape from that dangerous life-threatening situation.

The next day in meditation, I went to the Park and met them in my cabin there. I thanked them for saving my life and asked them what happened. As they replayed the scenario for me, I saw myself approaching that dangerous situation and, at the same time, my guides were approaching the same scene from above. One of them told me:

"We did not want you to go to the hospital, because you have things to do."

"Why did I not hit the other cars?" I asked.

"There is no left-brain explanation for what happened, Menev. There is only a right brain explanation! You did collide with three different cars: one in the middle lane originally behind you, one all the way in the right lane, and then, finally, one in your original lane. We were able to disintegrate the right side of your car during these three impacts. Your car just simply went through them without impacting their matter. At the same time, we created an illusion in your mind, and in the minds of all the drivers and people around you, that there was enough space and time for you and them to maneuver around the situation. But you know very well that there was neither the time nor physical space to do that without our intervention. The illusions we created also insured that everything and everybody was very calm. Nobody even bothered to get out of their car, except for that one guy well upfront in the right lane. He was on the borderline of our influence."

After the intervention by my guides in the very typical fashion of guardian angels, I was apparently overloaded with spiritually directed kinetic energy. The radio in my car and the broken lock on the door started to work again after a very long time of not doing so. In the evening

after the meditation, I simply told my defective printer:
"And now, please, you should work too!"
And it did. And my cellphone called Juanzetta several times
on its own.

Chapter 68
LURE OF THE STARGATE

"It always seems impossible until it is done." (Nelson Mandela)

I met Gardener in the Memory Room in October 2011. I emphasized that I was very humbled and thankful that such a powerful being as he wanted to talk to me.

"There is no more powerful or less powerful, there is only equal," said Gardener.

"But what about the Divine Structure of Consciousness?" I asked.

"The Divine Structure of Consciousness is just there to keep order. But you have free will and you can move about in the structure as you desire. Your movement is limited only by your skills."

"Why do people on Earth need to understand the beginning? Why do they need a beginning when there is no beginning?" I continued with questions.

"They are confused by time. Time was created in your space time universe for collecting experiences and Loosh. There is only the unlimited, albeit ever expanding or ever shrinking Now. Whether the Now is expanding or shrinking depends on the direction of the particular Loop of Creation."

"What is the relationship of thought and matter, Your Majesty?"

"Thought and matter are also in the loop, Jozef. Thought powers manifestation and manifestation is fueling thought. But the ultimate engine for the Loop of Creation is Pure Thought. Pure Thought does not have shape or form. It is pure. It is everything and nothing in the Now. Pure Thought is One and it connects everything. But you also have an infinite number of thought-manifestation loops. Once the Pure Thought releases a thought with a shape, form and intention, manifestation can begin, and the loop is in place."

"Is the Pure Thought the same as God?" I asked.

"Maybe. You can say so for now if you wish to," said Gardener.

At this point, I had been slowly coming to an understanding, and quite strong conclusion, that we as spiritual beings can end our spiritual existence by crossing through the Stargate to unify with God, the Source of Everything. But I still had some questions about that.

After I invited Gardener again to my Memory Room, we sat in armchairs. He took the form of my younger son. When I asked him why he did that, he said because my mind was quite occupied with my son, and he wanted to remind me that he also cared about my son. I felt a little uneasy seeing him in my son's form, and I asked him not to continue in that form. We were then vortexing outside of the station instead.

"Can I ask the ultimate question, Your Majesty?"

"There is no ultimate question but go ahead Jozef!"

"After we cross the Stargate and return to the Source, to God, do we still have our awareness, our identity?"

"I do not have personal experience about that, but I can tell you what my dear friend who is the Andromeda's Gardener has accomplished. But it would be second-hand information. I have not yet reached his level of determination."

"What is he saying, Your Majesty?"

"According to him, everything depends on your intention and your free will. After they have reached the highest state of knowing, many spiritual beings understand everything in their manifested universe. At that point, they usually decide to integrate back into the Ultimate Creator. They create intentions to dissolve into the complete Oneness where individual awareness and identity are not needed nor desired. Using free will, however, some of them not only set up the intention to experience complete unity with God again, but also keep their awareness and identity and to come back from the Stargate after that. But only very few can carry out those intentions. They experience a feeling of unlimited Love and peace in the Stargate that is completely overwhelming. They are simply unable to overcome it with their free will while present there in the Source of Everything.

The unlimited Love, power, and pure spirituality are also parts of every spiritual being in the moment of their Ultimate Creation. That is the moment when you separate from the Ultimate Creator into your spiritual quest as a newborn spiritual being. According to what my friend told me, your unlimited free will, powered by the unlimited Love from God, enables you to do whatever your intentions might be. That is why my friend from Andromeda was able to accomplish the rare achievement of coming back after experiencing complete Oneness with God. Then he could continue in his spiritual existence."

"Why don't you try that Your Majesty?" I was wondering.

"Well, Jozef, I like my present position very much because of a very few like you. It gives me a great deal of satisfaction and a strong reason to continue when I can answer many of those so-called ultimate questions that beings like you have."

"Your Majesty, I have to go back, my exercise is coming to an end. And my hand back on Earth is hurting me and I am losing connection with you."

"O.K., Jozef, go back. When you are deciding about reincarnation again, remember that the fastest development is only possible when you are embodied," said Gardener.

After I came back to the physical, I checked my CD player. When I had started to meditate it was 11:00 a.m. It was now 12:20 p.m. I had been playing the Starlines II Take Home exercise which is fifty-two minutes long. What happened to the missing twenty-eight minutes was a big mystery to me, so I decided to ask Gardener the next time what had happened to my CD and CD player. He explained to me that he had slowed down my CD by bending the time in my bedroom.

"Why did you do that, My Lord?" I asked.

"Because you needed more time to absorb, shape and bring

your ROTE back so that you could understand the answer to your question which was very important to you," said Gardener.

I was trying to use this opportunity for more questioning, but Gardener continued:

"I am not aware of many who have returned from a Stargate. There might be other Gardeners who have been able to do that since we have billions and billions of galaxies in our Universe. On your planet for example, we can talk about Buddha and Jesus who were two different physical persons, but only one spiritual being. Buddha was describing his reuniting with the Ultimate Creator and coming back from the spiritual world in the language of his earthly time. When Jesus was describing the return from a Stargate, he named the Source or God as his Father. That was the only way the people of his earthly time could understand it. But for most of those who might wish to come back through a Stargate, overcoming the instant bliss of merging with God is impossible. But I have already told you that before."

Chapter 69
SPIRITUAL CHILDREN

*"Someday I want to have children and give them all the love
I never had." (Marilyn Monroe)*

Another issue winding throughout the story is the
creation of thought forms in the spiritual realm by the human
minds of those living in the physical world on our planet.
Whenever we are thinking about an existing material or
energy form, we are touching and influencing them with our
minds. And when we are creating not yet existing forms with
our imagination and fantasy, we are also creating them in the
spiritual realm because we are shaping energy. Thus, this
implies that we should also be very careful about what we
create. Whatever we have created also exists out there. It
might be very tenuous and identifiable by only a few who are
involved, but it is there. When many people identify the
form, it becomes denser and denser. Once I asked Gardener
about this issue:
"On the Other Side, who are those fantasy or fairy tale
creatures that we have created with our minds? How about
the spiritual children created by our fantasies with our
partners?"
"They are not the spiritual beings in the true sense even
though they might behave so," said Gardener and continued:
"They can develop only by binding themselves to the
structures of their creators who brought them into the
existence. If you are talking about spiritual children, you are
that creator. If you keep them connected to your structure,
they can develop and enrich themselves and enrich you. But
if that connection is broken, they will be lost in the spiritual
realm."
I have two biological sons in my current physical life
given to me by my first wife Elena. And, for several years in
my second marriage, I helped to raise a stepdaughter whom I

loved as my own. I also had shared fantasies about other possible kids with my other female partners.

In November 2011, I had a dream in which I saw a little girl sitting on a bed. When she saw me, she started to smile happily and talk to me. I asked my guides in meditation who she was. They answered:

"Don't you remember that you wanted to have a little girl with Elena? But it never happened, and you never gave her a name in your fantasies. Now she has shown up in the dream to tell you how happy she was that you finally found her. That is why she was laughing so happily. From now on, you can call her Little Elena."

My second wife, Sasha, had a daughter from her first marriage, but she always wanted to have a son with me. We had shared fantasies about a future baby and gave him the name Benjamin. Later, during our separation, after hot sex in the kitchen, Sasha said she may have just gotten pregnant. I said:

"Fine, we shall have a little girl and name her Jumanji."

We had just come back to her place after seeing the movie with the same name and I desperately hoped that Jumanji could get us back together. Neither happened, but I have briefly met Benjamin and Jumanji on the Other Side during my spiritual travels.

Kate was my dear friend from English classes in Bratislava with whom I have had a brief sexual encounter. She also said afterwards that she could be pregnant. We joked about it during our nervous anticipation and talked about having a girl with the name Urshulka. Kate was an expert in literature, and she was spiritual at that time when I had no idea about it. I ignored her when she talked about her desire to come back as a dolphin and even tried to make fun of her in my arrogant ignorance. After the breakup of my second marriage, Kate and I met romantically at the Canary Islands. A year later in 1998, she came to the United States on a fiancée visa. But things did not work out. In November

2009, my guides told me in a meditation:

"We sent Kate your way twice. The first time we were trying to wake you up to help you understand the feminine part of your essence. The second time both of you misunderstood the importance of your relationship. You both reincarnated with similar intentions, and you were supposed to work together. But do not worry about it now, we rarely succeed with trying to have couples cooperating spiritually on the Earth the way we desire."

I met Urshulka in the Park early on in my spiritual journey in September 2009. She looked six to seven years old and was like a little Kate with her blond ponytail. She was very straightforward:

"Hi Daddy, you created me with Mommy, but you did not want me to come to the physical. If I could, I would find a good human body to get in to be close to you."

I met her again during Exploration 27 and we walked on the beach. She already had the ballet grace of her Mom in her walk. She said:

"Daddy, I am glad that you came again, and I am so proud of your progress."

She was also a little bit critical about the misunderstanding between me and Kate, so I just kissed her and said:

"Goodbye!"

Chapter 70
PLANTS, ANIMALS AND EARTH

"Do you have any idea how many lives we must have gone through before we even got the first idea that there is more to life than eating, or fighting, or power in the Flock? A thousand lives, Jon, ten thousand!" (Richard Bach in Jonathan Livingston Seagull)

The Love streaming to us from the Ultimate Creator is not destined only for us human beings; it likewise flows to all living creatures like animals, insects, plants and even bacteria. All living creatures have a place in the Divine Structure of Consciousness.

I started to understand this divine principle very early on during the Shaman's Heart program. After preparation with shamanic drumming, Byron asked us to go into nature and bring back something that would symbolize our connection to nature. I was hastily going around outside the Nancy Penn Center when I suddenly saw a root from a tree sticking out into the air. I broke half of it off thinking:
"Now I have broken the roots tying me to my old life; I am in a new awareness here; I am smart, I am right, and I am proud of myself."
I immediately heard a voice in my head:
"Is that your connection to nature? Did you ask for permission to break that root, and did you give thanks to your tree friend?"
I heard irritated humming coming from the tree. I turned back to the tree, apologized, and asked for forgiveness. Then I promised to come back. I left ashamed, but wiser.

During Lifeline, I decided to go visit my tree friend again. It was raining, and I was standing in front of the tree with an umbrella. I heard:
"Glad you came again."
I apologized and heard:

"No need to apologize again."

A stream of information was filling my mind. There is no need to hurt any living creature without a reason. When we kill other life, animal, or plant, it must be, so they can fulfill their purpose. Then, they can reincarnate again on a higher level.

"I love you my friend and I shall come again," I said before leaving.

And I was back again during Exploration 27.

"You represent all the plants on the planet for me, my friend and I have a gift for you."

I then fertilized the tree's roots with expressions of Love and respect:

"I am glad you came again. Yes, now we are devoted friends!" I heard the tree's voice in my mind.

A little later that day a little cricket whom I had rescued from the road the day before also appeared by the tree.

"Hey, buddy, I did not want to scare you yesterday; if I did I am sorry. I wanted to prevent your being run over. Tell me how it is to be a cricket?" asked I.

"Man, you are scared all your life that you will be eaten," I heard him say in my mind.

I wanted to explain to him that it was his purpose to be eaten, but I left instead.

Inside the building was a picture of a mother fox with four pups. The picture was talking to me about them. First, one of them was caught by a hawk, then the last one starved to death. They are all on the Other Side waiting for reincarnation. The mother vixen wants them to be foxes again; she feels she needs to do a better job next time.

In another exercise, we were connecting with the trees in the woods. I was standing in front of one in awe and surprised at how many topics I could discuss with her. I could talk about the branches and leaves, birds coming to visit, bugs and roots, about the wind and different summer and winter feelings, about the freshness in spring and tiredness in fall, about the sun, soil and togetherness with other brother and sister trees.

When I had gotten up that morning, my cricket was outside the door of the building telling me he came to say hello. He was happy because now he understood his place on the planet; he was telling me that one day he would become human too. All creatures seem to want to advance in their reincarnations to eventually become human. I felt that I had connected with all the crickets on the planet. I opened the door and he followed me in jumping into the building. I let him in because there was a cold October breeze outside.

Paul Elder, during a Lifeline informal evening discussion was talking about the merging of his consciousness with the consciousness of a lion hunting an antelope. Paul wanted to experience the feeling of being a lion. Then he reversed and entered the antelope to learn how it was to be hunted.

I was thinking about this during Exploration 27, and I decided to be a bird in my meditation. I saw a seagull sitting on a rock high above the seacoast. I merged with him, and it was pretty good to feel the beak, feathers, legs and blowing of the wind. I flew as high as my wings could carry me; I was Jonathan Livingston Seagull. I was enjoying the ride when an eagle suddenly attacked me. I managed to get out of the dangerous situation; I was just bloody on one side. I landed on a rock; my female friend perched next to me. She said: "Hi Jonathan, why are you doing that? It is very dangerous to fly like that!"
I answered:
"You know I have a funny feeling, that I am not just a bird, I am someone else; maybe I am a human."
"Jonathan, Jonathan, you never learn, you are just a bird like everyone else here," and she flew away.

Exploration 27 also had a lot of mediations about our Mother Earth. She is a living being indeed and, as such, she has her various organs. I discovered that her heart is in Sedona and the Grand Canyon is her aorta. Godly Love is flowing through the heart into her arteries. The consciousness of bacteria, plants, and insects, like armies of ants, swarms of bees, rainbows of butterflies, or even flocks of birds or schools of fish is tightly interconnected. The consciousness of each unit is intermingled with a structure much like a giant net. To keep the integrity and togetherness of each unit, these nets seldom leave the planet to go to the Other Side.

Chapter 71
STORY OF ALENKA

"You've got to the top of the ladder and found it's against the wrong wall." (Joseph Campbell)

Alenka and I started our loving relationship in the summer of 2003 while she was still working for the Voice of America as the Chief of the Slovenian Service. Both as journalists and Central Europeans, we had a lot in common and we developed a wonderful intimate life. As I have already written, we traveled together to many countries. I loved her children and grandchildren and she loved mine. It never really bothered me that she was several years older.

Where we were most different was in our individual outlook on religion or spirituality. Our differences sharpened when I started to go to the Monroe Institute. She refused to talk about dying and death. As a devout Roman Catholic, she always said that after she died, Jesus would take care of her. I gave up and respected her opinions and beliefs because she was a wonderful lady. The following story is the story of her transition into heaven and beyond.

It began in the year 2010 when she started to have very serious health problems. She had complications with a gallbladder removal from which she almost died, and then she had a hip replacement. She was always a jolly diehard optimist and believed that she had many years of life ahead. But the fragility of her health brought a consideration that her life might end much sooner than she had always thought it would.

She started to turn more toward hope through her religion. In September 2010, early in the morning, I was awakened from a dream by her euphoric laugh which I had never heard before. We were sleeping in her lovely apartment in Ljubljana, Slovenia. I tried to ask her why she was laughing so happily, but she could not answer at that time and later she told me she did not know. I decided to ask my guides about it.

They told me:

"She visited her heaven and Jesus was waving to her. She also laughed happily because she was surrounded by many angels radiating supportive and protective Love."

In October, she had a positive test for lymph node cancer with a biopsy scheduled for two weeks later. I cried like a baby when I heard it, even though I usually only cry in an altered state, (or any time that I hear our national anthem).

Three days later, in Starlines in the first exercise, I ventured into a Roman Catholic area of the Belief System Territories. I was immediately surrounded by a variety of bishops and priests telling me that they were ready and waiting for Alenka. When I tried to tell them that she would not stay there forever, they did not like it and asked me to leave.

In November, we learned that she had at least 25 lymph nodes infiltrated by the cancer which had also spread into her right lung. Two days later, after another visit to the BSTs, my guides gave me a warning not to interfere too much. As they said, heaven can be a temporary refuge for many people, and they must find their way out on their own.

One night in November, Alenka did what she had never done before, she described her dream to me in detail. In the dream, one of her deceased friends had invited her into a beautiful village with houses like she had never seen before. The village was connected by a bridge to a much larger town, and they could not see the end of it. They were just admiring the beauty of the scenery, especially the churches in both places. But they did not cross the bridge. This dream does not even need interpretation. Apparently, Alenka had been contacted from the BSTs in preparation for her transition.

Later in the evening, we were returning home discussing the movie "Hereafter" which we had just seen.

When I tried to emphasize the spiritual aspect of the movie, she said:

"I do not need to know what is on your Other Side. None of my friends are interested in something like that. I have my prayers and would rather just look at how wonderful it is outside tonight!"

She refused to consider any alternative treatments because she believed only in modern medicine, which had started in its genuine, yet vain, effort to destroy her already fragile body slowly through high doses of chemotherapy. I took her several times for treatments, and it was very hard to see her gentle weak body suffer so badly. She also refused to use the "Going Home" Hemi Sync collection of exercises that I had bought her from the Monroe Institute. This series is designed to help people with terminal illnesses. It was very hard for me to see her often suddenly cry out in the middle of the night, to beg "God, please let me die!" in an act of despair, and then to desperately pray to stay alive.

A month later in December, she was having a dream about being in a tunnel and not sure what she should do. In March 2011, after several heavy chemotherapies, her doctor excluded the possibility of radiation and surgery. She then started to have a lot of dreams about her deceased father and aunts and about colleagues and friends, Conrad, and Stanley. She saw her Daddy in blue striped pajamas in one of her dreams. She wanted to grab his hand, but her hand just went through his sleeve. She also learned in the same month that her daughter needed a kidney transplant. Frustrated, she pointed her middle finger toward the ceiling and said such words to her God that I cannot put in this book. I had experienced seeing similar anger toward God once before with my second wife, Sasha, after she was diagnosed with early-stage cervical cancer. Sasha had also turned her fear and frustration against God, saying she would not believe in Him anymore.

Some of you, Dear Readers, apparently also know

someone who is blaming God for his or her illnesses or other problems. I guess for them God is the guilty one, even when there is not really any proof that God is punishing anyone in any way.

When I later carefully questioned Alenka's beliefs, she apologized. Again, she was a wonderful lady, and I am writing this for you, Dear Reader, in the firm hope that in the distant future when your time shall come, you will sing your death song and die like a hero going home. You would merely just have graduated from this earthly school, and as a Graduate, you should be happy about a new upcoming life.

I decided that I had to help Alenka on the Other Side while respecting her faith and wishes here at the same time. I called for Timothy in my meditation. After thanking him for enabling me to communicate with Saint Paul, I asked him: "Can you please help Alenka with her transition to the Roman Catholic heaven when she expires on the Earth?" "I have to let her first meet with her dearest persons, with her Daddy and aunts. That is what she expects, and we do not try to influence normal transitions. She needs to spend some time with them. But I will repeatedly try to remind her that I am here to help her fly directly to heaven when she is ready. I shall tell her that the Slovenian Bishop Baraga will wait for her and she can even meet the Pope, Saint John Paul the Second."

I wanted to be at her side all the way up to her graduation moment of transition, which most people on the Earth call Death. But she angrily cut me off completely in August 2011 after she asked me about my developing friendship with Juanzetta. She stayed in her home with her wonderful son Mark taking care of her. As I learned later, she also took several trips to Houston to the MD Anderson Cancer Center in Texas, but obviously it was too late.

She finally called me again in January 2012 saying that "All is forgotten and forgiven." The next day I visited her with my sons. She seemed to be calm and getting ready.

But she still did not want to die, asking me repeatedly if I thought that she could still "Pull it off." She was always a fighter. After I saw her misery, I tried to ask Timothy for help to speed up her transition, if possible, in a little bit unusual way. But he was reluctant:

"We do not do anything like that, we have to let nature take its course, and your Alenka has to complete her earthly experience peacefully. It is a very unusual request from you. You don't want us to kill her, do you? However, you can talk to her, and I can advise you how you do it!"

When I tried, Alenka was popping up and down on the borderline between Focus Levels 21 and 22 as she was going in and out of her coma. I was trying to relay my message to her:

"You do not have to suffer anymore, Mucko" (her nickname in our relationship). "The time has come for you to go to heaven. Your body will not listen to you anymore. All who love you on the Earth have already told you Goodbye in their hearts. I love you very much and I will visit you when you depart from your body. You will help your family and friends to ease their worries and pain if you go. After you meet with your Daddy, Mom, Conrad, Stane, Francka and all the others you want to see, my friend Timothy will help you to find heaven. Saint John Paul the Second asked him to help you and Bishop Baraga will take care of you in heaven. You shall be happy and not suffering anymore."

But how much she was able to hear me in Focus 22 that I do not know. Two months later, one early morning in March, Mark called to tell me that Alenka had died. The night before the memorial service was very sad and demanding for me. I was waking up often with a strong itching all over my body and I knew that Alenka was with me. I was feeling her hands all over my body.

Finally, in the morning I felt a strong urge to meditate even though I had not had the intention before to do it. When I put the headphones on, I realized that the batteries in my player were unexpectedly completely dead. After I fixed them, I met her in Focus 23, and she was young and blossoming. She said she came to see me to say goodbye before the funeral service.

"I already met everybody I wanted to see. It is very easy here in the afterlife. Some of them were already waiting for me, and I just had to call the others and they came. Some of them live here like they did on the Earth, and some say they came from heaven. And I have a protector, Bucko!" she said, using the nickname she had given me and continued: "His name is Timothy; you know that one from the Bible and he is waiting to take me to heaven! I just want to go there after my funeral is over and stay in that heaven forever!"

She said how much she loved me and left. My itching stopped in an instant.

I was lucky to arrive at the funeral home while the casket with her majestic physical body was still open. I was able to touch her hand and forehead. The little white diamond cross I had given her for one of her birthdays was shining on the top of her chest. Crying overwhelmed me, and I quickly left after the service, wanting to be alone.

Later in April when I was in Panama at the Radisson Summit Hotel in the rain forest, I had a dream about speaking with Alenka over the phone. We were talking about how wonderful it was that we could now talk even though she was already on the Other Side. Our brains can portray a communication with the spiritual realm as a phone call.

It had also similarly happened to me ten days before the dream call with Alenka. I had received the telephone call from my deceased chief and friend, Miro, from the Slovak Service of The Voice of America. I was surprised and told him that he sounded very well and very young. He asked me to meet him, and we met at the market. He was indeed very young, slim, elegant, and well dressed. We hugged, and I was questioning the situation because I knew that he was dead: "Look into my eyes Miro. Can you see me very well

and clearly?"
He confirmed that, and we agreed to meet again before I
woke up.

In September, Alenka entered my dream, and it was
very vivid. She was young, slim, and pretty. She expressed
the wish to talk to me. After I woke up, I went into
meditation. I found her in the open space of Focus 25. She
wore a long burgundy dress with buttons all the way down
from the neck to feet. She wanted to apologize for not having
listened to me more when I was telling her about heaven.
"I thought you were crazy, but you were right. Heaven is
quite different from what I expected it to be," she said.
"How is it that you are here in this space? Did you leave
heaven?" I asked.
"No, but they sometimes recommend for us to go out of
heaven for a little while, when they see we might be bored."
Then, we had quite a long private conversation going beyond
the purpose of this book. I tried to persuade her to go to the
Park with me. But even though she considered doing it, she
said she felt safe in that heaven despite being disappointed
and bored.

Time passed, and I unexpectedly ran into her again in
November 2014 in the last free flow exercise during my
second Starlines II at the Monroe Institute. The exercise was
long, and I had some free time to spend and decided to go see
what was new in the Park. I was walking around the lake and,
suddenly, I met Alenka there.
"What are you doing here, Mucko, how did you get here?" I
asked with some surprise.
"Well, some guy came to our heaven, he called me out and
started to talk to me and he talked me into coming here,
Bucko," answered Alenka and continued:
"Only, when we came here, he told me that he learned such
tricks at your Monroe Institute. And you know what, I really
like it here for the time being. It is very interesting here, but
I am ready to go back to Earth and live a whole new life

there. I want to be there again."

"Wow, just as you always needed Mucko, someone else had to tell you. You always believed what others told you more than you believed me or even yourself. But I am very happy that you finally found a better place."

"Bucko, I have to apologize to you that I called the Monroe stuff "satanic shit" and for wishing bad luck to you and to your new woman. Is it good with her? Do you love her?"

"Yes, I do. And I am happy that I finally found her. She has been my Soul mate throughout the ages."

"And is she a good fuck?"

"Why are you talking like that, Mucko?"

"Because you always liked to talk dirty, you little bastard! Just kidding, but I wanted to remind you of our beautiful times together too," added Alenka with a wide, joyful and happy smile.

And then I heard the signal to return to the physical and told her goodbye:

"I wish you good luck, Mucko, and do not rush back to your beloved island of Pag. Think about that a little bit more, please!"

And I left knowing that she was happy and safe.

Chapter 72
AVATAR

"Minds are like parachutes - they only function when open."
(Thomas Dewar)

I had another powerful dream in January 2012. Juanzetta and I were in the dream taking part in a program like those we attended at the Monroe Institute. During the break, I went outside of the building and approached a walkway up above on a flat elevation. When I looked toward the walkway, I saw two identical Juanzettas walking there. The second Juanzetta was following the first one, keeping the distance of about fifteen feet with every step. Both Juanzettas wore identical long white summer dresses and banded straw hats on their heads. I knew I had received proof of something, but I was not sure what had needed to be proven. I expressed desire to both Juanzettas to merge again into one. Apparently, they received my wish and the Juanzetta walking in the back started to walk faster towards the one in the front and they merged. I was thinking what a wonderful experience of proof I had just had and woke up. I asked my guides in a following meditation what kind of proof I had received in my dream. Here is the message:

"It was the proof that we and you and Juanzetta and all people on the Earth are multidimensional beings. You saw her in two dimensions simultaneously. We now call it proof because you had already experienced it before. Remember when you saw two of yourself in the armchairs at your workplace a little while ago? At that time, you were seeing yourself in two dimensions simultaneously. But you did not understand it then because you were still obsessed with your effort to get out of your body in a specific way. Be aware that experiences like this can last only for a moment. Seeing into two dimensions at the same time requires a lot of special energy, and we can do it for you only when it has an important meaning and purpose. When it happened at your workplace after your seeing two of you, they immediately merged, did they not? The same happened with the two Juanzettas. But this time, we were able to trigger your active participation and you asked them to merge."

"Can you tell me where we were?"

"You were studying consciousness in another dimension. But the second Juanzetta you saw in the back was from yet another dimension."

The next day after only two hours of sleeping, I had another powerful dream. Juanzetta and I were somewhere, and we knew that a catastrophe was coming and that, together with all the other people there, we were supposed to die. But I told her to hang onto my body and I started to fly. I was slowly gaining height and speed and soon, I was in full control of the flight. We both were enjoying it tremendously. She was looking at me and I told her:

"I have to tell you something - I am an Avatar!"

But she was not surprised at all. We landed on a treetop, and I woke up. I followed up with my meditation and met Gardener.

"What did my dream mean, Your Majesty?"

"It means that you are an Avatar and now you have to digest it. I do not intend to tell you much more."

"What do Avatars do?" I ignored his response.

"They speed-up human progress."

"Can I repeat my flying experience from the dream now?"

"No, I cannot do it for you now. The Universal Law of steady spiritual progression applies to Avatars, too. I do not want to, nor can I break it," said Gardener and disappeared.

Three days later, respecting and understanding his sudden departure, I decided to call someone else, and I thought about the Cosmic Lady Ruala. She showed up in an instant and I expressed my surprise:

"How is it, lovely Cosmic Lady, that I was able to find you so quickly and easily at your place?"

"I will tell you a secret you do not know yet, Menev. Thought is identical with consciousness; it is the same thing. When you study consciousness on Earth, you people mostly believe that thought is the tool of consciousness. Not so. They are not separated. God is pure thought, as you know indeed. When you project your thought correctly toward me, you are with me because your thought is you, and a thought of yours is your consciousness."

"Can you tell me more about multidimensional seeing, Cosmic Lady?"

"You project your thoughts in multiple different directions, yet you keep them connected through you. You can spread yourself like a tree with many branches and leaves, yet you keep all of yourself connected to your tree body and roots. With you in your two armchairs and the two Juanzettas, you projected your thoughts in two directions. But you have to understand that you are at the beginning of the beginning of the building of these skills."

"Who are those who are able to do such projections into many dimensions?" I asked.

"Avatars can do that. And you are an Avatar, just still a sleeping Avatar. His Majesty could not tell you more, because you were just waking up. Most people on Earth believe that reality is only that which they can see, hear, smell, taste, or touch. But reality is multidimensional, and you can understand it only if you can have a small peek and can grasp at least a little bit of it. By doing these projections, you understand not only the multidimensional nature of being, but also the parallel universes and the universes within universes."

Chapter 73
ONE AND MANY

*"Our duty, as men and women, is to proceed as if limits to
our ability did not exist. We are collaborators in creation."
(Pierre Teilhard de Chardin)*

Well, I had been told that I was an Avatar, so I
courageously decided to deepen my inquiry about everything
that came to my mind. I still wanted to know a lot about
beginning and end or no beginning and no end, and about the
connection between Ultimate, Created and Manifested. Many
of the human beings who believe in God often ask who or
what was there before our Ultimate Creator. At this point in
our journeys, Juanzetta and I were pondering that God had
always been there and always would be. But also, there might
be the certainty that our Universe came into existence at
some point and could cease to exist at some point. I found an
appropriate time for meditation and called on His Majesty
Gardener. He waited for me in the Memory Room, and I
asked:
"How should I understand the development of God, Your
Majesty?"
"The idea of the development or expansion of God has been
created by God for the smart ones like you. This idea is an
illusion necessary for fueling the processes of manifestation.
You cannot widen or expand the Absolute or Ultimate. But
you need an engine to run the manifestation. According to
that illusion, God would desire and need development. You
have been able to get close to God as only a very few have
been able to do. Remember what you learned in Gateway,
that you will be allowed to get close to God, but you will not
understand who God is and what the Ultimate Creator's
intentions are. And no one in the manifested universes will.
We simply do not know why God creates."
"Then why not just quit, Your Majesty? Does it mean that all

of the universes, us, the Earth, everything we might recognize, are just an illusion?"

"Yes and no. You have two choices as your Hamlet said, to be or not to be. If you choose to continue as a spiritual being, then your question has just been answered. You will exist in your manifested Universe, and you will eventually be able to understand everything in it. But you cannot understand the essence of God, which is outside of all universes, even though the Ultimate Creator is present everywhere in all universes. If you choose not to exist anymore, then your question does not need to be answered. You will not exist, and the question will not exist either."

I came back to the physical quite confused but determined more than ever to never give up asking questions.

The next time I met Gardener, I asked him how I should understand our separation and our unity with God. Here is what he said:

"In the shaping of energy and matter, you have what you might call separation and you have manifestation. For the mind, there is no true separation from God. Even though it looks like you are separated, you are always connected. God or Consciousness is always a whole, it is One. In manifestation, you create Many."

"What is Nothing, Your Majesty?"

"Nothing or emptiness or void is everywhere and stands between consciousness and energy. Energy and matter are the same. Energy is Many, and Consciousness is One. When your holy books say that God created the Universe from Nothing, it means that the intention of the Ultimate Creator reached from the One through the Nothing into the local Many, and Energy and Matter were manifested. When you are reaching for God from your manifested form, you are crossing back to the Source through the Nothing. That is why meditators are trying to reach emptiness or void in mind. That way you can open a direct channel to God."

"Can I now go back to my previous conversation with Your

Majesty? Again, are we and our Universe also just an illusion? Are we real?"

"It depends on how you observe it. What is truly real is Consciousness, because it is One, always was and always will be. The universes and you come and go. There are Many, so they must be temporary illusions. Only One exists in the eternity of the Now and, therefore, only One is real."

"Can we say then that consciousness is analog, and energy and matter are digital, and that all digital is just an illusion?"

"You can say so, even though you can say it better. You can say that all energy, matter, universes, and your body were created. The One was not created; the One exists, and the One does not need creation. Indeed, that is why we wonder why creation exists. Again Jozef, we do not know why creation happens," and His Majesty closed our conversation.

Chapter 74
REMINDERS AND WARNINGS

"Wisdom that reaches beyond intelligence can be accessed only through heart." (Joseph Chilton Pearce)

I soon realized that I was being pulled more and more into deeper and revealing discussions about spirituality. I had never intended nor expected that something like that could happen to me. It was fascinating and traveling into the spiritual realm became not only a habit, but also kind of an addiction. Sometimes I felt like an ant in a fly trap or a hypnotized frog crawling into a snake's mouth. Yet, I was blessed to be able to get such marvelous information and teachings from higher beings. But soon I learned that it was not supposed to be a free ride. I was apparently chosen to become a conduit and messenger for their intentions.

And they started to remind me about my mission, usually through dreams. I was having dreams about not being able to put my stuff and belongings together in time when I was supposed to leave home for the trip. And, I am continuing to have these kinds of dreams even now when I am writing this book. When I inquired about them, I was told by either my guides or star friends that I could go home only if I put my matters in the physical plane into proper order. Other kinds of reminders were interpreted through dreams about marriages. It was explained that I had to marry myself with my mission.

Then, I was also dreaming about looking for a new apartment, which according to my guides and stars friends meant the necessity of creating a new peaceful environment for my work. I clearly understood that all of that was about their urging me to write this book.

I also tried to understand more about why and how I got on this road. I asked about some of my old dreams from my earlier life which I had recorded without knowing why I was doing that. I was told that some of them were designed to kick-start me onto the path of spirituality. I allegedly did not react, and they had to wait until the proper time came.

I had now finally discovered my real purpose in this physical life. I even realized that they wanted me to stay healthy and sane and fully equipped for the task I was chosen to do. I had a dream in April 2012 documenting such an effort. Someone in my dream was either exchanging or fixing my brain. I saw my brain taken out of my head, but I was fully aware in the dream and functioning normally. I was urging them to put my brain back into my head because the time for functioning without it was running out. I later met Starman in meditation and asked him what that dream meant. He told me:

"We needed to cleanse and refresh your mind and fix your interface and buffers. They had gotten too polluted."

"Polluted with what?" I did not understand.

"You started to worry too much about your body. Do you remember your broad band receiving from Starlines II? Well, recently you have slowed down. Don't you feel that you don't meditate as easily now as before?"

I had to admit he was right:

"Yes, I do feel that. What did you fix, how did you do it?"

"We took your mind completely out of your brain and straightened it up. But you saw the process in reverse. In your dream, you saw your brain being taken out of your head. Obviously, we cannot do that. But when you were waking up, your mind returning to your brain was producing an interpretation we also could not control. When your mind was outside of your brain, it took the shape of your brain. What we did with it I cannot explain to you, you would not understand. Also, do not worry about your health too much, because you are healthy enough for the job."

I was also receiving warnings, apparently letting me know that sometimes I was trying to go too far with my questions, especially when inquiring about God. Another dream illustrated such warnings. I saw everything in the dream like it was in a movie, but I was also one of the actors. I was in a group examination in a class and the topic of the test was "Who can best explain who God is." But my pencil did not want to write, and I did not have another one. When everybody finished, the teacher read the results name by name. When he read my name, he said I would do the test later.

Then, he called the four students who had the best scores and lined them up in front of the blackboard. Instead of praising them, he pushed the button next to the blackboard. The floor opened, like under gallows, and all four students disappeared through the hole. He said that would happen to anyone who falsely believed that they could explain God.

Then, he called two other students and said the real contest would be between those two and him. But suddenly two other participants, a man, and a woman from the class, ran toward the blackboard and pushed all three of the "real contestants" into the hole. Then, all the scenery disappeared and no explanation about God had been given.

Chapter 75
CANALING

"Every happening, great and small, is parable whereby God speaks to us, and the art of life is to get the message."
(Malcolm Muggeridge)

Everything that was happening was very exciting, but also a little bit frustrating. His Majesty Gardener wanted me to write my book, but he was not giving me the entirely clear answers I always expected from him. I was discussing this dilemma with Juanzetta and, jokingly trying to be funny, remarked:
"I do not know what that Son of a Bitch wants from me." Obviously, I did know what he wanted and soon I did not feel very well about what I had said.

In the second half of April 2012, Juanzetta and I spent a nice week in Panama. I had always dreamed about retiring somewhere where there is a lot of sun and sea and where the cost of living is cheaper. I considered Panama to be such a place. Juanzetta suggested that we go there first to see. On the second day in Panama City, I realized:
"I am not going to retire here for sure!"
But seeing the Panama Canal was a fascinating treat.

After returning, I had one of my reminder dreams in which I had to clean my office, but the task was above my abilities. Later in May, Gardener showed up in a vortex form in my meditation at Alpha Squared on Focus 42. I asked him if we could go sit in my Memory Room. He said:
"No, we do not need to do that. I prefer non-form communication. You would be distracted by trying to see how I look even though you have already understood for a long time that it does not matter. You know that I am here with you, so go ahead with your questions."
"First, I must apologize to you, Your Majesty, that I called you Son of a Bitch. I was just joking. Please forgive me."

"Jozef, you can call me whatever you want, and you do not need to apologize. What you said then does not have any significance in this communication now and it is not even an issue. Even though we here on the Other Side also have egos, they are of a different kind; our egos are spiritual egos. On your planet, you have a physical ego."

"What is the difference?" I asked.

"Your ego in the physical world must be strong and sometimes rude for you to survive in your dense environment. My ego has a different purpose. As you know, my spiritual essence can be very much dispersed. Ego helps me to keep my concentration on the tasks I would like to accomplish. While for you it is a tool for survival, for me it is a tool for effectiveness. By calling me a Son of a Bitch you did not hurt me at all. I am immune to that kind of talk since I do not share your sensitivity."

"When I was in Panama, Your Majesty, towards the end of the trip, I received the thought that channeling should correctly be called canaling. Is that so?"

"Yes and no. I sent you that thought, and you misunderstood it a little bit. Not only did I send you that thought, I also sent you to Panama with Juanzetta. Your intention to go there to see if you could retire there had only a secondary significance. The main reason was what you just said, to understand canaling. Yes, many psychics and mediums are channeling. But you, Jozef, communicate with us through canals rather than channels. Channels are discovered, and canals are created. You create canals. Just think about what you saw and enjoyed in Panama.

Imagine the whole complex of the Panama Canal. Imagine the Caribbean Sea as the physical world and the Pacific Ocean as the spiritual realm. The lakes in between them represent hypnagogic states. The locks at critical places are buffers. The mules pulling the ships are like tools helping you to get from the physical to the spiritual side through hypnagogic states. The ships traversing the canal carry information, guidance, Love and Loosh. They also carry the ROTEs that you are trying to bring back from the spiritual realm to the physical. Now you can understand that the ships can only accommodate a limited amount of information, guidance, Love and Loosh. If your ROTE were too big, it could not go through the canal. You understand that when ships are too big, they cannot go through canals. You must either break up the loads and put them into smaller ships or build wider canals. It is very similar with our communication. Think about it Jozef!"

Chapter 76
BIRTHDAY

"The way I see it, you should live everyday like it is your birthday." (Paris Hilton)

On June 11, 2012, on my birthday, in a meditation, Gardener came to my Memory room. He said: "I have a birthday gift for you Jozef. You always wanted to see my face, so I am going to show it to you today."
When I looked at my teacher, I saw a face I had never seen before. That face did not remind me of anybody's face I knew. He was an older age with a rather oval face, and he was dressed in a tunic. His whole look was antique.
"Surprised, aren't you?" He said and continued:
"You won't see Socrates, Einstein or Beethoven. I chose an indifferent face, because I am all those men, and many others like them. I am all of them and they all are me. Thus, for me to choose a face reminding you of someone else would not be appropriate for the occasion. I chose an antique outfit because, in your society, wisdom is often associated with the antiquity from which wisdom started its march forward."
"What is the significance of my birthday today, My Lord?" I asked.
"I'll show you Jozef. Look at me now!" said Gardener.
And I looked at him again and saw myself like in the mirror.
"You have a birthday and you have reached the wisdom stage. You are me and I am you. That is the significance of your birthday, and that is my birthday gift for you."
I would have liked to ask him more questions, but he stopped me and said:
"Surely you do not want to talk about apocalyptic stuff on your birthday, do you?"
I remembered that I had received the message five days before that we might be for God what one cell in our body is for us. We do not worry about one cell; we worry about the

whole body, or at least about our vital organs. I used the opportunity to ask Gardener about that. He said:

"I sent you that message, so we could discuss it today. Look, God is not micromanaging the life of anybody on Earth, just like you are not micromanaging the life of one cell in your body. The Ultimate Creator is managing only the important parts of the whole, like you are moving your limbs or affecting other parts of your body with your thoughts and actions. God is managing universes and multiverses, dimensions, and membranes and, sometimes galaxies. But I also want you to understand that, at the same time, everything is in every cell of your body and every cell of your body is everywhere. Everything needs to be structured in sacred geometry to be able to function. All things need to be connected, organized, and moved all the time. So even though God is not micromanaging, the Ultimate Creator is present everywhere all the time in the ever expanding and shrinking Now. Happy Birthday, Jozef!"

And my beloved teacher left.

Chapter 77
LOCALITY OF CREATION

"The whole difference between construction and creation is exactly this: that a thing constructed can only be loved after it is constructed; but a thing created is loved before it exists." (Charles Dickens)

I could not wait to meet Gardener again. I wanted to ask more about matter and energy from a spiritual point of view and about the difference between material things and biological life. When I met him, he again had my form, and we were walking on the platform of Alpha Squared Station. I asked him:

"Is the total amount of matter and energy constant, or is it changing, Your Majesty?"

"You have to see it in relation to the Ever Pulsating Now. Sometimes, just locally there is more and sometimes there is less, so we could say that the amount is locally changing, yet we can still say that universes are stable. All creations and the collapses are local. Pulsations are also local, and they are determined by God's intentions and the production of the Loosh and vice versa. God is feeding on the Loosh. When the amount of Loosh reaches above critical mass, new creations are triggered. When the amount of Loosh declines below a critical mass in a specific locality, collapses follow."

"So then, how much matter and energy exist?" I insisted.

"You can comprehend and understand local, but you cannot absorb the essence of the unlimited sea of consciousness which is God. Likewise, you cannot absorb and fully understand the unlimited sea of manifested matter and energy. In order not to go crazy, you have to think local."

"What is local?" I asked.

"In this sense, local can be a specific universe or a dimension or even a galaxy."

"Thanks, Your Majesty. Another question I have is about

material things and biological life. I understand that both are the product of consciousness, right?"

"They are and there are generally only a few interventions of high consciousness into the entire process of evolution which follows after local creation. The intention of the Ultimate Creator is to allow matter and energy to develop and eventually enable the creation of biological life. As I told you, God intervenes into and creates only new universes, dimensions and eventually galaxies. The lesser Creators are those who intervene to start biological life when the conditions on a planet have reached a desirable level. They intervene again when the plant life is rich enough to support mobile biological units, like animals on your planet. And finally, interventions happen again when the animal life is rich and variable enough to enable the creation of creatures more self-aware and productive. And that leads to developed intelligent life like you humans are. Unfortunately, intelligent life often leads itself into self-destruction, which is sometimes accompanied by almost complete annihilation of the living conditions on such a planet."

I continued my inquiry two weeks later in July. We were in a completely pure white field. I asked Gardener about the Higgs boson. He said:

"What you call the Higgs boson is a tool of creation. It is a bridge between consciousness and manifested matter. But you can understand it only when you include both sides in your consideration. Then, you would not need the horrific amounts of energy your scientists are using trying to find it. They are looking at the issue from only one side. If you are in manifested matter, you must include consciousness; you cannot ignore its existence. If you are here where I am, you must understand the manifested Universe. And many here don't understand that world of yours. You can become a Creator only if you truly understand what manifestation is and when you are seeing in the material world fully."

"Does the boson have something to do with the

morphogenetic field?" I asked.

"Exactly! It is what the morphogenetic field is composed off," answered Gardener.

I looked around and saw an unlimited white sheet as thin as you can imagine and spreading in all directions as far as I could see. I think I saw the Membrane.

Chapter 78
STILLNESS AND MOTION

"While I thought that I was learning how to live, I have been learning how to die." (Leonardo da Vinci)

Next time, I asked Gardener to meet me in that same vibrational spiritual place very close to the infinite very thin white sheet I had seen. We were on the bottom side of the sheet, and I noticed bubbling coming down from it. We could see through the sheet and the upper side was clean and flat like a mirror.

"Where are we, Your Majesty? What is that white sheet?" I asked.

"That is the Ultimate Membrane, Jozef" answered Gardener.

"What does that mean?"

"That is here for you to understand the answer to your question about consciousness and motion. It is another way to look at the borderline of spiritual existences. Robert Monroe was here when he described the flow from the aperture, and you were here, Jozef, when I threw you into the Stargate. You just see it in a unique way now. Do you feel the breeze, and can you hear humming?"

"Yes, I do My Lord, but I also feel the pull to the other side of the membrane where nothing is."

"Stillness is very inviting, Jozef. But do not worry, you cannot get there yet. I could, but I do not want to go there yet either. You have only a very small part of your consciousness here, the rest of it spreads throughout spiritual and physical dimensions. Here both of us are like a bit of a piece of chewing gum being stretched from out of a mouth full of gum. My connection is wider than yours because of my wider and larger development. Your stretched connection here is very thin, but thick enough to absorb this discussion and the information I am sharing with you. Spiritual beings multi-vibrate on many different frequencies according to their multi-level spiritual structure. Only after you reach the Ultimate Graduation can you decide to cross into the Divine stillness. Before you can finally become still, you will vibrate on only one godly frequency. But that is far away, first you have to finish your growth and spiritual development."

"Is God still, not moving?"

"Only the Ultimate Creator's spiritual essence is still, but all of God's creations are in motion. You were still before you separated into a spiritual existence, and you can become still again after you eventually decide to cease your spiritual existence. I could cease to exist and be in ultimate unity with God, but I do not have the desire to do that whatsoever. I like to be on the move and in movement all the time," said Gardener.

I was very humbled and thankful because I realized that I just had touched the subject of the spiritual essence of the Ultimate Creator.

Chapter 79
AWARENESS AND BALANCE

"The first step toward change is awareness. The second step is acceptance." (Nathaniel Branden)

It seemed that my questioning was going well, thus, only two days later I asked my teacher to tell me more about our evolution. Gardener said:
"The evolution of a species is a product of the concentrated focus of their particular consciousness. Individual animals or other beings focus their wishful thinking in one common direction to enhance their abilities to survive and develop in their environments.   For example, animals are growing bigger teeth to have more successful hunting skills. But you must go back all the way to the creation of organic life to see when a new quality of consciousness effort has begun."
"How does it happen?" I asked.
"It happens by an intervention of the Creators. As you already know, these interventions are needed when upgrades to a higher quality of incarnations are desired. As I told you before, they happened on the Earth when the creation of organic life was desired, when the creation of the animal kingdom was desired, and when the development of an intelligent species such as you humans had been desired. But to think that only you humans are self-aware is not correct. All organic life is self-aware. Awareness was created by the intervention of the Creators. Awareness inspires intention and intention creates drive."
"When the evolution of a species ends, what happens next?"
"Species can stay in balance, or they can either change, modify themselves into another species or die out. Look at your saber tooth tigers. They became extinct because, in their greed, they grew their teeth so big that the teeth became useless and eventually killed them. They were unable to modify their hunting skills. And you humans, in a different

more sophisticated greed might have a similar destiny if you do not change. You are not keeping balance as most other living species do. The only way forward for you may be to change into another species."

Even though I completely trusted my teacher, I still wanted to know more and to have a second opinion. I took my ship from the Alpha Squared Station and headed to Sagittarius to look for Ruala.

"Welcome Menev, you haven't been here for a while. How can I help you?" she asked when we tuned into each other's vibrations.

"Madam Ruala, I would like to know more about the feminine and masculine aspects of spirituality, I would like to know more about gender."

"There is no gender here, Menev. God has no gender; I have no gender and His Majesty Gardener has no gender. You see me as female and you see Gardener as male, because you are with us now only as an observer and visitor. You see what you want to see."

"Then why do we have genders on Earth, Cosmic Lady?"

"Gender exists not only on the Earth, but on most of the planets in your universe. Genders are created in accordance with God's decision to use duality as a tool for development. But there is one significant difference between your Earth and many other planets. The duality is supposed to work in harmony and balance. That is the case on most planets, but not on the Earth. You developed a huge discrepancy when the masculine gradually took over almost completely. It is rare that it happens like that, because the Creators know from experience about such dangers. During the interventions, they are giving more powers to the feminine. The feminine is much more able to keep harmony and balance than the masculine. But beings on your planet, and especially you humans, have turned the destiny of your temporary home in the wrong direction."

"Is it too late for mankind, Madam Ruala?"

"No, it is not. It looks like two out of the three main criteria of balance have currently reversed their trend, and they have started to move back into the right direction as desired by God."

"What are they, can you elaborate, please?"

"Yes, there is a trend toward a better balance between feminine and masculine. The feminine is gaining strength on the masculine. The second good trend is that spirituality is also gaining strength in the minds of many people. These individuals can help mankind. You are one of them. But the deepening of the divide between your handling of your environment and nature continues. You still have a pretty good chance not to destroy yourselves, but you must start moving more toward nature again. By the way," continued Ruala, "can you imagine if there would be no gender on your planet? Juanzetta and you would not be able to complement each other like you can do now. And can you imagine not being able to make love and enjoy sex?"

"No, I cannot imagine that" I answered.

Chapter 80
SPICE OF LOVE

"We delight in the beauty of the butterfly, but rarely admit the changes it has gone through to achieve that beauty."
(Maya Angelou)

After such a challenge from Ruala, I followed up with a series of meditations about art and the ceremonies of lovemaking. Obviously, because of tuning into such a spicy topic, I also had some very spicy sexual dreams. I do not intend to present most of them here because they were more than private. Also, they could kind of stain the whole spiritual story a little bit for some of you, who are more sensitive on this topic. I shall try to include only what is relevant to the flow of my spiritual discoveries. And the Cosmic Lady of Love, Ruala, played a very active part in it.

We all have sexual fantasies and most of us keep them to ourselves. A very few of us can be brave enough to share them with a loved one or someone else whom we can trust. Many of us are often questioning ourselves to determine if we are not going too far in our wildest imaginations. And we also can have feelings of guilt. I asked Ruala about it in one of our sessions. She said:

"Your sexual dreams, images and fantasies, Menev, reflect your freedom. Sometimes your rather submissive nature is trying to carry and express guilt for all the masculine aggressions on the planet toward the feminine. And that guilt you are trying to carry is fueling your drive in your sexual wishes, imaginations and needs. But you cannot carry the guilt of the whole masculine aspect of the planet, unless every man would understand and accept what you are trying to point out."

Juanzetta's involvement in this issue began with a butterfly. She had a dream of being under a sun umbrella at an exotic beach. She saw a huge five-foot size monarch butterfly flying above the water. The butterfly suddenly changed into a myriad of small butterflies flying around and behaving like a cloud. She and I speculated about the dream thinking it might have something to do with the approaching end of our lives. As Anatole France once wrote, at the end of life we should be like butterflies: just make love, be beautiful and die. I had no idea that the butterfly dream would come up when I was not expecting it. After one of my spiritual sexual sessions with Ruala, she gave me little lesson:

"Duality and sex on your planet, Menev, were not created to give you people frustrations. But, unfortunately, many people are sexually frustrated. The main reason is that they are unable to communicate about their sexual needs, fantasies, and dreams. When love between two human beings is born and lovemaking starts to happen, the highest quality of Loosh is being produced. But as you well know, after a while the quality of such Loosh declines because people stop spicing it."

"What do you mean by spicing it, Madam?"

"Love is the spice of life; sex is the spice of love and ceremony is the spice of sex. As you see, Menev, there is a lot of spice in the entire process. You build it up in that order. First you find your love, then you start having sex, and then you bring ceremony into your lovemaking. Of course, you can destroy it in the reverse order. First, you start to have mere routine instead of the ceremony, then you stop being intimate, and finally, the love might be gone entirely. And even though the two of you, you and Juanzetta, are now two very gorgeous, beautiful butterflies, you still should cherish and take diligent care of all your spices by being aware of what I just said. However, it does not mean that you must act on all your fantasies totally, just like you would not put a full container of pepper on your favorite food. With a little bit of spice here and there, you can ritualize your lovemaking and accomplish a very, very high stage of looshing."

"You mentioned butterflies, Madam. Is it somehow

connected to Juanzetta's dream about the big butterfly?" I asked.

"It is, indeed. Do you remember walking on Campobello Island around the beautiful colorful flowers with butterflies on them? What caused you to stop and move closer to them when others in the group were ready to leave? You even took pictures of the butterflies. I gave you that impulse to go back to see them and to think about what they represent in your mind. And here is the interpretation of Juanzetta's dream for you: When her big, gorgeous monarch butterfly changed to a cloud of small butterflies, she spread the message of the wonderful butterfly type of Love at the end of the human life all around her and everywhere."

Chapter 81
BUBBLING AND ELOHIM

"Many of those who have explored within and discovered their true nature have made one of the most contentious and confusing of all mystical claims - the assertion "I am God!""
(Peter Russell in From Science to God, page 86)

In August 2012, Juanzetta and I had a wonderful experience when we saw the magnificent performance of "Totem" by the Cirque du Soleil. The show presented ten various stages of human development and progress from the primordial soup all the way up to the landing on the Moon. Seeing the tremendous athleticism and artistry of the performers, you might think that they are not normal people. But they are showing us how the human spirit can conquer the human body.

My night following the performance was full of mystical dreams with almost constant vibrations inside and outside all over my body. I was rising back and forth out of the primordial soup, feeling the survival struggles of every creature imaginable. Two days later, I called on Starman to have him explain and tell me more about my experience.

"You experienced some moments of your Ultimate Creation through bubbling. As you probably already understand, bubbling is the expression of God from stillness into motion. God as the Source of Everything is the stillness, and the separation of the Soul from the Source is enabled by bubbling. When God creates an intention to release a new Soul, the process can be very intense, almost violent. That is what was happening in your dreams. You know about the primordial soup and the beginning of the creation of biological life. Likewise, there is a primordial soup for the creation of souls."

After my conversation with Starman, I was pondering that the newly created souls who had just separated from God must still be very close to the Ultimate Creator. They apparently understand the real essence of the Source for a while. But, as soon as they start to execute God's intentions, they become busy with creations and manifestations, and they start to forget about their permanent home in the stillness from which they came. Such souls closest to God are known in some human sacred texts as Elohim. Two weeks after the conversation with Starman, I decided to ask my beloved teacher about them. I met Gardener in space and asked:

"Who is, or who are Elohim, Your Majesty?"

"You can use that name Jozef if you want to. You were an Elohim when you were consciousness without any form shortly after you separated from God through bubbling in the moment of your Ultimate Creation. At some point, you stopped and forgot about being an Elohim when you lowered your vibrations enough to start manifesting into the lower realms all the way down to your physical existence. You may become an Elohim again only after you have collected all your possible experiences and are trying to return to God, to your origin as a spiritual being. At that point, you will be able to absorb the whole structure of your existing consciousness back again. If you desire to bring it back home to the Ultimate Source, you again stop having any form. If you can accomplish that, then you can cease to exist as a spiritual individual if you wish to do so, and you can return to the Source."

"Are you an Elohim, Your Majesty?"

"Yes, I am, but I like what I do. I keep my vibrations intentionally lowered, even though I could go home at any time. But I like to be local," answered Gardener.

"What do you mean by that, My Lord?"

"When you are an Elohim, you are non-local, you are almost pure consciousness. But only God is pure consciousness. As an Elohim, you consciously localize yourself; you can go to any form-based reality, and you can work in any universe and galaxy. That is what I did."

"I would like to also know more about why we in the physical have the permanent and constant so-called monkey mind which often causes undesired activities and feelings. Can you tell me something about it?" I asked.

"The monkey mind, or brain noise, is a completely natural state of mind. It reflects the bubbling which is going on within you, and it is with you throughout all your spiritual existence. Even tinnitus reflects bubbling. You were created by bubbling, weren't you? When you meditate, and you are trying to reach Nirvana, Samadhi, or Satori or whatever you call that state, you are forcibly trying to stop the bubbling. When you reach that very temporary stillness, you are touching God. And, while it is very rewarding, it is still only a temporary illusion. To make it permanent, you must collect all your spiritual experiences and cease to exist in any of the form-based realities. As I said before, you can become an Elohim and you can go back home to your Ultimate Creator. You can, from time to time, conquer your monkey mind and visit God in a state of temporary stillness. Or you can utilize your skills and build a bridge for your final return," said Gardener.

Chapter 82
MISSION HAS BEGUN

*"The Earth is a very small stage in a vast cosmic arena."
(Carl Sagan)*

From June until October 2013 not much was happening. I routinely recorded my dreams and had several pathetic unsuccessful attempts to meditate. I was busy with my job and with my private life, while at the same time not feeling very optimistic about my ability to write this book. Then suddenly two things happened which triggered my new effort and determination.

Only when I got ready to write this chapter did I realize how much they were connected. In October, Juanzetta met with the medium, Cheryl Lewallen, and asked her for a reading. She told Cheryl only that she had a boyfriend, not describing anything else about him. In her reading, Cheryl saw a baldheaded man (Juanzetta's deceased husband Charlie) sending a message to Juanzetta approving of her having this boyfriend and encouraging her to help him with his writing. The image Cheryl saw was of the baldheaded man's outstretched hand holding another man in his palm as if he were being given to Juanzetta as a gift. This man-gift was sitting at a computer. Cheryl also saw a woman standing behind the man's computer and telling Cheryl that she was the mother of the man at the computer. Cheryl then identified the man's name as beginning with a J.

I asked Gardener in the following meditation about the significance of the reading:
"To tell you again, that you should move your ass," said Gardener.
"O.K. But it was not just about me, it was also about Juanzetta, and others involved, like Charlie and my mother, what about them?" I answered.
"First let's talk about Cheryl. She did not know about your

mission. But I thought that because she was a medium, it would not hurt to remind you through her that other spiritual people are waiting for your work, not only Juanzetta. Your message is also important for them, not just for regular folks. I know you would like to concentrate on inspiring everybody who would be interested regardless of whether they are meditating, praying, channeling, canaling, speculating, or just asking very simple questions. And Charlie is willing to help through Juanzetta any time she would ask."

"And what about my mother?" I asked.

"You have never asked about her previous lives, have you? You know about your life with your Dad when you were dolphins. But your Mom used to be your wife in one of your past-lives. She loves you not only as your mother, but as your lover and she wants you to succeed."

Later in the month I had the most beautiful dream I have ever had. It was exactly six years after Dr. Balbir Singh Sidhu placed a stent into my main "widow-maker" heart artery. In the dream, I was on the top of a flat hill accessible only by a foot path. A large structure was being built there. It looked like a large dome with the tower on the top and was constructed from clear pipes. When they finally put a spire on the top, it was finished, and I made a speech in front of the tower to the huge crowd of people gathered there:

"Let this beautiful machine built by the efforts of people of all races, ages, genders, ethnicities, religions, countries and different sexual preferences send the signal to our Ultimate Creator that we are finally unified and want to talk to God. Let the Ultimate Creator know that we have eliminated all violence, hatred and greed and we are ready to be one again with God. After all, God is in each one of us from forever to forever as the Source of All That Exists. Now we are sending the message to the Ultimate Creator that we have finally recognized our purpose and are begging God to come to us. And we are expecting to receive the Ultimate Creator's response."

Then in the dream we were sitting outside in sort of a makeshift restaurant, apparently waiting for a reception. While waiting for the celebration to begin, we were admiring the structure and were looking at the path winding like a snake up to it from the valley below. Someone suggested that maybe something like a cable-car line should be built to be used by the people coming up to see the structure. Others talked about two men who had created the public campaign to promote and protect the whole structure the way that everybody could understand its purpose and meaning, not just spiritual leaders, ministers, priests, imams, gurus, and other leaders. But someone else was insisting that it should be like a pilgrim's place. According to him, people should be able to reach the structure only after a long and demanding walk so that they would deserve to be there. Discussion started to be heated, so I stepped in and said:

"Listen my friend! This machine was built for everybody! You must understand that everyone should be able to get here, even the sick and handicapped and even those unable to move at all."

People around me nodded their heads in agreement. I felt obligated to finish my opinion because I considered it to be very important. I turned to the elitist guy and finished my talk:

"You should know that there is no difference in the value of people for the Ultimate Creator. God loves us all the same way regardless of what we do or do not do. Everybody here is as valuable and important as you, stranger!"

And I woke up.

The dream reminded me again of the magnificent movie, "Contact," based on the novel by Carl Sagan. Three days after the dream, I wrote the first chapter of this book.

Chapter 83
HEADING TO THE ROOTS

"The past explains how I got here, but the future is up to me, and I love to live life at full throttle." (Janice Dickinson)

It all began again with a dream in July 2014. At first, I was apparently screaming loudly from the dream, not knowing nor being aware of why. Then I dreamed that, in a dream, I woke up screaming in the house in the village, Láb, where I was born. The whole house and yard were completely empty, no furniture, no anything. I climbed up a ladder leading into the attic and saw that the attic was also completely empty. Nobody was anywhere. But the little garden behind the house was full of cars. I realized I had to run away because they were chasing me. We had previously lived in the house and now we had been replaced by someone else who apparently was getting ready to move into it. I understood that they should not find me in there and that they could come at any moment. I immediately ran out of the house even though I was naked and had no clothes, no wallet, nor anything.

In about a week after this dream, Juanzetta and I were supposed to take a trip with the Charles E. Flowers Society on the Viking Pride ship, sailing on the Seine from Paris to Normandy and back. Juanzetta's deceased husband, Dr. Charlie Flowers, was the deeply admired long time Chairman of the Department of Obstetrics and Gynecology at the University of Alabama in Birmingham. His residents continue to make professional and recreational trips every year in his memory. After the river cruise, she and I planned to go to the largest and most rural canton of Switzerland, called Grisons in English and Graubünden in Swiss German. I wanted to look for the place where I used to meet Gardener when I was incarnated in the 15th century as Menev. I had no doubt that my dream had been sent by Gardener.

I went immediately after the dream into meditation. Gardener created a place for us. We were sitting in modern round chairs facing each other and he took my form. I was looking at myself just like in the before mentioned dream. He told me:

"Now that you know how things work here on the Other Side, the time has come for your personal reflection. I am glad that you have decided to go to the roots of your spirituality on the planet where we used to meet. There is a deep connection between the place where you were born into physical life on your planet and the place where you were born spiritually. Now you can find that place and understand that connection. The empty house in your dream means that all that you considered to be important in your previous life is not important anymore, including your childhood, your family, your friends and everybody and everything. All of that shall be replaced in the newly cleaned and emptied house of your mind by a new understanding of your cosmic essence. Your screams were not the screams of fear but the screams of joy. I shall meet you in Grisons at or near the place where we used to meet in your earthly time when you were Menev. Look for a small shack on a hillside overlooking a meadow around the place called Zuoz."

I finally got to do a meaningful meditation early in the morning when the Viking Pride was anchored on the Seine in the town of Vernon. When I reached the space of Focus 27 and TMI-There, I realized that, besides the connection to my physical body, I had an equally strong connection to the Source through a stream of information that was coming to me about my new understanding of the cosmic essence. I was already feeling the strong connection to Gardener which I usually felt only when reaching much higher vibrations. I felt that he was already talking to me. And, when I reached Focus 42, two vortexes (one Gardener's and the other one mine) were engaging in a magical dance, splitting, and merging again. I heard his voice:

"When you are traveling spiritually, you are like a spider on a web. The web is your spiritual structure, and as you discovered today, your connection to the Source of All That Exists must be equally as important in your earthly life as your connection to your physical body. That is the core of your new understanding of your cosmic essence. This trip you are taking is more spiritual than you ever expected. Indeed, you are going to your spiritual roots on the Earth. Just think about it. You the Viking, Skjoerg the Shaman, are on a ship with the name Viking Pride, and you are actually coming to the same place you visited when you were Skjoerg!"

And I did not even fully realize what he had just said. My questions were pushing me into another direction.

"How is it Your Majesty, that I could already feel your presence in Focus 27? Why were our vortexes merging and splitting again?" I eagerly asked.

"You as The Roter started the practice of advance roting. While a ROTE is basically a ball, it can change to any form; it can stretch and disperse, and you can grasp it in any form. That is what you did because, as you know, there is no time here. Our vortexes were merging and splitting because I am you and you are me. When you communicate with me, you do not even have to worry about which vortex is whose," said Gardener. Only now, I reacted to what he had said earlier:

"Did you just say, My Lord, that I had been here in Normandy as a Viking Shaman?" I was expressing my little doubts.

"The experiences you have had in meditations so far were of you as a young shaman. When you were older, you were following the berserkers more and more because you were curious about new lands. You were here, and you were in a place called Rouen. But you can ask Skjoerg directly to tell you more about it."

"Shall I see you in Switzerland, My Lord?"

"You shall feel my presence in Grisons all the time from the moment you step out of the train up to the moment you step into the train again when leaving," he answered, and we parted.

Two days later in the early afternoon, I was showing the palm of my right hand to Saul, one of the guests on the Viking Pride who specializes in surgical operations of hands. I was pointing to the little fatty bumps I have in my palm. "Those are from Viking times," said Saul.

I then realized that I was being mysteriously reminded to look for Skjoerg the Shaman. I found him later in the afternoon in meditation while the Viking Pride was majestically sailing on the Seine. He was brief but clear: "I am glad that you are repeating our trip from the ninth century. I will tell you what happened to us. We were sailing up the river from the town you call Rouen toward the town of Paris. Later, you and I were killed during the siege of Paris. And I am sending you the proof that I am telling you the truth. Check your right hand!"

The palm of my right hand and fingers started to hurt so badly that I had difficulty to come back from my meditation in an orderly manner. While I was counting down to C1, my hand was violently trembling and shaking.

Chapter 84
IN MENEV'S COUNTRY

"Follow your bliss and the Universe will open doors for you where there were only walls." *(Joseph Campbell)*

After the Flowers Society meeting was over, Juanzetta and I took a train to Chur, the Capital of the Swiss canton Grisons (Graubünden), with the intention to look for the place where I had met Gardener during my Menev incarnation. We settled in Chur in the ABC Hotel at 8 Otto Strasse. As I was falling asleep, I was intensely inviting Gardener to come see me. Shortly after, I woke up in a hypnagogic state and I saw a silhouette on the left side of the balcony window. The situation felt almost the same as when Timothy had entered my room in Selge Beach in Turkey; but at that time Timothy came on his own, and this time I had invited Gardener.

I clicked off and fell back asleep but woke up again and decided to go into meditation. I met Gardener at Alpha Squared on Focus 42, and he had the same form as the silhouette I had seen in the balcony window. I also had a silhouette form, and we had no faces. Gardener said that faces did not matter. I invited him into our room in the hotel. We flew instantly in and sat in black leather armchairs. The chairs and our spiritual bodies were glowing together. Now my whole experience in Grisons became pure bliss just as Gardener had promised, and it continued to be so until we stepped into the train to go to Munich.

"Why did I really have to come here, My Lord?" I asked.

"So that you can show an example and tell people what they can accomplish when they truly follow their intentions and their bliss. This trip is a very important part of your testimony about your spiritual journey," answered Gardener.

"How can I find the exact place where we used to meet?"

"As I told you, it is near a place called Zuoz. It is on the side of one of the roads around the town and you must find it. But I cannot tell you the exact place on your physical plane as I would have to be fully on your planet in a physical body. You must find it yourself and you must go by feelings. You shall know when you are standing there on a hillside which goes sharply down into the meadow below in the valley." And my teacher returned into the depths of space, and I went back to bed.

In the morning, we rented a car, a Ford Focus (!) and Juanzetta drove me south from Chur, and then east toward Zuoz. I was eagerly scanning the countryside all the time. After several hours while passing Saint Moritz, we realized it was late and we needed to go back to Chur. It was getting dark; we worried about a safe return to the hotel and forgot entirely what we were doing there. We hastily turned to the left shortly before Zuoz to take a shortcut via a small twisty mountain road. We were occupied with conversation, when Juanzetta suddenly said:

"Look at that little shack, I wonder what it could be!"

"It is Menev's place."

I said it seemingly jokingly, and we continued over the hills and scattered mountain villages. When we had gone too far to return, I suddenly realized what I had said. We did not see anything else even remotely like it.

The next day, we decided to approach the area from the northern side. After Juanzetta drove past Davos and Zernez, we headed up through Ober Engadin Valley, passed through beautiful Zuoz and decided to take the same mountain road as the day before. When we reached La Punt-Chamues-ch, we turned right and headed up over Albulapas toward the village of Preda. Rain had just started pouring when the shack appeared again on the right side of the road. I asked Juanzetta to stop a bit before reaching the place, stepped out of the car, looked up at the sky and asked the rain to stop.

The rain stopped instantly. I crouched down

overwhelmed by crying. I knew I was at the place. Several large boulders were around the shack and the hillside was sharply descending into a green valley with a fresh stream still partly hidden by fog. Shaking took over all my body. It took me a while to be able to go back to the car and continue the ride back to Chur.

The next morning, I met with Gardener at the Alpha Squared Station. I told him:

"I am very humbled and thankful to Your Majesty for enabling me to see our place. I cannot thank you enough, My Lord."

"I am glad, Menev Jozef, that you found it. You are more determined than I expected. We used to meet at that roundish boulder you saw. You were coming there to meditate the way I taught you and you always called me from there. Now, by connecting your present with your past, you have reached the state when your spiritual journey on the planet Earth is complete. But you still can and will have many more spiritual experiences in the process of polishing all that you have learned. The quest never ends."

"What should I do now, My Lord?"

"We promised each other on that rock that when the right time in the right incarnation would come, you would spread the message of love, humility and compassion all over the planet. By showing the way, you can help everyone to venture on the similar spiritual road just as you have. You have found the right physical body, the right environment, the right tools and your Juanzetta. She is your rock. Support her, cherish, and protect her for the rest of your physical life and beyond. You know how much she has accelerated your effort. I love you both!"

"We love you very much Your Majesty and we thank you for all that you have done. I promise to finish my job and fulfill our pledge made on that rock all those centuries ago!"

Chapter 85
JUANZETTA'S HEART

"A joyful heart is the inevitable result of a heart burning with love." *(Mother Teresa)*

It took me a while to get back to meaningful meditation again after the experiences on the European trip. I was sometimes wondering if I should also travel to Rome to try to have a deeper connection to my Plautus incarnation. I realized that it would not be necessary. I could find and study a lot of information about him. Plautus was a very famous public figure, and his life is richly documented. I was thinking of how to continue in the spiritual journey, if at all. And, like several times before, I had the feeling that I already had accumulated enough stories for my book. I was thinking about the conclusion of the whole journey. But as Gardener had emphasized in Grisons, the quest never ends. And then something happened again which gave me new energy and direction.

After some time had passed, I finally decided to say thanks for the wonderful European experiences to my dear teacher and I went into meditation in September 2014. When I approached the Alpha Squared Station platform, I saw an elevator coming down and expected to see Gardener stepping out. But when the door opened, to my surprise Juanzetta stepped out.

"What are you doing here Sweetie, it is such a delightful surprise to see you here!" I said in awe.

"I am Gardener, Menev," said Juanzetta's form:

"I took her form to remind you how it all started to happen between the two of you. You know, Jozef, we have many spiritual students like you on many planets, but only a few of them have support like you are getting from Juanzetta. I was not kidding when I told you that I was jealous that you have her, Jozef!"

Now I had completely forgotten that I was supposed to thank him for my trip. Something inside of my right ear started to beat wildly: Bum...bum...bum...

"What is that Your Majesty?"

"I brought you the beat of Juanzetta's heart, Jozef, to remind you that her heart is beating for you all the time!"

Then I started to be aware of the Hemi Sync as never before. Sounds were wandering and wobbling all around in my head as if something or someone were howling in there, from left to right and back, from top to bottom and back and across.

"And what is that My Lord?"

"I modified your Hemi Sync for the moment so that you can experience The Bubbling of the Ultimate Creator through the cacophony of your physical Universe. I warn you; you might soon feel physical discomfort. God has feelings also and they are going through the Ultimate Creator's heart. When God has too much discomfort or any reason to stop the activities anywhere, then the bubbling stops in that time and space too. When the activities stop, annihilation happens. Then, creation can start at another place and time and in another bubble. God is always keeping the Source's heart in harmony and joy."

And I had discomfort indeed. Water started to pour out of my right ear and my left hand was paralyzed in temporary pain. After this experience, it was obvious that when Juanzetta asked me if I would accompany her to the Starlines II program at Monroe Institute that I simply replied:

"Of course!"

Chapter 86
WITH OLD BUDDIES

"One of the most beautiful qualities of true friendship is to understand and to be understood." (Seneca)

The Starlines II program, facilitated by Dr. Franceen King with the assistance of Lee Stone and Andrea Berger, was held in November 2014. I was very curious as to what it could bring me when taking it for the second time. Things started to happen very soon. I received the first interesting information from Starman, when we were instructed to inquire about the distinction between the vibrational levels of Focus Levels 34 and 35. He told me:
"We higher beings have to know what we want when we are approaching your planet, Menev. Some intelligent species from the universe just want to observe you, others are thinking about incarnation, and we must be very careful about it. If we just want to observe, we must establish ourselves in the safer vibrational distance of what you call Focus 35. If we are not paying attention, we can slide into Focus 34 and become earthbound. The temptation from your planet can be very strong because of all the goodies you have. If we cannot resist them, we incarnate. It has happened to me several times, even though I already knew all the struggles and sufferings that would go with it."
"You don't want to come back anymore, Starman, do you?" I asked.
"Sometimes I still think about it, but right now it is not a good situation on your planet. But you are a very interesting and enticing species indeed. And the food and sex there are so gooood!"
Another one of my old friends whom I met again at Starlines II was Mister Q. It happened this time during a time traveling exercise in the Portal Room with a teleporting device. After browsing for a while, I zoomed and focused in

on Mister Q doing one of his favorite past times, checking the primordial soup on our planet.

I teleported myself to the place. He curiously looked at me and said:

"You are not Captain Picard, but you look familiar to me, who are you? Did we meet before?"

"Yes, Mister Q, you were giving me a lot of advice early on in my spiritual journey and I apologize that I am not in contact with you so much anymore. I am very busy with my travels and work."

"It is O.K. I like for anybody to come here besides all those Star Trek folks. They sometimes bore me with all those crazy costumes and questions. We can talk if you want to."

"Mister Q, I would like to ask you some questions."

"O.K. go ahead."

"How did it all begin; I mean life on our planet? You must know because you seem to be an expert. Are you pondering about our planet all the time, Mister Q?"

"Well, I am also spending a lot of time in the Akashic Library. Life can begin on any planet in two ways. The Creators, or Terraformers as you might call them, can receive permission from the Ultimate Creator to create biological life from inorganic matter. The process is very complicated and requires a lot of Dark Matter which acts as a facilitator.

It can take millions of planetary years to create even bacteria. Or they can bring life from outer space by comets or asteroids. It is quicker, but it negatively affects the originality and uniqueness of life on the new planet. In the case of your Earth, both happened because you received so much variety from so many different environments. That is why you now have so many kinds of flora and fauna and different races of humans. And once the seeds of biological life are planted, no one can stop them, not even the Terraformers who brought them in."

Just for the fun of it, the next time I called Hadien because he liked to show me the things in our universe. He said he would show me two very different planets. The first one of them was inhabited by giant beings who looked like white worms. They were the only creatures living there, but they were intelligent beings who were very aware of their existence. Everyone had both genders and they had built a very sophisticated underground system of tunnels and chambers where they lived. The surface of the planet was flat and dry with only four kinds of plants, and only one of them with giant leaves was edible. The worms had developed a very complex system of small tunnels under the plants. The tunnels were used to hold the water which they obtained from deep inside the planet. The planet was circling around its red star close enough to have the light needed to nourish the plants. Hadien told me that once a being incarnated there, it was very difficult to build up the necessary spiritual velocity for leaving the system. The lifespan was very short and recycling into the non-physical world and back was also very quick.

He then took me to a very complicated planet. The beings there had gotten rid of all their biological organs, bodies, and limbs, and kept only their brains. The Brain-Beings were using complicated robotic bodies with a variety of wheels, arms, hooks, and other parts. The main work on the planet was to grow nutritional beans under the ground. Their robotic bodies extracted nutritional fluids from the beans for the brains.

Meanwhile, the Brain-Beings were constantly occupied with entertainment of all kinds. They held competitive physical gladiator-like games and games using multidimensional projections of artificially invented creatures who were fighting and deceiving each other. They had given up sexuality. The order to keep only brains became the basic law of the planet. Spiritual escape from this planet was also very difficult. They could keep their brains by regenerating them and keeping them alive for thousands of years.

Most of the inhabitants who died were eagerly waiting for reincarnation and hastily ran back when new brains became available. They grew new brains by using DNA from dying brains. When the new brains reached the proper size, they cleaned them by erasing any residual memories, which then enabled the beings waiting for reincarnations to enter them.

I was a little bit disgusted by both visits. I thanked him for an interesting outing but was very happy to rush back into the physical world of my beloved Earth.

Chapter 87
COUNCIL OF STAR FRIENDS

"You are never alone. You are eternally connected with everyone." (Amit Ray)

Thanks to all the wonderful participants at my second Starlines II, I felt tremendous energy and strong high vibrations inside and all around me. It was obvious that I wanted to use this opportunity to see what my Master Teacher could still have in store for me. Our first conversation was very short. I wanted to know the relationship between consciousness, intention and thought. Gardener told me:

"Supreme consciousness is first because it is the One and it is stillness. It is the Source; it is God. Intention is created from the stillness as a driving force which shapes, and forms thought. Thought can move energy and energy can move matter. Any manifestation, as you already know, Menev Jozef, starts with an intention which is created from the stillness by the power of One."

Before another inquiry, I also tried to fully sort out my understanding of the relationship between the I-There Cluster, the Bonded I-There Clusters, and the Infinite Sea of I-There Bonded Clusters. All of them are mentioned in Robert Monroe's books. It seemed obvious to me that I needed to clearly understand this issue before I could call upon my teacher again. The following is my understanding based on what I had already learned.

The I-There Cluster is an elementary component of Global Consciousness or One or God or Source. It is at the bottom of the tree of the hierarchical Divine Structure of Consciousness. The I-There Cluster is the hovering Higher Self of spiritual being incarnated on a planet. I can have many different I-There Clusters or Higher Selves in many parallel time and space universes and in any time and space universe.

My Higher Self can be horizontally connected to all my other I-There Clusters and to the I-There Clusters of any other spiritual beings, thus forming the Bonded I-There Clusters. My Higher Self is also vertically connected to many levels of my Higher-Higher Selves all the way up to my Ultimate Higher Self.

The very well-developed spiritual beings on the Higher-Higher Self levels can form different bodies of thoughts, which can be described in our earthly terms as Councils. One of their purposes is to help spiritual beings at the lower vibrational levels. I have visited some of them during my travels described in this book. The Infinite Sea of Bonded I-There Clusters, described by Robert Monroe, is the Divine Structure of Consciousness of all the spiritual beings separated from God after being created by the Power of One. If I would cease to exist as a spiritual being, all my I-There Clusters or Higher Selves, Higher-Higher Selves and my Ultimate Self would disappear and would dissolve unstructured back into the Source. And in his book, Robert Monroe described watching some of those chunks of the Infinite Sea of Bonded I-There Clusters disappear from time to time.

After this contemplation, I simply decided to call my most important Council of Higher Beings into my Memory Room. I wondered who would show up. Here they came: Gardener, Hadien, Ra, Ruala, Starman and Mister Q. And yes, Kamaláska showed up too.

"Are you surprised, Jozef?" asked Gardener.

"Yes, I am, My Lord. What was that council which I faced for the first time so long ago?"

"That was just another council. You can ask for as many types of councils as you want. It is not necessary to be strictly tied to any council or even to give it a name like Cluster Council, Galaxy Council or whatever. But I thought if I put together all of us whom you call your Star Friends you would appreciate it. You can call us the Council of Star Friends now if you want. And we are ready to help you as a Council if you want, or just on one-on-one meetings as we have been doing so many times before."

"Thank you so much, Your Majesty and the whole Council of Star Friends, I am very humbled."

Chapter 88
STRINGS AND IMMORTALITY

"Logic will get you from A to B. Imagination will take you everywhere." (Albert Einstein)

I decided to continue one-on-one with Gardener. When I met him again, I immediately started in with my questions:
"How many dimensions does our Universe have, Your Majesty?"
"Thirteen, Jozef," he answered very simply.
"Why is our universe expanding at an accelerated rate?"
"Your universe is very young, Jozef, it is still unwinding and the Love in it is generally still overcoming fear, greed and hate. Also, there are plenty of novelties for our Boss!"
"What are the vibrating strings and why are they different in each universe?"
"Everything in all manifested universes is composed of strings. They are created immediately after a Big Bang and they rapidly multiply like viruses or bacteria until they are brought under the control by dark matter and dark energy. Then the unwinding of a newborn universe slows down and reaches the stability necessary for the creation of livable and hospitable planetary systems. Thus, new life and civilizations can be born. String shapes and vibrations are different for each universe because they carry the unique intentions of the Ultimate Creator for particular universe."
The next time, I wanted to know how it was possible for Gardener to travel instantly throughout time and space. Said he:
"Look Jozef, as you already know, everything manifested is quantified, or, as you say, digital. Even electrons cannot choose their distances from the core of the atom; they can only jump up and down by defined quantified distances. I am using some of my many manifested forms and bodies and

they are quantified and digital. My manifested form is defined by The Code of Manifestation which is very similar to the DNA code in your biological bodies on Earth. Sometimes creating my form in the lower vibrational dimensions requires a lot of energy. If I wanted to use the same form in another space and time, I would have to use even more energy. I prefer to move my form from the original space and time by using the technology which you would probably call quantum entanglement. What I do is take just a small sample of the Code of Manifestation with me. The sample contains the core information of everything that I need to clone my whole form in the new space and time."

"I have wanted to ask you for a long time, Your Majesty, why you have not incarnated on our planet. Can you tell me?" I asked.

"Of course, Jozef. I have incarnated on many similar planets and the result was almost always the same. I learned repeatedly what I already knew. The price I had to pay for the repeated experiences was also the same with all those sicknesses, pains, depressions, and other struggles I would encounter. I came to the point where it was not worth it because I was not encountering anything new anymore. But now I see that your planet may be able to offer something different because of people like you. Let me think about it. I might try it out!"

"How did you reach immortality, My Lord?"

"Every spiritual being is immortal, Jozef. What is important is not whether we are or are not immortal beings. What is important is awareness. Most beings, when they incarnate, forget who they are and, thus, they are not aware of their immortality. They become stuck. Imagine that your toe or finger is clamped to a large object you cannot move. That is like the situation the stuck beings are in. They can cut the toe or finger off, have pain, and become theoretically free. Such beings can leave, but they have lost their completion. Afterwards, they must go back and finish the incarnation they left without completion. There are many things you can only do when you are a complete spiritual being. Only complete spiritual beings can accomplish a return to The Source. Therefore, many spiritual beings would rather avoid incarnations on biological planets."

Chapter 89
DIMENSIONS AND UNIVERSES

"Dark matter is where the whole spiritual aspect of our Universe is housed." (Juanzetta Flowers)

I felt afterwards that I needed to move closer to questioning about global and infinite reality. The next time I met Gardener, I simply asked him if he could tell me more about the bubbles.

"Bubbles are manifested universes created from the stillness of God by God. They are created by acts you call Big Bangs. From an informational point of view, bubbles are like the ROTEs you know so well. When they burst into existence, they contain all the necessary information needed to enable them to spread into space and time. These universes can function immediately after being created. I mentioned the ROTE to you, because the bubble-universes unwind in an analogous way to how you would unwind a ROTE. And they have a specific number of dimensions reflecting the intensions of the Ultimate Creator," said Gardener.

"Do they have any hierarchies or structures between them?" I eagerly asked.

"No, they don't. They are parallel. But they can bump into each other, and they can overlap. When you are living in one of them which is overlapping another, you can perceive it sometimes, like being aware of a parallel universe."

"Then, again, what is local and what is universal Your Majesty?"

"Local is what is happening in your particular bubble where your I-There Cluster is located. That is the local perception in your bubble. A universal perception travels across the bubbles and it is how you can perceive the universal reality of the Infinite Sea of Bonded I-There Clusters."

"What are dimensions, My Lord? What is the difference between dimensions and parallel universes?"

"Dimensions are local because they are inside of a particular bubble-universe. Remember, as I told you, the Ultimate Creator creates bubbles with different amounts of dimensions which can range from zero up to an infinite number. Parallel universes are in different bubbles. Do you recall, Jozef, when I played The Cacophony of your Universe into your headphones? At that time, I could have also played to you The Cacophony of Big Bangs and Big Annihilations, but you would not have understood it. But maybe you would now!"

I had a lot to think about. The next time I met him, I thanked Gardener and praised him for all the information he had given me. And I also expressed a lot of love for my Dearest Teacher. But then I asked again:

"My Lord, I am trying to understand multiverses, can you tell me more?"

"Multiverses are multiple overlapping bubbles, Jozef."

"Are the parallel universes and multiverses the same entities with just a different name?"

"You can say so."

"Do bubbles have a variety of sizes?"

"Yes, they do. When they are thriving by respecting and multiplying the loving intentions of the Ultimate Creator, they grow; otherwise, if they are not doing that, they shrink back. The bubbles-universes are pulsating. When they shrink too much, Big Crashes and Big Annihilations happen, and the universes are sucked back into the stillness of the Source. They completely disappear."

"Can another bubble be created in a bubble itself?"

"Yes, it definitely can. If everything is going as the Ultimate Creator-God intended, then the Creators governing bubbles can create bubbles within bubbles or new universes inside existing universes. But such Big Bangs are very local, and they can happen only after the permission of the Ultimate Creator has been given. It is only a temporary creation, and the permission can be revoked."

"How is it possible, that you know all of that, Your

Majesty?"

"I am constantly visiting The School of Creators and I would rather not tell you any more about that at this level of your development, Jozef!"

But the next time when we were vortexing around the Alpha Square Station, I continued with what I thought of as my sometimes rather aggressive questioning:

"Your Majesty, what is holding everything together, like all the bubbles-universes, as well as everything between them and inside of them?"

"Gravity and time are local, and they are maintaining the balance in the bubbles. However, anomalies in the local gravity fields and times can destroy complete planetary systems and civilizations. Anomalies can be of two different kinds: holes in gravity and time and the extreme concentrations of gravity and time in other areas. That is why the Ultimate Creator constantly creates and maintains Dark Matter and Dark Energy as a necessary tool to keep all manifestations together. Both Dark Energy and Dark Matter are partly still and partly in motion. But they are very flexible, and they can correct the anomalies both between the bubbles and inside of them. Dark matter is more local and acts as a cosmic balancer and glue inside the bubble of a universe. Dark Energy is more global, but it also operates as a balancer and glue between the bubbles of universes."

"What does God derive from all of this, My Lord? Why is the Ultimate Creator doing all of this work?"

"Jozef, since you have gotten all the way up here, I can tell you that God feeds not only on the Loosh, but also on novelty. Both are infinite and everlasting reasons for creating. They fuel the inspirations and intentions and are the driving forces for God."

"Your Majesty, can you tell me anything about Terrence McKenna's theories about the end of our Universe? According to him, our Universe was supposed to cease its existence in December of 2012 A.D. due to the novelties reaching the ultimate limit. But nothing happened, My Lord!"

"Yes, it did happen, Jozef. Indeed, Terrence McKenna was right! It happened in a parallel universe in another bubble and that Universe was annihilated! God had no reason to keep a bad universe alive!" said Gardener, now in my form with a big smile on his face.

He left me pondering once again. While pondering still in an altered state, I realized the tremendous possibilities and powers of our human minds. We can discover parallel universes with our thoughts because there is no time, and everything just happens now. All of that is not only possible, but natural, because of the bubbling by the Ultimate Creator. Our tremendous Universe is just one little bubble, no more than a grain of sand upon the infinite shore of an infinite sea, as Kahlil Gibran said. We can live in a parallel universe free of the mistakes from our current local space and time and be happy there without any limitations. I have visited parallel universes many times and lived multiple happy lives in them in my dreams. But that is for another story.

Chapter 90
LIGHT BODY AND RAMA

"Love, praise and gratitude, arising from your heart center in silent expectancy are the three Ascension Attitudes, those focused attitudes of mind that exalt your feelings toward the Christhood level." (Ruby Nelson in Door of Everything)

One of the most wonderful and exciting spiritual places of the Starlines II program, inspired by Dr. Franceen King, is the Spa in the Alpha X Station in Focus Level 49. It has a Subatomic Particle Accelerator. When I arrived there, I felt two light taps on my shoulders from behind. I turned around and was greeted by Ruala and Starman. They looked at me and, without saying anything, they completely undressed me and pointed to a spa chamber. They followed me in and then positioned me in the middle of the room, made sure that my body was fully straight up and that all the vortexes of my chakras were blissfully rotating in their colors from the bottom red to the top white. In an instant, the room was full of small fairy-like bodies flowing around me and all of them had colors corresponding to the chakra levels. I was immediately overcome by a blissful feeling. It traveled in waves repeatedly from the bottom of my spiritual body to the top and back.
"Who are you my dearest ones?" I asked in excitement.
"Don't you know Jozef? We are your friends and friends of your friends. We were at your wedding to your ISH. We have come again because you are ready for the next step. We are now going to create your Light Body!"
Streams of particles started to flow from their bodies into my body through the chakras, red to red, orange to orange, yellow to yellow, green to green, blue to blue, purple to purple and white to white.
And again, uncontrollable crying had overcome my physical body. Tears were pouring down my cheeks and my

whole physical body was vibrating and shaking. I was so extremely joyful that I was barely able to thank my friends at the end of the exercise. After my expressed gratitude, they disappeared in the blink of an eye.

Naturally, I decided to use my new light body immediately. My meditations using the chakras significantly changed. Both the crown and the base chakra started to have little pilot light flames on the top and bottom of the axis of my body. I understood I could use them as if my body were a missile. I stepped onto the platform of Alpha X station at Focus Level 49 and saw several ramps with small booths like phone booths. I chose one with the sign for Light Body Travelers and stepped in. I was asked to express my intention. I asked to visit the galactic core and started to count down from ten to one. The flames under my base chakra shot out like the burning fire of a missile.

Then, at the speed of thought, I was approaching the galactic core and hearing the millisecond pulsar. The stars were spiraling with me, and they were getting closer and closer to me. Time was running faster and faster. Suddenly, I was in a compact yellow spiral stream, and I felt very, very heavy. The yellow stream was pulling me into the black hole. But I did not panic; I knew I was in control. I did not want to get sucked into the hole. I pushed myself backward out of the spiral. I was starting to see stars around me again, and they were moving farther and farther away from me, and time was slowing down. When I had left the spinning, I could hear the millisecond pulsar again. I landed back in the booth on the ramp, and the flames coming out of my base chakra changed back into the little pilot light flame. I came back into my physical body.

During the next Subatomic Particle Accelerator exercise, we were supported by the Palenque sounds in Hemi Sync. Near the middle of the exercise, my base chakra vortex started to be bigger again, but the crown chakra vortex was a little bit smaller. My light body slowly moved out of my physical body at the crown chakra, and in a slow loop entered my body again at the base chakra. Then the entire process continued in a sequence of loops. My light body changed into a stream of pure white light. The loops were changing their size in synchrony with the Palenque sounds from headphones. A loop smaller than the check unit had deeper sounds and those bigger than the Nancy Penn Center building had higher sounds. When the Palenque sounds ended, my light body stopped rotating and the base and crown chakra pilot light flames shrank back down to their normal size.

In one of the next exercises, we were exploring the future and I was determined to see how I would be using my light body. When I reached the Portal Room, I set up the intention to see Earth in the year 3650 A.D. I was zooming in on our planet trying to see South America. But there was a smaller island there instead of a continent. I zoomed over the coast and found only a coastal village with very simple life. People were fishing and collecting fruit. I was sad and wanted to see what was happening to me at that time. I knew I was somewhere deep in space far away from Earth.

I expressed the intention to find myself. Then I was being shot deep into the distance. I found myself inside a huge asteroid sized cigar shaped ship which was slowly rotating to have artificial gravitation. It was a home which I shared with my Juanzetta and several other couples. We each had young male and female human bodies for our use. They were free of any pain or sickness. We used them for our enjoyment and pleasure. We alternated; sometimes I was a man and sometimes I was a woman. Likewise, Juanzetta could also use the body of the opposite gender whenever she wished. We had a beautiful home where we had whatever we liked and could use.

We also had several tools which helped us enjoy our trips throughout the universes. One of them was a huge ball with the diameter of the average human body. It was a ball of time that helped us choose time loops for our trips. We also had maps of the universes which we had visited or planned to visit. Our trips were initiated by our intentions and tools. We traveled by using a bender of space and time. It looked like a giant bed sheet. We marked the position and local time of our ship and the local time and position of the place where we wanted to go. We traveled in our light bodies, which had no genders. We stepped in and folded the bender sheet so that our home and the desired destinations touched. Then our intention changed into an instant tremendous flash of light almost like a little Big Bang. Our light bodies appeared in an instant at the desired destination, where we safely stored our bender for return. We were always guaranteed to be able to come back to our home on the ship we had created together.

Our trips served three different purposes, observe, help or incarnate. We were immortal because we lived in the Now. But we also understood that if we should choose to reincarnate, we would have to experience physical deaths again. However, we would not necessarily have to be together in our physical bodies in those planetary incarnations. When one of us died, the other one would just hang around that planet and wait until we could go back home to our ship together.

We visited planet Earth quite often since it was where we had initially reconnected again and were able to become Light Beings. Sometimes we sentimentally visited The Monroe Institute in the first half of the 21st century A.D. of earthly time. But we also liked to go there in the late second half of that century to admire the huge complex of modern buildings spreading out over the foothills of the Blue Ridge Mountains. The Complex at that time was called the "The Monroe Planetary University of Consciousness." It was a very busy place that was teaching and inspiring thousands of students of consciousness from all over the planet. We would walk around in our spiritual light bodies and give students energy and inspiring thoughts. And then we would go back home.

When I was sharing this story in the group, I realized that our home looked like a cylinder described in one of the books written by the magnificent Arthur C. Clarke, participant Brooke reminded me of the title. The book is "Rendezvous with Rama." Thus, Juanzetta and I decided to call our future home "Rama."

Chapter 91
REWARD

Then I fell at his feet to worship him, but he said to me, "You must not do that! I am a fellow servant with you and your brothers who hold to the testimony of Jesus. Worship God, for the testimony of Jesus is the spirit of prophecy."
(Revelation 19:10)

Even after such a wonderful experience, I still felt that something else was needed to complete my spiritual journey. The teasing and tickling secret of the Stargate was giving me new energy. I was especially inspired by the experiences of other participants. Terry found out that nothing was on the other side of the Stargate, and Karen saw only blackness. Juanzetta saw a nursery with incubators full of newborn universes. Several other participants saw the Stargate simply as a possible choice for the end of the road.

A tremendous opportunity arose on the last day of the program. Franceen suggested that we try to focus our intention during the group trip throughout the Earth Core by using not only the group energy but also the support and energy of our Earth, our Mother Gaia. I met everybody in the Earth Core, and we were all propelled together in one slingshot technique to the platform of Voyager 8. Participant Frank loudly called in his distinctive Brooklyn Italian accent: "Is everybody here?"
He counted us and made sure all of us were there. He assumed the leading role and said:
"Now everybody, get around that crystal and charge it and think about staying together forever!"
When we got to Alpha X on Focus 49, Frank reminded us: "Remember after you do your stuff, we meet here again, and we go back to Earth Core together!"

The support of the group and Mother Earth gave me tremendous courage. When I met with Gardener, I told him:

"I love you dearly, Your Majesty, I praise your spiritual knowledge and appreciate with great gratitude all that you have done for me!"

"What's up, Jozef? What is it this time?"

"Well, My Lord, can you go with me to the Stargate, please?"

"You already know what is there, I do not think it is necessary for you to do it again. Anything else?"

"No, Your Majesty, but please take me to the Stargate again. Please…" I was begging.

Surprisingly, he agreed. We immediately appeared there, and I could see the aperture and feel the breeze coming out.

"O.K., what now, Jozef?" asked Gardener.

"Can you please slingshot me in there as you did before?"

"No, I will not do that. You should be now able to slingshot yourself. I am sure that if you want it so much you can do it!"

I started to twirl like a dervish, and when I felt that I had reached the velocity needed for a slingshot, I directed myself into the Stargate. The same thing happened as before, I just heard a buzzing sound and was surrounded by complete darkness. I decided to challenge it and stay there longer than before. I waited. After a while, I started to hear a sweet seductive choir of gently angelic female voices:

"Welcome home…welcome home…welcome home…"

"I do not want to come back home yet!" answered I.

"Stay!...Stay!…Stay…!" an even more seductive whisper started to take my powers slowly away.

"No, please don't do this to me…don't do this to me..." I was begging.

"Freeze!…Freeze!…Freeze!…" they continued.

My spiritual form started to be denser and denser, and I was not feeling my vibrations anymore. I suspect that the vibrations which were creating the high density of my form had started to reach the frequency of God, which is perceived as stillness by us spiritual beings.

"I still have my physical body!"

I bravely but barely pronounced the magic sentence. A big flash of light followed, and I was back outside of the Stargate where Gardener was waiting for me. He looked surprised, and said:

"You really have guts man!" Then he asked me in a rather friendlier tone:

"Did you find something new in there, Jozef?"

"No, Your Majesty, but I am confident that I can always come back out before they can freeze me!"

"Do not call me Your Majesty or My Lord anymore, Jozef! From now on I want us to be friends, and my name is Michael! And now I shall take you on a trip!"

Our forms changed to pure light, and we flew to the end of the Universe. But Michael did not stop there, and I hastily followed him through the membrane. When we passed through it, our forms changed again. I looked at Michael and his body had wings. I looked at myself and I also had wings, even though mine were a little bit smaller. I looked around and saw bubbles of universes everywhere. We enjoyed flying inside of them one after another. When we were inside each one, we changed into pure light again. Some of the universes had yellow clusters of galaxies and stars like our universe, while others had clusters of different colors - white, green, orange, pink and even blue.

Before we flew inside or outside of them, I always kissed their borderline membranes. I was kissing the universes again and again!!! I tremendously enjoyed it and wished that it would never end. But then, I heard the call in my headphones to get back to the group. I thanked my wonderful long-time teacher and now, new friend, Michael. But, before heading back to my physical home on the Earth, I kissed the bubble of the dearest universe, my own and our home, before I entered it. Then I continued at the speed of thought into our Milky Way and back to join my meditating friends.

I landed on the Alpha X platform, where everybody

from the group was already there. Frank again coordinated our entering Voyager 8 for the flight back to Earth Core where we grounded our energies.

We had all gained knowledge from our trip and brought it back to our Mother Gaia for the benefit of all mankind. When we cooled down, we returned home to the Monroe Institute. I heard the beautiful soft voice of Darlene Miller in my headphones reciting Robert Monroe's poem: "There is no beginning, there is no end…"

Chapter 92
GOODBYE

"There are no goodbyes for us. Wherever you are, you will always be in my heart." (Mahatma Gandhi)

I could not wish for more than what I had just received, the highest respect from my beloved teacher who was now asking me to be his friend. I knew I would now have to say goodbye to him because, otherwise, I would not be able to finish the writing of my story. I wanted to limit my meditations to a bare and very occasional minimum. The first thing I did was to visit with my guides and tell them that I would not be around for a while.

Then I headed to the Park to the Planning Department to see what there was in store for me. They only had a very thin file with the label Guardian in Waiting. I was told by the lady in the office that, if I would successfully finish my current mission on Earth, there would be no more plans for me to stay in the Earth Life System. All information about me in such a case would be sent, as she said, "higher." But, if I would fail, they would call me again for planning my next reincarnation. When I asked her, who had given them the instructions, the lady looked at me with a serious expression on her face, and said:

"A very, very high developed spiritual being."

Then she leaned to me and whispered into my ear:

"He comes here very seldom, but everybody knows him, and they call him Michael."

I talked to Michael again several months later. He appeared again with his form having wings. When I asked him why he came like that, he said:

"That is how many of you people on your planet perceive us, especially in your Christian culture. However, you know that I am an inter-universal being like many of my peers. I am Gardener in many other galaxies in different universes, but

we also operate in between them."
We were talking about inter-universal topics, bubbling and the magic of creation. I asked him:
"Michael, what is the Ultimate Membrane? Is it part of the Source, or is it a part of manifestation?"
"It is both and neither. It depends on where you are as an observer. If you are in a manifested universe, it is the last frontier you can reach when going back toward the Source. It is The Skin of God."
"Is it still or is it in motion?"
"Both. It stays still when there is no intent of creation. When an intention to create is initiated, parts of the Ultimate Membrane start to vibrate. Likewise, when vibrations that are coming toward God during an annihilation need to be frozen, the movement in that part of the membrane stops."
I did not want to try to correct my dear friend or argue with him about the vibrations being frozen. After my experience in the Stargate, I am now sure that the freezing of vibrations is just an illusion created when the traveler's frequency is tuned to the frequency of God. And it is perceived by the spiritual beings as stillness.
"What is the membrane composed of and how thick is it?"
"It is composed of strings only and normally it is homogenous. When God has an intention to create a new universe, a knot of creation forms in the membrane, strings modify and then burst out into the Big Bang of a new universe. On the contrary, when a universe ceases to exist, it enters the membrane in the form of a knot of compressed strings and then dissolves and freezes into stillness. The Ultimate Membrane's thickness has no limit. And it is everywhere, because the strings are everywhere, unlike the membranes between dimensions in the universes which are infinitely thin. You cannot reside in them. You are either in one dimension or the other. The crossing of the dimensional membrane or the border of a universe is instant."
"Michael can the existence of what we call the Other Side

be proven by physical means on our planet?"

"No, it cannot be proven in the physical world. Everything in the manifested universes is digital, with the membranes separating the dimensions. Only a developed and stretched consciousness, which is always One, can penetrate through them. Manifested forms can cross membranes temporarily, but they cannot attain the properties of dimensions other than their own. If they want to cross into another dimension permanently, they must cease their existence in the dimension they occupy. The people on your planet can occasionally see forms from higher dimensions in the physical, but such forms cannot stay in the physical long enough to be considered a permanent presence. If you have in mind scientific proof of the Other Side by any of your five senses, it is not going to happen. It would contradict the Basic Law of Separation in Creation as set up and established by God."

"Creation is Separation!" I told myself, now also clearly understanding how the spiritual One creates the manifested Many.

"How is it possible then, Michael that I can travel in my form into different dimensions?"

"You don't do that Jozef. What is traveling into different dimensions is your consciousness. When you cross into another dimension, you are using the vehicle of another manifested form of energy. However, it can look identical to the form you were using in a previous dimension. The process is very similar to changing horses on very long rides in your physical world. Most of the time you are doing it subconsciously and not even knowing that it is happening."

The last time I spoke with Michael was in June 2015. It was the last day that I could still revoke my decision to retire from my service with the Federal government of The United States. I have had a very good ride. Working as a radio journalist, I had received the Voice of America Gold Medal in the year 2003. Then as an engineer, I received the award as Technician of the Year in the Central Recording of Operations Department in the year 2015. I was struggling with the departure from VOA, and I told him so. Said Michael:

"It is always difficult to break the chains of today, Jozef. But think about the freedom you shall have tomorrow. I am glad you came to see me, because I miss you, Jozef. But I do understand that your meditations now would interfere with the writing of your book. Your book shall be everywhere. You can observe people and their reactions without even being recognized. And then you can depart Earth permanently and come home and be with me all the time, if you wish so."

He also warned me to be aware of some very powerful deceiving spiritual beings who had lost their connections to God in the Divine Structure of Consciousness.

"You call them Fallen Angels in your culture," he reminded me and continued:

"They are especially interested in strong spiritual beings such as yourself. So be aware please, even though I am not truly worrying about you and them. Love thy enemies and opponents, Jozef. Express empathy for them and you shall have no real and dangerous enemies and opponents."

Then Michael invited me again for another ride through the bubbles of universes. This time, however, when I tried to make my wings smaller than his, I could not. Our forms were completely identical. I tremendously enjoyed kissing the universes whenever I could. After the ride I told him:

"I love you Michael and thank you for everything!"

Answered he:

"I love you, Jozef. Remember that I am always here for you!"

With that, suddenly both of our very high vibration forms jumped into each other like when two birds would hit each other in full flight in the middle of the air. Our forms merged in a giant flash of light and, immediately, I saw a small dot disappearing at the speed of thought into the distance. I was slowly and calmly returning to my physical body and thinking with a little sadness:

"Goodbye Michael!"

Then remembering the Native Americans saying I corrected myself:

"Goodbye is a lie Michael, because you are always with me."

EPILOGUE

"I looked at the skies, running my hands over my eyes, and I fell out of bed, hurting my head from the things that I'd said."
(From the song "I started a joke" by the Bee Gees)

O.K. Wow!
"And now it is the end of the made-up fairy tale," some or many of you might say, Dear Readers.
And some or many of you can also say:
"He is now even claiming that he is an Angel with the wings!"
I am not claiming anything. I have just told my story exactly as it happened. Whether I am an Angel or not, that I shall leave for you to ponder about, Dear Reader. Angels are messengers after all, and I am certainly a messenger of some kind. But an Angel? Gee, I don't know!

I must congratulate you, Dear Reader, for you have gotten to the end of the narrative without any incident or harm. Whether you think that what you have just read is a revealing and inspiring book unlike any other ever written, or you just consider it all made up, welcome! I, myself, often must wonder about what I have written, and sometimes I struggle a little bit trying to understand my own story fully. In any case, it was a heck of a ride! Yet I must remind you again, Dear Reader, this book was not written to prove anything to you or anybody; it is a story, and I am a reporter.
The British psychologist Richard Wiseman views paranormal experiences as very sophisticated and very interesting illusions where, for one reason or another, we are kidding ourselves about those experiences without realizing it. You see, Dear Reader, I am even trying to help you fortify your doubts if you have them. But before you judge, remember what I have written in the book. Meaningful meditation, driven by intention, is like a box of chocolates; you never know what you are going to get, as his smart

Momma was teaching Forest Gump.

You are welcome to challenge and contact me. I will always gladly respond as time constraints and circumstances would allow. But I would also like to welcome those who would try to help me extend the message to anybody willing to listen, because I have no doubt many of you, like me, want to spread it around. As Barry Gibb suggested when talking about the very spiritual song quoted at the beginning of the epilogue:

"Someone might find the meaning of it."

And Robin Gibb concurred:

"The listeners have to interpret it for themselves."

If you are on my side, let's look for more meanings together. If more human beings on our beautiful planet would venture out of their physical bodies and go inside the universal mind, they would discover the eternal and unconditional Love that abides there. And the world would be a better place. As the great Mahatma Gandhi said:

"Be the change that you wish to see in the world."

It is much easier to get on the spiritual road than you might think. You do not have to spend thousands of dollars as I did at the Monroe Institute, and you do not need to have a guru or master like you might see in the movies. You do not have to get up every day very early in the morning to meditate as I did for years. It is good, however, to have someone or something helping you on the way. It is not necessary to use Robert Monroe's Hemi Sync, there are plenty of other good tools available everywhere.

You only must learn to have a clear mind, a clear heart, and a clear intention. Remember that, at the core, every meditation is similar. You can always apply and adjust the Monroe Protocol, as I have described it, into your own conditions and routines, or you can use other techniques or suggestions from literature or the Internet. And do not worry too much about the so-called monkey mind. Even such a master and spiritual leader as His Holiness, the 14th Dalai Lama, Tenzin Gyatso, would tell you that the monkey mind will always be there. You only must move most of your mind out of your body, and you are there, on the Other Side. After you develop a routine, you shall quickly learn to recognize whether you are still mainly in your body or whether you have already moved into the higher vibrations of an altered state of your mind and into a spiritual reality.

We are multidimensional structured beings. As such, as Wynn Free said on Coast to Coast, we can be in our physical bodies and in many other dimensions and parallel universes at the same time. If you decide to join a meaningful group of like-minded individuals with a spiritual teacher or helper, you can progress even faster. But be aware of frauds and those who just want your money and obedience; there are plenty of them around too.

If you feel that you might be spiritual, respect people who think otherwise like layman skeptics, scientists, or pure atheists. The best way to talk to a challenging skeptic is to ask him or her questions with full respect regarding his or her own beliefs and opinions. Once I asked my skeptic friend if he would believe in extraterrestrials if someone would tell him that a UFO had just landed on The White House lawn. He answered that he would have to see it for himself. And even then, he would suspect that it was a hologram. And when the little gray men would walk out of it, he would believe for sure that they were just actors.

Scientists and skeptics are governed by the five senses; subsequently there is no extra sensory perception or simple sense of knowing that they would recognize as legitimate. They must have proof by utilizing only the five human senses. Anything else for them does not exist. There is a story of a contemporary scientist who was trying to build a time machine so that he could visit his deceased father whom he loved very much. He said in his comment about a spiritual time traveler currently visiting our planet, first, he would have to see his time travel box machine. Traveling in a time machine box was for him probably the only way to accomplish his wishes.

The progress of humanity shall continue to be somewhat limited until science recognizes and includes consciousness into its very important and valuable work. And the mainstream media must stop ignoring spiritual explorers and making fun of them. A worldwide public and open discussion about consciousness and our true essence is overdue to happen.

There is not a slightest doubt in my mind, that the essence of All That Exists is not physical but spiritual. All parts of our planet now seem to be connected through the Internet with most of us holding tremendous computing, researching and creative powers in the palms of our hands. But if you want to find your spiritual essence as I did, you must go inside your own Soul; no current computer or any other so-called intelligent machine can do it for you. And no other human being can do it for you either. Rahasya Poe once said on Coast to Coast:

"If you're just feeding off somebody else's experiences, you are not getting nourished."

Our consciousness is neither matter nor energy. It is a driving force of Love fueling our free will and intentions, and it was given to us by the Ultimate Creator.

If you are a skeptic or fundamentalist thinker, consider the possibility that your beliefs and knowledge could be somehow limited. Think about the possibility of opening your mind to something entirely new, different, and exciting. You might be skeptical primarily because you have not had any spiritual experiences yet. You will not have an experience only if you do not want to have one. But if you are open to try, you will have one sooner or later. And imagine what you can do, not only on the Other Side, but also on this planet and in your physical life when you finally get your proof. You are striving for proof, aren't you?

You will become more connected not only to the

Oneness of God, but you will start to like people more and will have more empathy and compassion. You will learn how to be much more present in the Now, and you shall be enjoying every moment of your physical existence on our planet with a new quality. You will build new conditions for your life on the Earth which will serve you to better understand the complexity of your spiritual essence. For sure, extraordinary achievements by human beings happen because we have extraordinary brains, but also because of the ability of our brains to connect to a spiritual reality. Our brain is only a tool carrying a small part of our essence and helping us to live and pursue happiness on this planet; the rest of our essence is residing outside of our brains.

What happens to you after you die depends upon you only. You can decide whether to keep your identity or not, decide where you will go, whether and when or where you will reincarnate or not. You can think about better planning for your next life. As my Dad often used to say wishfully about his somehow complicated life that he was not satisfied with:

"If I would be born again…"

You can even consciously end your entire spiritual existence. A spirit or Soul cannot be destroyed unless he or she wants to be. Because you are eternally connected and one with God, moving closer and closer to the Source will make you more and more composed of godly essence. It appears to me that the only choice you cannot affect is your transition to the spiritual world. It is going to happen irrespective of whether you do or do not believe in it, you don't like it, or you don't even want it. If you believe that your physical death means the end of everything, you might be surprised that it does not. And as George Noory likes to say, if that is the wrong anticipation, you simply will not know about it and you will simply cease to exist. So?

But if the anticipation is right, then you shall be ready. There is no reason for you to have any fears of any kind, because after physical death you only change, and you get closer to your true home.

You are an unlimited and timeless being. That knowledge should give you an incredible freedom that you did not even know you had. So finally, make yourself free, discover your wings as I did, kiss universes and fly throughout the bubbles of creation! Lastly, do not forget to kiss Our Universe when returning to your physical home on our beautiful precious planet Earth!

"Now joy is mine through my long night, I do not feel the rod, for I have danced the streets of heaven, and touched the Face of God!" (Cuthbert Hicks: The Blind Man Flies, 1938)

GLOSSARY

AFFIRMATION - verbally expressed determination to achieve an altered state of mind and effectively execute meditative intention

AKASHIC RECORDS (LIBRARY) - records of all that has happened, is happening and will happen in manifested universes

ALPHA SQUARED - an inter-stellar non-physical space station used by the Monroe Institute's spiritual explorers

ALPHA X - an inter-galactic spiritual station with a light spa and a Subatomic Particle Accelerator

ALTERED STATE OF MIND - when the human mind is communicating more with a spiritual environment beyond the physical body than with the physical body itself

APERTURE - an opening leading into the Stargate and the unlimited consciousness of God

ASTRAL BODY - part of your consciousness not residing in your physical body, but still having a form like your physical body

ASTRAL PROJECTION - when you successfully direct your consciousness to be mostly out of your physical body

ATLANTIS - a former island empire on Earth now in a non-physical realm where many of its suddenly departed post-catastrophic inhabitants live in a non-physical copy of their former environment

AVATARS - very highly developed spiritual beings who are helping humans to speed up their spiritual progress

AYAHUASCA - a soul wine used by shamans and their students for trips into an altered state

BASIC LAW OF SEPARATION - a principle defining the essence of manifested universes being separated from the uniqueness of God

BELIEF SYSTEM TERRITORIES - a complex variety of vibrational spaces where the souls of physically dead people reside and are under the direct influence of other spiritual beings

BERSERKERS - an elite group of Viking warriors often going into battle while in a trance

BIG ANNIHILATION - when a universe is sucked back into the stillness of the Source and completely disappears

BIG BANG - creation of the new bubble of a new universe by the intention of the Ultimate Creator

BIG CRASH - opposite of the Big Bang when a universe shrinks into the process of annihilation

BINAURAL MUSIC (BEATS) - alternative acoustic way of stimulating the brain used to induce an altered state of mind

BLACK HOLE - a gateway into different galaxies, clusters or even into different universes

BONDED I-THERE CLUSTERS - interconnected I-There clusters (Higher Selves) of spiritual beings incarnated in or attracted to planetary systems, galaxies, or local universes

BUBBLES - universes with local space and time created by God

BUBBLING - a process of God's expression from stillness into motion and manifestation

BUFFERS - storages of information during the transferring of parallel spiritual realm batches into a serial interpretation for your brain

CANALING - communication by humans with spiritual beings through pathways created by the humans as opposed to channeling, which is when channels are discovered and not created

CHAKRAS - energetic centers in the human body which enable the exchange of energy and information with nonphysical spiritual realms

CHEC UNIT - Controlled Holistic Environmental Chamber at Monroe Institute which provides isolation from light and outside sounds

CLUSTER COUNCIL - a governing body composed of very high spiritual beings who are guarding the balance and development of the spirituality of inhabitants incarnated in a cluster of galaxies

CODE OF MANIFESTATION - the key that is enabling manifestation into different space and time like the DNA code in biological bodies on Earth

CONSCIOUSNESS (also MIND) - our spiritual essence, different and separate from matter and energy, but which enables us to manipulate them using the power of intention

CONSCIOUSNESS ONE (C 1) - when your earthly mind is mostly present in your physical body

COSMIC LOVE - unconditional Love supplied by the Ultimate Creator which is expected to be cherished, magnified, and returned to God from all manifested living beings

COUNCIL OF GALACTIC GUARDIANS - a governing body composed of very high spiritual beings guarding the balance and development of spirituality of inhabitants incarnated in a galaxy

COUNCIL OF STARS FRIENDS - a group of high spiritual beings helping the author of this book in his spiritual journey, chaired by Gardener

CREATORS - highly developed spiritual beings close to God who can manifest planetary systems and conduct terraforming

DARK ENERGY- the global balancer and the global glue between the bubbles of universes

DARK MATTER - the local cosmic balancer and glue inside the bubble of a universe

DEMONS - spiritual beings who have lost their silver cord connections to God

DERVISH - a member of the Sufi order who is using energetic whirling dancing for bringing his consciousness into an altered state

DEVIL - a malicious powerful spiritual being without a connection to God

DIMENSION - a distinct spiritual vibrational space between membranes separating it from a lower vibrational space and from a higher vibrational space

DIVINE STRUCTURE OF CONSCIOUSNESS - a hierarchical tree-like structure of interconnected spiritual beings maintaining their connections to God

DNA - a molecule that carries the genetic instructions used in the growth, development, functioning and reproduction of all known living organisms

DOPPELGANGER - an apparition or double of a living person

EARTH LIFE SYSTEM (ELS) - the physical and spiritual space where the Soul is significantly more bound to our physical planet than to a wider spiritual reality

ELOHIM - the highest spiritual beings who are close to God shortly after separation from the Source or before the final return to Source

EMOTIONAL CLEANSING - the process of removing unwanted conditions from your mind before you can effectively utilize an altered state

EMPTINESS - a meaningless void perceived by the meditating mind as a blackness

EVER PULSATING NOW - the process of the expanding and shrinking of local bubbles of universes in no time

EXPECTATION - a wished for but usually not guaranteed result of your meditation

EXPLORATION 27 - a program at the Monroe Institute dedicated to the study of the vibrational level of Focus 27, where the Park is also located

EXTRA SENSORY PERCEPTION (ESP) - the ability to perceive information other than just by the five senses

FACILITATOR - a certified teacher and spiritual helper at the Monroe Institute

FALLEN ANGELS - unfriendly spiritual entities who have lost their connections to the Ultimate Creator

FINGER OF GOD - acknowledgment of connection and recognition from the Ultimate Creator when a new human being is conceived

FIRST TIMERS - spiritual beings who have finished their first earthly incarnations
FLOW - the stream of information while meditating when a canal is created
FLYING GRIZZLY- the author's first spiritual guide who appears in that form
FLYING POTATO - a local transfer vehicle seen in Atlantis
FOCUS LEVEL - a loosely specified spiritual area of the mind in an altered state according to the model developed by Robert Monroe
FOCUS 10 - when your body sleeps, but your brain is awake, and you have reached a basic altered state of mind
FOCUS 12 - when your awareness in an altered state widens and enables you to communicate with non-physical realms
FOCUS 15 - an altered state of mind with no time perception
FOCUS 21 - an altered state of mind on the borderline between the Earth Life System and the vastness of the Universe
FOCUS 22 - a spiritual vibrational space where the souls of people still living on Earth can temporarily pop-up for a variety of reasons
FOCUS 23 - the lower astral plane, a very dense spiritual vibrational ring around our planet where most of the recently departed souls (physically dead) of people reside
FOCUS 24 - the lower vibrational space of the Belief System Territories where less developed souls with a strong affinity for very manipulative collective belief systems reside
FOCUS 25 - the middle vibrational space of the Belief System Territories where souls with an affinity for mainstream religious and ideological systems reside
FOCUS 26 - the higher vibrational space of the Belief System Territories where souls with a loose affinity for like-minded non-religious or non-ideological communities reside
FOCUS 27 (also the PARK) - the spiritual vibrational space inhabited by souls who have overcome the lures of the lower vibrational levels and are getting ready for further conscious

development

FOCUS LEVELS 34 AND 35 - the spiritual vibrational spaces immediately beyond the Earth Life System, a platform for starting voyages beyond the planet and deep into the galaxy and beyond

FOCUS 42 - the spiritual vibrational space well beyond the Earth Life System, yet still local in a planetary and galactic sense

FOCUS 49 - the inter-galactic spiritual vibrational space, yet still local to our Universe

GAIA (MOTHER GAIA) - our planet Earth as a living organism

GALACTIC CORE - the center of the galaxy with a gateway into another galaxy or universe

GANESHA - a Hindu god with an elephant head, a big belly and four hands, the Lord of success and the destroyer of evils and obstacles

GATEWAY VOYAGE - the first fundamental life changing meditative program at the Monroe Institute

GARDENER - Milky Way administrator of the Loosh and the author's main spiritual teacher

GENERATORS OF MANIFESTATION - spiritual devices producing a strong force for pushing intention into energy and matter

GENERATORS OF RELEASE - spiritual devices producing a weak force for releasing experiences and the Loosh into consciousness

GHOSTS - the souls of departed people residing in a lower astral plane and, occasionally, slightly and temporarily manifesting in the physical

GOD (SOURCE) - the formless, timeless, and unlimited power of creation, the unlimited sea of interconnected consciousness

GRADUATE - a spiritual being who has finished the process of reincarnation and education on a planet

GRATITUDE - appreciation and thanks for information

received from non-physical realms

GREAT EMITTER - the source of universal unconditional Love beyond the Stargate, outside of the manifested universes

GROUNDING - the process of calming down and bringing your vibrations from a spiritual activity down into the physical environment

GUARDIANS - the higher spiritual beings securing the safety of our planet and her purpose as intended by the Ultimate Creator and the Creators

GUIDE (also GUARDIAN ANGEL) - a spiritual entity always willing to help you in an altered state and in your physical life

GUIDELINES - the Monroe Institute's program focusing on the development of relations between you and your inner self

HADIEN - the author's spiritual star friend from a different galaxy who appears in a pyramidal form

HEARTGATE - an oversized activated heart chakra receiving Love directly from God

HEARTLINE - a program at the Monroe Institute dedicated to the spiritual study of the human heart and emotions

HEMI SYNC - the patented Monroe Institute's audio technology which produces different tonal sounds into your left and right earphones to achieve an altered state of mind

HIGHER SELF - the part of your consciousness residing permanently outside of your body that is always willing to help you in your physical and spiritual journey

HIGHER-HIGHER SELF - the consciousness of a spiritual being containing multiple higher selves

HYPNAGOGIC STATE - the borderline between the asleep and awaken state

IMMORTALITY- the essence of all spiritual beings who are mostly not aware of it

INFINITE SEA OF BONDED I-THERE CLUSTERS - all loosely interconnected Bonded I-There Clusters

INTENTION - the driving force of creation and a tool of

manifestation and manipulation

INTER-DIMENSIONAL GENERATOR - a device for generating the energy needed to enable crossing a dimensional membrane

INTERFACE - a part of the third eye enabling communication with the spiritual world

INTERGALACTIC COUNCIL - a governing body composed of very high spiritual beings who oversee big areas of the Universe

INTERNAL SELF HELPER (ISH) - your personified internal power and guide always willing to help you when you ask

I-THERE CLUSTER - a "hovering" Higher Self of a spiritual being incarnated on a planet

KAHUNA - Hawaiian wise man, woman or Shaman

KAMALÁSKA - the author's Internal Self Helper in female form, who is more than a friend but less than a lover

KARMA - an account of your actions, including previous lives, influencing your current life and your spiritual value

KUNDALINI - a hidden energy sleeping at the base of the spine, coiled like a snake waiting to be unleashed

KUNDALINI MACHINE - a spiritual device in the Park helping souls who are recovering from earthly traumas to quickly connect to their Higher Selves

LAST TIMERS - spiritual beings planning to leave the Earth Life System permanently after they have finished their education on Earth during their last reincarnation

LAW OF KARMA - the universal principle of raising or lowering your spiritual value in harmony with Love or in contradiction with Love

LEMURIANS - the inhabitants of a former continental empire on Earth

LIFELINE - a program at the Monroe Institute dedicated to helping the souls departed from Earth by spiritual explorers still living on our planet

LIGHT BODY - the highest vibrational energy body further

transformed into light form with the help of a Subatomic Particle Accelerator

LIGHT SPA - a chamber enabling transformation from the high vibrational energy body into a light body

LOCAL KARMA - your spiritual value in the effort to become a Graduate and reach the velocity needed to be able to permanently leave a planet

LOOP OF CREATION - the flow of the creative intentions of God into the manifested universes and back

LOOP OF LOVE - the flow of Love from the Source through your Heartgate and then back to the Ultimate Creator

LOOP OF SOULS - the intertwining bond between soulmates enabling them to repeatedly incarnate together

LOOSH - a non-form substance created by the emotions and experiences of sentient living beings and flowing to God

LUCID DREAMING - when you know in a dream that you are dreaming

LUCIFER - a malicious powerful spiritual being who voluntarily severed his connection to God

MACHO - a spiritual being called on by the author with the intention to suppress his own ego

MANIFESTATION - the process of creating or affecting a physical or other form-based reality by using the power of the mind

MC SQUARED - a Monroe Institute program dedicated to confidence building and psychokinetic practices

MEDIUM - a person with abilities to see the past, present, and future events of a person by tuning into the spirit energy surrounding that person

MEMBRANE - the distinct borderline between distinct levels of spiritual reality and dimensions

MEMORY ROOM - a non-physical chamber for explorers containing the tools and devices for enabling communication with the Akashic Library

MENEV - the author's most important reincarnation on planet Earth as a folk healer in Rhaeto Romansh Switzerland

MICRO-WORLD - the manifested physical reality we discover when our mind is moving more and more inside elementary particles and their components

MIND (CONSCIOUSNESS) - our spiritual essence distinct and separated from matter and energy and enabling us to manipulate them

MIND OF THE BODY EXPERIENCE - when you know that most of your earthly mind is out of your physical body

MIRANON COLORS - a set of channeled colors helping the imagination to rise through the vibrations from Focus 15 to Focus 21

MISTER Q - a higher spiritual being with interest in the origins of planets and living biological beings

MIZU NO KOKORO - a Japanese expression for the peaceful mind being like calm water without any disruptions

MONKEY MIND - a natural state of mind in the awake state with scattered thoughts of all kinds

MONROE INSTITUTE - a non-profit organization in Virginia dedicated to the study and research of human consciousness

MONROE PLANETARY UNIVERSITY OF CONSCIOUSNESS - the future name and mission of the current Monroe Institute in the late second half of the 21st century

MONROE PROTOCOL - one of the reliable ways to get to an altered state

MORPHON - a spiritual official in the Recovery Center in the Park who is assisting spiritual explorers when they carry out Soul retrievals

MORPHOGENETIC FIELD - the field of thoughts created by everything in existence

MULTI-DIMENSIONAL - being able to operate simultaneously in different dimensions of the universe or universes

MULTI-EYES - the spiritual tools for simultaneous seeing into many different dimensions and universes

MULTI-TELEPORTER - a spiritual device enabling very high beings to do simultaneous teleportation into multiple spaces and times

MULTIVERSES - multiple overlapping bubbles of universes

NON-FORM BEINGS - highly developed spiritual beings free of the need to have any shape or form to be aware of their essence and actions

NON-VERBAL COMMUNICATION - the exchange of information between spiritual beings in a no time environment, usually by exchanging balls of information

NOW - the ever-present moment with time not having any dimension or locality

ONENESS - all spiritual beings interconnected with the Source and with themselves

ORBS - beings from another dimension manifested on our physical planet as small slowly moving lights

OTHER SIDE - the expression commonly used for the non-physical reality of a spiritual realm

OUT OF BODY EXPERIENCE - when you are aware of your astral non-physical body being temporarily separated from your physical body

OVERSEER (JESUS or JESHUA) - the highest known spiritual being very close to God, highly respected and admired by anyone whom the author met during spiritual travels

PALENQUE - a Maya city state in southern Mexico that flourished in the 7th century

PARALLEL UNIVERSE - the overlapping space and time in different bubbles of created universes

PARK - a spiritual vibrational space for conscious recovery of souls from the traumas of physical reincarnations and for planning their further spiritual development

PERSONAL CLUSTER COUNCIL - a temporarily created ad hoc body of higher spiritual beings for helping any spiritual being who asked for it

PLAUTUS - a Roman comedy playwright and the author's

third most important reincarnation on planet Earth
PORTAL ROOM - a non-physical chamber enabling teleporting into a different space and time
PROTECTION BALLOON - an energetic protective barrier around your spiritual body form when traveling in an altered state
PSYCHIC - a person using extrasensory perception (ESP) to identify and process information hidden from the five known human senses
PSYCHOKINESIS - the ability to move physical objects on Earth with the power of the mind
PULSARS - very dense cosmic objects used by super-intelligences for identifying and correcting dangerous imbalances in the physical universe
PURE THOUGHT - a source for creation of a thought with a shape, form and intention
QILIN - a mythical hooved chimerical creature known in Chinese and other East Asian cultures
QUANTUM ENTANGLEMENT - the technology used by high spiritual beings to create the Code of Manifestation for teleportation into a different space and time
QUANTUM UNIT - the smallest known possible amount of any existing manifested physical entity
RA - one of the spiritual beings who are enforcing the divine order in The Universe
RAMA - future spiritual and physical home which the author shares with Juanzetta and other higher spiritual couples in the depth of the universe
RECOVERY CENTER - a place in the Park, where many souls departed from the Earth recover from their planetary traumas
REINCARNATION - when your Soul is embodied again in physical form for another physical life
REMEMBER - a command in an altered state for helping to remember an experience
REPEATERS - spiritual beings who repeatedly reincarnate

on Earth

REPTILIANS - unfriendly spiritual entities who lost their connections to the Ultimate Creator

RESIDUAL CONSCIOUSNESS - a part of the mind remaining in the physical body during an out of body or near death or altered state experience

RESONANT TUNING - aligning your vibrations with a variety of the frequencies of the Universe

RESONATOR - a spiritual tool for aligning with the Universal Harmonic Frequency of the Universe

RETRIEVAL - a process of helping stuck souls to move on into a higher vibrational space by spiritual explorers still physically alive on Earth

ROTE (RELATED ORGANIZED THOUGHT ENERGY) - a ball of information exchanged between communicating higher spiritual beings

ROTER - a spiritual explorer routinely communicating with higher realms using ROTEs (balls of information)

ROTING - creating, exchanging, and processing ROTEs (balls of information)

RUALA - a higher spiritual being appearing in female form helping the author to understand the feminine part of his essence and Cosmic Love

SATAN - a malicious powerful spiritual being without a connection to God

SCHOOL OF CREATORS - a gathering spiritual place for the Creators (Elohim) who are very close to God

SCREEN OF MANIFESTATION - a tool for the unwinding of a ROTE

SECURITY REPOSITORY BOX - a storage for a variety of subjects and influences which could disrupt your meditation

SHADOWS - substances created when consciousness starts to manifest or when matter and energy start dispersing into consciousness

SHAMAN - a traditional intermediary between physical and spiritual worlds

SHAMAN'S HEART - a former program at the Monroe Institute dedicated to the blending of traditional shamanic practices with Hemi Sync technology

SILVANA - a planet for processing the Loosh in our galaxy

SILVER CORD - a connection (pointer) between the physical and astral body and between spiritual bodies on different vibrational levels

SINGULARITY TRANSFER POINT - a spiritual point through which consciousness from our time and space can immediately move to any other time and any other space

SKIN OF GOD - the Ultimate Membrane separating God from manifested universes

SKJOERG - the author's second most important reincarnation on planet Earth as a Viking shaman

SLINGSHOT - a spiritual technique for a rapid increase in vibrations by using the combined spiritual energy of a group of explorers and the Earth Core energy

SOUL - the organized consciousness of a timeless and multi-dimensional spiritual individual

SOUL STRETCHING - when consciousness anchored in the physical body is projected to an intended target

SOUL TRADERS - malevolent spiritual beings offering deceiving deals to human souls residing in the lower vibrational areas of the BSTs

SOURCE (GOD) - the formless, timeless and unlimited power of creation, a borderless sea of interconnected and universal consciousness

SPECIAL PLACE - a non-physical place created by a Monroe Institute student for use when he or she wants to meet with spiritual guides

SPIRITUAL BELT (RING) - a spiritual space around our planet where the souls of the departed reside while still overwhelmingly bound to the Earth's physical environment

SPIRITUAL CHILDREN - thought forms in the spiritual realm created by the fantasies of lovers

STARGATE - a gateway, a portal out of the stars and out of

the manifested universes into the infinity of the spiritual Source

STARLINES - the Monroe Institute's program dedicated to communication with spiritual entities beyond the Earth Life System

STARLINES II - the Monroe Institute's program dedicated to communication with galactic and inter-galactic spiritual entities

STARMAN - the author's spiritual star friend who has experiences from reincarnations on the Earth

STRINGS - elementary units of manifestation created immediately after a Big Bang and which rapidly multiply like viruses or bacteria

STRONG FORCE - it is produced in generators of manifestation and pushes the flow of intention from consciousness into matter

SUBATOMIC PARTICLE ACCELERATOR - a spiritual device in the spa of light for helping a high energy vibrational body to be transformed into a body of light

SUPER-LOOSH - the purified high quality Loosh, Super-Love, giving the Ultimate Creator a reason to manifest more Big Bangs and Universes

TELEPORTER - a spiritual device in the Memory Room enabling a mind's projection into a different space and time

TERRAFORMING - a process executed by the Creators for preparing a planet for the introduction of sentient biological beings

THOUGHT FORMS - energy forms in the spiritual realm created by human minds

TIME BALL - a spiritual tool enabling access and shortcuts into the past and future across the bubbles of universes

TIMELINE - a program at the Monroe Institute dedicated to the study of time and its influences on people

TIME WHEEL - a spiritual tool enabling access and shortcuts into the past and future in local universe

TMI-THERE - a non-physical copy of the Monroe Institute

in the Park

TOTAL KARMA - the sum of the karma accumulated from all your I-There Clusters in your effort to become an Ultimate Graduate and reach the Stargate

ULTIMATE CHOICE - when a spiritual being as an Ultimate Graduate can decide whether to return to God or stay in the manifested universes

ULTIMATE CONCEPTION - when a spiritual being is born by separation from the Source

ULTIMATE CREATOR - God, Source, timeless and borderless consciousness

ULTIMATE GRADUATE - a spiritual being who has reached the state where he or she has learned everything that was possible in the manifested universes

ULTIMATE HIGHER SELF - the complete consciousness of a unique spiritual individual having only one unique silver cord connection to God

UNIVERSE - a local space and time bubble with a defined number of dimensions and flexible boundaries manifested by the power of the Ultimate Creator

VIBRATIONAL LEVEL - a quantified specific frequency of a spiritual energy body oscillation

VIMANA - an intercontinental Atlantean aircraft

VORTEX - an energy form of a spiritual being forced into spinning by intention

VOYAGER 8 - an inter-dimensional spacecraft used by the Starlines program participants for spiritual travels

WEAK FORCE - it is produced in generators of release and pushes the Loosh from matter into consciousness

WORMHOLE - a spiritual tunnel beyond space and time connecting two different black holes in different galaxies and universes

ACKNOWLEDGEMENTS

It is my pleasure and duty to express profound thanks to the individuals who inspired me to get on the road of spiritual and metaphysical exploration and supported me during the process, and which finally led to the publication of this book.

First, I want to thank my dear Slovak friend Peter Ondris, who inspired me first to emigrate to the United States, and later to start my spiritual journey; to my Colleague at the Voice of America, Native American Eugene Taylor, who led me to the Monroe Institute and William Buhlman. I also thank William for helping me with my first steps on the road.

My many thanks for guiding my spiritual development and for many inspirations go to the Monroe Institute facilitators Karen Malik, Lee Stone, Patty Ray Avalon, Byron Metcalf, Paul Elder, Dr. Joe Gallenberger, Skip Atwater, Dr. Franceen King and Penny Holmes.

The biggest gratitude however belongs to my beloved wonderful wife Dr. Juanzetta Flowers. This book, My Love, would not be possible without your constant encouragement, countless advice, spirited conversations, and complete understanding. I thank you for the repeated editing of more than 15 versions of the script, suggestions for improvement, and for correcting my English and grammar. Your unconditional love is unwavering, and I love you so much!

Thanks also go to Barbara Lee, Dr. Kay Knowlton, and Ravi Chhabra for reading the first version of the script and giving your opinions. A special thanks to Beth Gundersen for reading the manuscript, and for her brilliant suggestion to include a Glossary.

And finally, I need to list people who indirectly encouraged and helped me through their books on self-publishing and website design after I wisely and early on abandoned my attempts to find a willing agent and traditional publisher. They are Dr. Andy Williams, Sarah McHarry, Helen Sedwick, Rick Smith, Mike Taylor, and Tim Grahl.

REVIEWS AND MESSAGES

Dear Reader, if you enjoyed this book, especially if it affected your thinking about life and afterlife, please consider leaving an honest review or opinion on Amazon.

Also, please help me to spread the message about the book around to your family, friends, colleagues, and everybody you know who would be interested. I would appreciate if you would use any means possible, such as word of mouth, phone calls, texting, emailing, social media, placement of information about the book on Internet, contacting and informing the press, magazines, media, and public organizations.

I will also appreciate your comments, opinions, messages, and questions sent through my websites or directly to the emails below. If you wish to make them public, tell me so and I will gladly quote them publicly when opportunities arise. I can also publish them or their parts on my website. If you would desire a private answer, I shall fully honor your request.

howtokisstheuniverse.org
howtokisstheuniverse.com
jozefsimkovic.com
howtokisstheuniverse@outlook.com
jsimkovic@howtokisstheuniverse.org

Printed in Great Britain
by Amazon

18655972R00193